RAISED ON ROCK

RAISED ON ROCK

The autobiography of Elvis Presley's step-brother

DAVID E. STANLEY
with
MARK BEGO

MAINSTREAM
PUBLISHING PROJECTS

First published in Great Britain in 1996 by
MAINSTREAM PUBLISHING PROJECTS LTD
7 Albany Street
Edinburgh
EH1 3UG

ISBN 1 85158 852 3

A catalogue record for this book is available from the British Library

Typeset in Sabon
Printed and bound in Great Britain by Butler and Tanner

Dedication

To my father, Master Sergeant William J. Stanley – thank you for giving the other side of the story and the courage to write it.

To my mother, Davada May Presley – I hope you understand that I could only find myself through what I lost as a kid, my father.

To my sons, Austin and Tyler. You shall know the truth and the truth shall set you free. In reading the pages of this book you must understand that I am not proud of the mistakes I have made.

Contents

Acknowledgements

David Stanley thanks the following people for their help, assistance and support in writing this book: Tony Seidl, my agent; thanks for your help and support both professionally and personally. Mark Bego, my co-writer; it took a while Mark but we finally got it out there. Billy and Ricky Stanley, my brothers; thank you for helping me survive this ordeal. Jennifer E. Stanley, for helping to close that chapter of my life at last. John Dawson, my dear friend, many thanks for help with the photo selections. Curtis Head, my buddy; it was all those cold beers and cheeseburgers that got me through. Peggy and Don Bakel, my friends, for their personal support and for providing the room from which the book was written. All my associates at DKB Advertising & Public Relations in Dayton, Ohio, especially Jamie Kenny, Deb Giarratana and Marty Kelly. Much love and many thanks for your help in this endeavour. Also, Lynn Bruce and Catherine Lennon, many thanks for your additional editing and support on galley proofs and photo layouts.

Mark Bego and David Stanley would also like to thank the following for their help: Edie Fadal, Charlie Moniz, Lynn Moon, Marie Morreale, Bill Campbell and John Beaton.

Introduction

In 1960 when my mother, Dee Stanley, married Elvis Presley's widowed father, Vernon, my life changed forever. I was four years old when I found myself moving into the larger than life world of the King of Rock and Roll and living in Graceland Mansion. Elvis Presley, some 20 years older than me, had become my big brother.

From that time until 1977 I grew up amidst all the major events that defined Elvis's life – from his greatest glories, to the demons that haunted him. I was there in 1962 when my future sister-in-law Priscilla arrived at Graceland as a child not much older than me and had lived at Graceland for eight years before my niece Lisa Marie was born in 1968.

I grew up on the backlots of movie studios, attended many recording sessions, and at the age of 17 I dropped out of high school and toured with Elvis as his personal aide and bodyguard. I was there with Elvis, hanging out backstage when the rock royalty and stars came to visit – including the Beatles, Led Zeppelin, Eric Clapton, Alice Cooper, Elton John, Three Dog Night, Frank Sinatra, Sammy Davis Jr., Barbara Streisand, Tom Jones, John Wayne, Raquel Welch, and Ann-Margret – to name a few.

I endured the stress of watching Elvis develop his self-destructive vices. I was amongst the first to discover Elvis's lifeless body on 16 August 1977 and I stood on the steps of Graceland, and watched 17 years of my life being carried out in the back of an ambulance.

With Elvis's death, I was out of Graceland as fast as I had moved in. As a part of his entourage, I had once been treated as visiting royalty. Now all I had to show for it was drug addiction, a ninth grade education, and my memories.

I was relentlessly pursued by the press, and I remained candid about the controversial circumstances that surrounded my big brother's death. From the very start, I publicly testified that Elvis's death was a result of a self-induced drug overdose. Elvis had lived a lie, and now he had died a lie. This revelation sent shockwaves not only through the Presley estate, but the world as well.

Like a Tennessee Williams play come to life, I witnessed the power struggle for Graceland and the whole Elvis empire which commenced after Vernon's death in 1979. Now that millions of dollars of estate money were at stake, I was amazed at the way Priscilla convinced me how she would stop at nothing to get what she wanted.

As a result of my bizarre upbringing and unusual circumstances, I turned to religion. I became an Evangelistic preacher, a voice for God, but, because of the distorted perspective of life instilled in me from the Elvis years, I soon began to feel like a predator in the pulpit. Although I was convincing as a preacher, my private life was filled with lies and deception. I had created my own façade: a by-product of the Presley environment.

Now that I am 41, I am just coming into my own as a person. When Elvis was my age, he was poisoning himself, and hastening his own self destruction. As I've become older, overcome the negative traits instilled in me by the Presley environment and dealt with what I saw, I have come to understand why he was the way he was.

Raised on Rock is the story of my relationship with my world-famous step-brother. It shows how out of touch with reality life with the Presleys made me become. In writing these memoirs I have remained unfrightened and objective as I look back on my life at Graceland, and its aftershocks. I examine the disposable lifestyle and façade-laden ideology of Elvis Presley and describe how, by mimicking the negative traits of my older brother, it nearly cost me my life.

I tell for the first time how Elvis's distorted world introduced me to sex, drugs and manipulation. I reveal Elvis's post-Priscilla affairs with young girls, and his strange liaisons with their families.

I also tell of my controversial relationship with Priscilla Presley, and how she has become mesmerised by the Church of Scientology. The story comes full circle into the 1990s when my millionairess niece, Lisa Marie Presley, rebelled against her mother and married Michael Jackson.

Perhaps the most delicate part of my entire story is the description of the deceitful triangle made up of Vernon Presley, my father – Bill Stanley Sr. – and my mother – Dee. Vernon acted as if he was my father's best friend until he got what he wanted: my mother. My father died in February 1991 and, armed with a rare copy of his memoirs which he left to me, I have attempted to recount this episode for the first time.

In this book I look back on my life, to tell the larger-than-reality story of what it was like to be part of rock and roll's first family. Starting with the affair between Vernon Presley and my mother, this is a classic story of how power and money can corrupt. The Presley family used their money and clout to get what they wanted, often ruining lives along the way; somehow, I survived.

David Stanley, 1996

1

Near Death in Baton Rouge

I had been going on tours with Elvis since 1972. As time went by, they were becoming increasingly harder to go on, and the concerts more and more difficult. On 31 March 1977, we were in Baton Rouge, Louisiana, preparing for a show, and Elvis, who normally weighed about 175 pounds, had by this time ballooned up to nearly 250, a result of his medication throughout the years.

Things were not going well for him, he had dramatically increased his daily dose of medications, had begun gaining further weight and was not feeling at all healthy.

Just getting him on stage was a job in itself. At this time it wasn't uncommon for him to be completely disoriented. We had just done a concert in Houston, Texas, and he walked out of his dressing room and he looked at me. He had a glazed look in his eye. He put his arm around my shoulder and said, 'David, where am I?' That night, my brother Ricky and I had to keep him from falling off of the stage.

The show in Baton Rouge was going to be totally routine. It entailed getting him up in the afternoon and letting him eat what we called 'his breakfast'. He would watch the television show *The Match Game* and we would sit there talking. At this point in his life he was really down.

You would say something to him such as 'Good morning, Elvis,' and he would snap back, 'What's so good about it?' He had a really negative approach to everything and you could see by the look on his face that he was extremely unhappy. If he had been checked out by a psychiatrist, they would have diagnosed him as being clinically depressed. He knew that he was failing in a lot of areas of his life, and finally realised he was addicted to prescription drugs.

The weeks leading up to that particular day in Baton Rouge had been pretty bad. Throughout 1975 and 1976 he had given some really lousy shows. Elvis had been admitted to different hospitals several times for 'fatigue'.

The drugs that he was taking had virtually taken over his life. We had already been through a couple of situations where we had to physically pull food out of his throat to keep him from choking and there had been times when he had taken too many pills and had passed out on the floor.

This started as a typical day. I went to his room at the Hilton Hotel at about 4 p.m., knocked on his door and said, 'Hey, it's time to get up.'

I had already ordered his breakfast, which normally consisted of two pounds of very crisp bacon, burnt toast, eggs and cantaloupe or honeydew melon. He ate a tremendous amount of food at this point.

With his prescription drug intake, he made John Lennon and some of the other cocaine and LSD-taking rock stars look like angels. Although he had a very serious drug abuse habit he would never openly admit it. To him they were 'medicine'.

This particular engagement in Baton Rouge was one of 14 concert dates in 14 different cities, one a day. He wasn't like my ex-step-nephew Michael Jackson, who will go out and do two concerts and then rest for three days.

This was a tour in which we would do a show, get into his aeroplane, fly to the next city, go to bed, wake up the next day and do it all again. This time around, the speed and uppers he was taking to counteract the sleeping pills that he also took, were failing to revive him. Elvis was literally burning himself out. At the time I was 21 years old, and it was wearing me down just to keep up the pace.

On that particular afternoon, through his slurred speech, Elvis said to me, 'I'm not getting up. Get me Dr Nick.'

My room was right next door to Elvis's. It was my responsibility to make sure that he was up, to make sure that his food was there, to ensure that he had taken his medications and to see that he hadn't taken too much.

I was what I called a 'lifer'. I was one of four or five people whose assignment was to sit in Elvis's room to watch him sleep and make sure that he didn't choke to death or stop breathing. His sleeping pill intake had escalated from two, to four, to eight, now it required 11 different narcotic pills just to put him to sleep at night.

Thanks to his staff doctors, these were legal pills. That way, he could look in the mirror and tell himself that he wasn't a drug addict. He abhorred 'street' drugs or anyone who used them. He was on 'medication' so he could somehow justify his out-of-control habits.

He was really disillusioned with his former 'Memphis Mafia' members, Red and Sonny West. Red had been to high school with Elvis and he was capable of looking Elvis in the eyes and saying, 'You're doing too much dope.' Following an aborted 'intervention' to get him off drugs, Elvis fired them. They were trying to save his life but he saw this as betrayal. He no longer had anyone in his inner circle who would stand up to him, whom he would actually listen to. Now that they were gone he was surrounded by gutless 'yes' men who were able to turn their heads away while he slowly poisoned himself.

If it wasn't for us 'lifers', who would literally pick him up and drag him from room to room whenever he had to go to the bathroom or be anywhere, he would have died years before. We weren't like the other tour employees such as Lamar Fike, Jerry Schilling and Joe Esposito, who were the glory boys who were just around for the high-profile tours like this one. We were around no matter what he was doing, whether it was a tour, or just a normal day at Graceland. He had to be watched 24 hours a day.

When Elvis refused to get out of bed that afternoon in Baton Rouge, I went and found Dr Nick. I stood there watching Elvis talk to Dr Nick, and I was really getting fed up with the two of them. The doctor's real name was Dr George Constantine Nicholoulos, but he went by the name of 'Dr Nick'. Behind his back I referred to him as 'Needle Nick' because of all the additional prescription drug injections I watched him administer to Elvis over the years.

Today's scenario wasn't uncommon. We had been down this road before. When Elvis refused to get out of bed, Dr Nick would simply give him a dose of speed. He was one of many doctors whom Elvis used for these purposes. In a pinch, Elvis was not above getting dental work done, just so he could have the prescription for painkillers.

I went and got Joe Esposito from his hotel room and told him that Elvis didn't look well and that he wouldn't get out of bed. We went back to Elvis's room. The sight of Elvis lying like a drugged-out beached whale was a devastating one.

Elvis was the icon of my life. He was the King of Rock and Roll. My mind flashed back to the first time I saw him on stage in Las Vegas in 1969, so glorious and above reproach. Now, here he was lying on this huge bed in his suite, unable to get up. I felt so disillusioned, knowing that he had done this to himself.

This particular concert date was a coliseum show. Over at Louisiana State University, there were 20,000 fans in the stadium waiting for Elvis. J.D. Sumner and The Stamps, one of Elvis's opening acts, were currently on stage warming up the crowd. His background group at the time, the Sweet Inspirations, had already performed their set.

One of the concert coordinators, Tom Hewlett, telephoned and said to Joe Esposito, 'Tell Elvis, "You'd better get out of that bed, buddy. You've got 20,000 screaming fans over there, and if they don't get a show, we're going to get sued."'

When he did, Elvis looked up and told Joe, 'No, I can't get up. I just can't do it – I'm sick.'

I turned to walk out of the room, disgusted by the pathetic mess Elvis had turned himself into. I was furious with frustration by now. As I was leaving, Dr Nick was coming into the room. I stopped him in the doorway and said, 'You know you're killing him, don't you?'

I had to go over immediately to the coliseum and give the boys and all of the management people over there the message that Elvis wasn't coming. After word spread throughout the crowd the scene became bedlam. I had to have a police escort to get me out of the stadium.

When I got back to the Hilton, Elvis was still in bed, semi-conscious. I walked over to him and said, 'Elvis this is chicken shit. Dr Nick is killing you with all those drugs.'

When I first started working for Elvis as a teenager I really enjoyed it but I soon realised something was wrong with the whole picture and that Elvis was truly a self-destructive individual. As I look back to that evening, to my life, and the effects that Elvis has had on it, I can honestly say that that night was the beginning of the end of the Elvis Presley saga.

From the hotel, we went straight to the plane, the *Lisa Marie*, fuelled it, and flew right back to Memphis and checked him directly into the Baptist Memorial Hospital. The official record claimed that he was suffering from 'fatigue'. If we hadn't admitted him to the hospital the promoter of the Baton Rouge concert would have filed a massive lawsuit for breach of contract.

We checked Elvis into the hospital and I had to deal with my own problems. I was truly pissed off at Elvis for becoming this pathetic person I didn't know anymore.

There was no question that Elvis's mental state at this time was one of self-destruction. I am not naturally a self-destructive person but during this era I saw the beginnings of similar traits within myself and was trying to fight the temptation off.

Yes, it was true that Elvis loved being up on stage. But at the same time, he loved his drugs even more. That night the drugs were more important than the planned stadium concert and the 20,000 screaming fans. They were important enough for him to check himself into the hospital the second we got back to Memphis. His stardom no longer made him happy.

I had moved out of Graceland long before and lived at an apartment complex around the corner from there. Once Elvis was safely checked into the hospital my job was officially 'done' for the time being. I had a certain amount of responsibility and I had my comfort level. Once he was checked in, and the security guards were in place, I went home to the apartment I shared with my first wife, Angie.

I was so upset that I began drinking heavily. I then proceeded to take a handful of Valiums with the Scotch. I was still so mad when I woke up early the next morning that I got out a pair of handguns and began firing them.

Poor Angie woke up from a sound sleep that morning to the sound of gunfire as I shot round after round into the ceiling of my own living room. She thought I had lost my mind.

Then I got into my car and drove around the block to blow off steam. In my rage I lost control and smashed the car into a tree. My brother Ricky lived in the same apartment complex, and, as luck would have it, the tree I hit was right in front of his apartment. He called an ambulance, and checked me into hospital.

That afternoon I was lying in my bed with intravenous tubes in my arms. I was distraught. This hero of rock and roll, and this hero of mine whom I had known since I was a kid, was really screwed up. And, prior to this whole fiasco, I had already witnessed several nightmare scenes first hand. Now, here I was, so affected by it that I found myself in a hospital bed, flat on my back.

Later that night the door creaked open and there stood Elvis. His room was just down the hall from mine.

He said, 'What are *you* doing in here?'

I looked at him and said, 'I'm in here for the same reason that you're in here.'

'What do you mean?' he said as if he didn't have a clue what I was talking about.

I said, 'Obviously, you've done something that you don't like. Well let me tell you Elvis, *you* have done something I don't like.'

For 17 years, since the day I moved into Graceland, I had looked up to him. He was my friend, my idol, my brother, and the man who meant the most to me when I was growing up.

He was literally killing himself with all the drugs he was taking, and now he could no longer deny that I knew. He couldn't look me in the eye after that. Unable to say anything, he turned around and slowly walked out of my room. This was truly the beginning of the end.

2

My First Family – Bill and Dee Stanley

As I have already stated, the marriage of my parents was virtually destroyed by the Presley family. Although I was much too young to know all that was going on at the time, the events taking place around us were altering my destiny forever. I cannot honestly say for sure that the marriage of my natural parents would have survived if my mother had never met Vernon Presley. However, once Vernon and Elvis Presley entered the picture, the world I was to grow up to know started being shaped for me.

To understand who I am, where I came from, and to appreciate the marriage that Vernon Presley destroyed, you have to first meet my parents and know about their relationship. From what I later learned about it, it was stormy at best – even from the very beginning.

My father, William Jabe Stanley, was born on 1 September 1922 in Wilmington, North Carolina. He was the youngest of five children. He lived with his parents and siblings in a shabby unpainted house outside of town. He grew up very poor, wearing only patched hand-me-downs for clothes and rarely wore shoes as a child.

My grandfather Stanley held three jobs just to make ends meet. He was not only the sheriff of Brunswick County but he was also the local postmaster and he worked in a sawmill.

When my father was six years old, my grandfather was involved in a gory accident at the sawmill. One of his legs got caught in the belt of the saw and was literally ripped from his body. Although he survived this horrible accident and was fitted with an artificial leg, he was never to hold another steady job. As my father was later to explain, 'He started drinking, and I don't remember him ever being sober after that.'

My father had just started school that same year but no one in the family seemed to care whether or not he received a proper education. They were only concerned about the fact that it was against truancy laws for him not to be in attendance each morning.

Having replaced his three jobs with full-time drinking, Grandpa Stanley would come home at 2 or 3 in the morning, drunk, bored and wide awake. To entertain himself, he would wake my father up from a sound sleep, make him play draughts (checkers) until dawn and then send him off to school. My Dad grew to hate his father for his drunken disregard and for the fact that this one-legged man would beat him with his walking stick if he dared to doze off amid a game, or if he took too long to make a move on the draughts board.

My grandmother was a little mousey woman who never once stood up to her husband for fear that he would become physically abusive towards her. She never stood up for my six-year-old father, and accepted Grandpa's wilful temper as law.

Hating his home life and resenting his parents, my father retreated into an emotional shell that he drew around himself, like a hermit crab seeking shelter. He learned that his only defence was to spend as little time at home as humanly possible.

His best friend in school was a young boy his own age, named Vernon Teague. Vernon's father was a policeman and his mother was an outgoing woman who was warm and friendly – everything Grandma Stanley was not. At the Teagues' house, Dad was spoken to and treated like a normal person. There was always a place set at the dinner table for him and he was made to feel like a member of their family, so after a while he began spending as much time over there as he could.

My father's older brothers and sisters left my grandparents' home as soon as it was possible. The minute my Uncle Tate could enlist in the Navy he did so, simply to escape from the intolerable atmosphere in the house. My father couldn't wait until he had the opportunity to do the same thing.

Aunt Pearl married and moved away to Richmond and Uncle Earl landed a job in the same town. When my Dad was 13, Earl and Pearl came to his rescue. They moved him to Richmond to get him away from his physically and mentally abusive father.

However, after a year of alternating between sleeping on the sofas of Earl and Pearl's separate households, Dad moved with his parents to Baltimore, where they would be near his oldest sister, Nodie. He landed a job in a box factory and each week he handed over his hard-earned wages to his ungrateful parents. He grew to resent them greatly.

At the box factory he met a man who was older than he was and the man told him stories of his experiences in the Fifth Infantry Regiment of the Maryland National Guard known as the 'Dandy Fifth'. It sounded like fun and could ultimately mean more time spent away from his parents. Although he was only 15, he lied about his age and talked his way into the 'Dandy Fifth'. This led to Dad meeting and associating with many guys from all walks of life. One of his buddies suggested that Dad take a job where he worked – at a local hospital. This led to Dad working in the emergency room as an orderly. Without anything much for an education, at the age of 15 he began bettering his lot in life.

Although the United States didn't officially enter World War II until December 1941, in February of that year, Dad's National Guard regiment was mobilised into active service as part of the famed 29th Infantry Division. For the next three years, he was in constant training, preparing for the United States' inevitable confrontation with Hitler's Third Reich.

Dad had once thought it would be fun to join the service, but it had now turned into a life and death situation. His baptism-of-fire came on D-Day, the invasion of Normandy, a battle which helped turn the tide of the war in Europe. He was later to recall in his memoirs, 'At three in the morning on 6 June 1944 we were off-loaded to LCM crafts, about 36 feet long, each holding about 40 men. Each of us occupied about one square foot and carried over 125 pounds of equipment. We circled for one and a half hours in the storm, then headed for the beach. One hundred feet from shore my landing craft hit a sand bar. Thinking we were on a beach, the coxswain dropped the ramp, which was a signal to disembark. We ran into 12 feet of water. There was widespread panic. The weaker and non-swimmers drowned. The war ended for them 100 feet from the invasion on Omaha Beach. The shock, fear and reality of what happened is indescribable. When my feet touched the beach, I made my way to the shore, stumbling and pushing the bodies of my American comrades aside. There was only one way to go – ahead. Machine-gun fire hit the water, the dead bodies became sandbags and protection. Not one American son could ever be prepared for this.'

During intensive fighting in Northern France, Dad was wounded in both knees by German machine-gun fire. He was hospitalised in England, awarded the Purple Heart and was decorated with a Bronze Star for his valour at Omaha Beach. After three months of recuperation in England, Dad was returned to active duty in Cherbourg, France. His time there was shortened by the massive German offensive through Belgium's Ardennes Forest. He was transferred to the front, fighting with the Fifth Infantry Division, pushing the Nazis back into the Rhineland during what became known as the Battle of the Bulge.

Because of his heroic actions in Normandy, Northern France, and the Ardennes, General George C. Patton hand-picked my father to be one of his personal bodyguards. Dad spent the last months of the war with Patton's Third Army, crushing what was left of Germany's Third Reich, liberating the death camps, and seeing the atrocity of Hitler's madness at first hand.

After Germany's surrender in May 1945, Dad was soon shipped back to the States and stationed at Ft. Campbell, Kentucky as an MP – a member of the Fifth Infantry Division's Military Police. Standing six feet two inches tall, big, brawny, and driving his first car – a snazzy 1939 Buick – Dad was the cock-of-the-walk, a catch to any American woman he met.

One night, in a local bar, Dad was called upon to break up a drunken disturbance. There was a pretty girl at the bar that night who made quite an impression on him. She was a small blue-eyed blonde with a warm smile and an exciting and outgoing manner about her. Her name was Dee and Dad knew right then and there that she was the girl for him. Well, he was right, because she was to become my mother.

My mother had a difficult background as well, and she found out at an early age how to live by her wits to move upward in life. She was born Davada Elliot on 19 June 1925 on a small tobacco farm outside Clarksville, Tennessee, nearly 50 miles from Nashville. Her father, James Wright Elliot, and her mother, Bessie May Heath Neely, had each previously been married and divorced from their first spouses. They each came to their marriage with young sons. Mom's older half-brothers, William Elliot and Richard Neely, were six and ten when she was born. With her blonde hair and blue eyes, she was the family's 'darling' child, doted on by her parents and protected by her brothers.

After her mother became sickly and bedridden, a change came over her father. A pretty young girl was brought into the household and late at night little Davada was often awakened by the sounds of her father drinking and carousing with the new housekeeper late into the night. Along with the drinking he also had quite a temper, and my mother was later to recall, 'My father frightened me, but he would give me anything I wanted.'

Mother was just five years old when her own mother died. At first she went to live with one of her aunts in the nearby town of Waverly. A year later, Davada went back to live with her father, who would often leave her alone in the house at night to go drinking and partying until the early hours.

While Davada was still a young girl her father turned over a new leaf and turned to the church. He was stern and uncompromising when it came to raising his young daughter. By the time she was a student at Lone Oak Central High School she had grown up to be quite a beautiful girl. Standing five feet three inches tall and with her blonde hair and blues eyes she could turn heads wherever she went. She soon learned that her looks and her charm were to become the keys that would unlock many doors in life.

According to her, 'I liked excitement, and I always got bored easily. I don't think that I could have ever married a local high school boy and settled down in my home town. I wanted to travel and there were so many things I wanted to do. All my life I knew that I was going to be something.'

She decided early on that she was destined for great things and she wasn't going to settle for anything less. She made a vow that sex wasn't something that she was going to get involved in until she found the right man who was going to take her away from her repressive home town. She was later to recall, 'When a young lady gave herself in those days, it was the only thing she had to give and was supposed to be the greatest thing in the world. I could never let a man take me lightly and just go to bed with me. It was going to come very high.'

She wanted a lot out of life and she was determined to get it. 'I was convinced that if there was ever a woman in the world destined to be happy then it was me,' she claims.

Dee was always a little girl who wanted the world and everything in it. She wasn't afraid to ask for whatever she desired. She once walked out into a corn field at night, looked up at all the stars and said, 'God, I want it all.'

By the time she was 17, both of her brothers had moved north to Detroit, where they had found jobs at the Ford Motor

Company. Right after her high school graduation, she packed her bags and headed for the Motor City.

After several months of independence in the big city, she returned for a visit to her father. However, when she returned to Clarksville she was no longer smalltown Davada, she was now 'Dee', mistress of her own destiny.

During her visit she went out with one of her best friends, Jean Elrod. At the bar they chose a fight broke out and Bill Stanley and one of his buddies were called in to break up the disturbance. After the bar room brawl was over and done with Jean arranged for Dee and herself to have a double date with the two handsome soldiers from Ft. Campbell, Kentucky. Originally, Dad's friend had asked Dee to be his date but Dad convinced him to switch dates and go out with Jean.

For the date the guys took the girls to the local county fair, where they rode the rides at the midway. Dad was totally enthralled with her, recalling 'Dee laughed a lot and talked constantly. She kept things going for us. I never had been able to carry a conversation. She seemed to dance from one place to the next, and watching her was like seeing a bird in motion, occasionally lighting for us to catch up.'

She was quite taken by him as well. Bill was a combat World War II veteran with a chestful of medals. He had gone from a 15-year-old nothing to a master sergeant and he ran the whole military hero gamut. How could she not be impressed with him?

They made plans to see each other the following night. When he arrived to pick her up he was startled to find that the place she wanted to go dancing that evening was completely 'off limits' to military personnel. Risking disciplinary action from the Army, although he had only known her 48 hours, he found it impossible to say 'no' to her.

They dated steadily for eight months, and then Dad was scheduled to be shipped back to Europe, assigned to the First Infantry Division to be stationed in Bremerhaven, Germany. Mom tried to pressure Dad into marriage but he didn't feel that he was ready for that, especially since he was being shipped across the Atlantic again for an undetermined length of time.

Mom went back to Detroit and picked up her big city life, expecting to hear from Dad any day. He never wrote to her and several months passed. Eventually she decided to marry someone she met in Detroit. She informed her father of this. When Bill Stanley finally did write to Dee, Grandpa Elliot figured that there was no need to pass it on to Dee, since she was already engaged. When she found out that her Dad had burned Bill Stanley's letter to her she was furious.

Since Dad never heard back from Mom, he figured that it was all over between them and proceeded with his own life in Germany. One afternoon Dad went to the movies with a couple of his buddies and was taken aback by a couple of the girls who were working as ushers. After the movie was over, Dad introduced himself to the pretty blonde girl whom he was most impressed with and asked her out on a date that evening. She told him that her name was Mollie and that she would only accept his offer if he came home with her to meet her family beforehand.

Dad agreed and went with Mollie to her house nearby. There he was introduced to Mollie's brother and mother. Her brother was polite and pleasant but her mother gave him the cold shoulder. Dad surmised that she was bitter towards all Americans because she had lost her husband in the war, and he did not take offence.

Mollie was gentle and good to Dad and he became friendly with her brother. Eventually, even Mollie's mother warmed to him. In time, Dad felt like a welcome member of Mollie's family. However, just as things were going smoothly between Dad and Mollie, he was sent back to the United States where he was to be stationed in Harrisburg, Pennsylvania.

On a 30-day leave, he returned to Clarksville and was reunited with Dee. They resumed their relationship for several months and Mom spent quite a bit of time in Harrisburg with Dad. Again he received word that he was going to be shipped overseas. This time, he was to be in the south of Germany, far from Dee, and also far from Mollie.

His plans were changed at the last minute and again he resumed his relationship with Mollie. Although they talked about marriage in the months he spent in Bremerhaven, Dad never got around to taking that big step. The next thing he knew, he was reassigned to the post in the south of Germany, and once again he was separated from Mollie.

In the beginning of 1948 Dad was shipped home and was stationed at Camp Pickett, Virginia. At the time he was the non-commissioned officer in charge of parades and ceremonies for the candidates who were awaiting assignment at the Officers' Training School.

Dad was lonely, and spent most of his off-duty hours with a couple of married military buddies and their wives. His pals constantly bugged him about looking up his old girlfriend Dee, of whom he spoke so fondly. At their urging he got in contact with her and purchased a bus ticket for her to come for a visit. Little did he know, but his buddies had conspired with Dee, and together they had a surprise for Dad. He went with his two buddies to pick up Mom at the bus terminal and was startled when his friend drove the car they were all riding in straight to the office of the army base chaplain to make plans for them to be married.

Three days later, on 6 February 1948, my Dad married my Mom with full military honours at the camp chapel. Only hours later their marriage was off to a rocky start. After several drinks at the wedding reception, Dad found Mom in the embrace of a young lieutenant, who appeared to be taking the tradition of 'kissing the bride' a bit too far. Having had several drinks himself, Dad threw the lieutenant to the floor and promptly knocked him unconscious. From all reports I have had on the marriage of my parents that was to be the nature of their marriage: drinking, fighting and bitter misunderstandings.

Mom was later to say of Dad's excessive drinking, 'Bill never drank or even smoked a cigarette until he went through seeing his very best friend in the war get killed (which happened during the Normandy invasion at Omaha Beach). His head was completely blown off, and Bill was right there. It made him start drinking.'

After two months it was announced that the camp would be closing and Dad was transferred to Army Ground Force Headquarters in Fort Monroe, Virginia. He was assigned to the post of boat captain on base commander General Mark Clark's private yacht.

After eight years in the military Dad was used to life in the barracks, but he wanted to give Mom everything that neither of them had when they were growing up. They moved to base housing and Mom threw herself into entertaining. According to Dad, Mom went from running up bills they couldn't afford, to bills they couldn't pay, to bills that she never told him about until the collection agencies started calling. Without taking anybody's side in the matter, Mom wanted everything that she never had, whether Dad could afford it or not. She would frustrate him and he'd storm off and have one too many drinks to forget about the whole incident.

According to Dad, Mom was very wilful and loved to party until all hours at the local bars and clubs near the base. More than once he would accuse her of getting too friendly with the other soldiers on the base, and they would fight bitterly. Mom announced that she was pregnant and they thought that a baby was going to magically repair their marriage. When Mom went into labour prematurely, they both blamed each other for the loss of their first child.

When it was clear that things were not working out for them, Dad arranged to be relocated to Fort Campbell, Kentucky. He felt the change of scenery would be good for both of them and they could give their marriage a new start. They moved in with Dee's father and step-mother, and Dad hoped that they would become a tight family unit. He was horrified to find that his young wife and one of her girlfriends were hanging out at night in several of the local bars that were off limits to enlisted personnel.

My mother has always been an independent thinker. If she has ever wanted anything she has simply gone out and got it. She wasn't about to sit at home in the evening with her parents, bored and lonely. Dad would get mad at her and would storm off and begin drinking. Again he put in for a transfer, thinking that getting Dee away from her high school girlfriends would be a good move. However, life at Camp Breckenridge didn't resolve their marital problems either. With that, Dad put in for a transfer to Korea, where he would head alone, hoping that time away from each other would be good for both of them.

Apparently he thought that he had a better chance fighting with the North Koreans than he did fighting with my mother. Dad planted Mom at his mother's house in Baltimore, and headed for the battlefields of Korea.

It didn't take long for Dad to find himself back in battle. He was assigned to the First Cavalry Divison as a Platoon Sergeant. He would later recall that the war in South-east Asia was a totally different ball game to war in Europe. He recalled, 'Patrolling was difficult. The North Koreans and Chinese crawled like ants through the jungle and countryside. They covered themselves with bushes and leaves. It seemed as if bayonets suddenly came from these bushes and stabbed you in the back. We were ever leery and afraid. Preparing for battle was the toughest. We watched as thousands got themselves ready by drinking *sake*, beating drums and tin cans, waving guns and sticks, yelling at the top of their voices. They would become deathly quiet for a few minutes, then come running down the hillside like sheep. We had to cut them down as they came within range. They kept coming. We didn't dare allow them to overrun us. Many brandished sticks; there weren't enough weapons to go around. When the battle ended, thousands had been killed. Somehow they were always replaced. Another thing that bothered me was the number of young people and even kids amongst the thousands of dead. It was like nothing I had ever seen before.'

Dad was later to complain that all the time he was in Korea he never heard from Mom. He was transferred to Japan in 1952 as a harbour captain at a boat company in Yokohama. While there he studied the martial arts and eventually achieved the level of black belt in Judo and Karate.

In Yokohama he received a letter from his mother informing him that Dee had long ago moved out and was now living with a church deacon's family. Dad decided to send for Mom and take another stab at their marriage.

Mom arrived on the USS *Anderson*, which was a troop transport ship. To celebrate her arrival in Japan, Dad took Mom for a night of dinner and drinking at the Dependents' Club with several of his friends. According to Dad's version of the story, 'While at the club, several of the chief petty officers from the *Anderson* came in and took seats at the table next to us. During the evening the drinking became heavy at the sailors' table and they asked permission for Dee to dance. Their conversation was beginning to run foul, and they persisted in requesting my wife's company on the dance floor. I asked them to please watch their language, reminding them there were ladies present, and refused them Dee's company to dance. One of the more rowdy of the group asked why I had any objections to their dancing with Dee since they had no trouble getting her to dance with them while on the ship during the crossing. This comment ended in Dee not dancing at all and the chief with a broken jaw. One of his friends, coming to his rescue, ended up with a broken arm.' Well, Mom and Dad's marriage clearly picked up right where it left off.

Nothing was going to stand in the way of Mom getting whatever she wanted in life, and the only way Dad knew how to end a conflict was to punch someone's lights out and have a drink. Apparently, their way of life was to battle bitterly and then to reconcile and begin all over again. That first year in Japan, Mom again became pregnant. On 18 January 1953, she gave birth to my oldest brother, William Jabe Stanley, Jr. Two months later, she was pregnant with my other brother, Richard Earl Stanley, who was born in December 1953.

After Japan, Dad was to be stationed in Seattle, Washington, but first he was given a 30 day leave. As Dad explained it, 'We visited her brother and sister-in-law in Huntsville, Alabama. Dee's brother was an extremely religious man, and in the days we spent there, I saw that he was a good influence on Dee. So I went to the Pentagon and had my orders changed to stay in Huntsville. I decided this would be a turning point in our marriage, that I would refrain from drinking at all, and had high hopes we would again come together and be a tightly-knit family unit. Dee was a natural born party-goer and was not thrilled with my change-over, but with her brother's influence she settled down and we began to knit together. Our lives took an upward curve.'

Dad was commissioned to Warrant Officer, transferred to Fort Eustis, Virginia, and Mom was once again pregnant. Eight months after they relocated to Virginia, on 30 August 1955, Mom gave birth to me: David Edward Stanley.

Looking back on the year after I was born, Mom claimed that Dad drank too much, which made her unhappy. Dad claimed that to get even Mom spent more money than she and Dad made in income, essentially driving him to drink. Again Dad felt that a geographic change was what his family needed if his marriage was going to survive.

With that, he requested to be transferred back to Europe. Dad, Mom, Ricky, Billy and I flew to Bremerhaven, Germany, where we boarded a train for Orleans, France. I was only a year and a half old at this point. Along with another military family we all moved into a French chateau, which was divided up into apartments. At first, the change of scenery seemed like a good thing for my parents. But soon they were battling with each other.

According to Dad, Mom insisted on spending too much money entertaining the neighbours in a gregarious fashion. She ran up bills that were so high that Dad was told by his commanding officer, 'Pay the bills or stand court martial.'

Things really came to a head on Thanksgiving Day of that year when Dad decided to take all of us for a family dinner at the NCO club on base. In the chateau in which we were living the heating was provided by kerosene burning heaters. As we were about to pull out of the driveway, Mom asked Dad if the heaters had been turned down or not. While we all waited in the car, Mom ran back inside to check the heaters. She quickly returned to the car and off we went.

When we returned to the chateau, black clouds of smoke were billowing out of the windows and from underneath the doors.

Mom had turned the knobs up instead of down. When the smoke cleared, they were horrified to find that everything they owned was ruined. The five of us then moved to a tiny apartment with only two rooms. Dad later recalled, 'Our meals had to be taken downstairs at the club. There wasn't room for three small kids to play or move around. Dee and the three boys were cramped in the two rooms all day. There was no play area for the children to get outside; besides, the weather was too cold.'

Dad would come home from work and Mom wanted a break. So, he would babysit us and Mom would go downstairs to the enlisted men's nightclub on base.

After a year in France, Dad put in for another transfer. He had liked life in Germany and made arrangements to move us to Bootsbach. To fight the boredom, Mom would throw dinner parties and insisted on hiring a maid. Again, Mom was restless, and Dad was too busy and preoccupied to fight with her.

At this point, Mom and Dad began enlisting the maid they hired as a babysitter for my brothers and me and they would go out on the town together. Dad was later to explain, 'Dee was anxious to get out on the town once again. So we began our rounds of night-club hopping two or three times a week . . . I found my time pulled between a socially-minded wife and three boys I loved dearly. I felt obligated to keep up with my wife.'

On one of their nights on the town, Mom mentioned to Dad that there were rumours that there was a show business celebrity stationed on the same base. Word had it that it was that popular young American singer everyone was talking about: Elvis Presley.

3

My Second Family –
The Presleys

At the same time that all of these events were happening, there was another family history unfolding. This was the Presley family, and little did anyone suspect it at the time but this was the family that I was to become part of, to be educated by, and destined to grow up in. How could anyone have predicted that Elvis Presley's family was to become my own, and that my father, Bill Stanley Sr., was destined to become but a distant stranger to me, whom I was to see only once or twice every couple of years?

From everything that I know about Vernon Presley, his son Elvis, and the whole Presley clan, there could not have been a more unlikely group of people destined to become show business royalty, cult-worshipped entertainers, or multi-millionaires. However, that was exactly what was to happen. And, who could ever have foreseen that I was going to end up raised in the circus-like atmosphere that they were to create around them?

The Presley family was even less well-off than the household that my father grew up in. Through old emigration records, Vernon Presley could trace his family tree back to the 1740s, when an Anglo-Irishman by the name of David 'Pressley' first came to North America, landing in New Bern, North Carolina. His grandson, Andrew Pressley Jr. is known to have fought in the Revolutionary War, and it was David's great-great-grandson, Dunnan Pressley Jr. who first migrated to the state of Mississippi, in the mid-1800s. According to court records from this era it is known that although Dunnan married Martha Jane Wesson in Fulton, Mississippi in 1861 he also had another wife and set of children whom he had abandoned in North Carolina.

By 1862, Dunnan and Martha had two infant daughters, Rosalina and Rosella. According to family legend, the girls' grandparents took Martha and her two daughters to church one Sunday and when they returned from the service Dunnan was long gone, having abandoned them to return to his first family. Little Rosella was to grow up and become Elvis's great-grandmother. Never married, Rosella kept her Pressley name and eventually bore nine illegitimate children. Rosella and her brood would support themselves as wandering farm hands, picking up work, and moving onward whenever times became rough. Eventually they settled in the vicinity of East Tupelo, Mississippi.

One of Rosella's sons, Jessie Pressley, married Minnie Mae Hood in 1913 and they had two sons – Vester and Vernon. With jet black hair, and a penchant for flashy clothes, Elvis's grandpa Jessie also loved to drink whiskey, and often spent the night in the local jail, sobering up after a night of brawling in the local bars.

Elvis's mother, Gladys, whom I never met, also came from a wandering family who started out in the Carolinas and eventually migrated to Mississippi. His great-great-grandfather, John Smith, was listed in the 1850 census as a resident of Atlanta, Georgia. In 1874, his son Obe Smith married a widow by the name of Ann Mansel, and they settled in Saltillo, Mississippi, north of Tupelo. Amongst their children, was the second-born child, Robert Lee Smith, Elvis's grandfather. According to the records, he married Octavia Lavinia 'Doll' Mansell. It has long been suspected that Robert Lee and his bride were actually first cousins, and the children that they bore can blame many of their maladies in life on this fact.

Robert and Doll's children included Elvis's mother, Gladys Smith, and her three brothers. Tragically, none of them was to live to see the age of 50, and emotional and drinking problems seemed to run rampant amongst the boys in the family. Of her brothers, Tracy was born deaf and could never speak properly, and Travis and Johnny were both heavy drinkers who died young. It is no mere coincidence that Gladys was to die at the age of 46, and her son Elvis was to die the year he turned 42.

As a young girl in the early 1930s, Gladys Smith landed a job as a seamstress at the Tupelo Garment Company. She earned $13.00 a week for sewing shirts together on an assembly line. She was 21 years old when she met and fell in love with a handsome, blond, curly haired, 17-year-old farm worker by the name of Vernon. Nearly illiterate, it was Vernon who mistakenly dropped a letter 's' from the family name, thus altering it to its present spelling of 'Presley'. Vernon was later to mis-spell Elvis's middle name of 'Aron' on his tombstone as 'Aaron'.

According to people who knew her, Gladys was an imaginative and outgoing person who had fallen head-over-heels in love with Vernon. They both lied about their ages on their marriage certificate, claiming that she was 19 and he was 21, and on 17 June 1933, they became man and wife. For the first year they were married, Vernon and Gladys lived with his parents, the Jessie Pressleys.

Gladys discovered that she was pregnant in the spring of 1934 and Vernon began making plans for them to move into their own house not long after that. Vernon at the time was working for a cattle and hog farmer by the name of Orville S. Bean. He secured a $180.00 loan from Orville, and with the money purchased the lumber and supplies to construct a two room 'shotgun' cabin. Located on North Saltillo Road, the cabin was known as a 'shotgun' structure because one room led to the next in such a fashion that every item in it could be struck by the bullet of a single shotgun if fired from any direction.

On the bitterly cold morning of 8 January 1935, Gladys went into labour. She had never seen a doctor regarding her pregnancy up until this point, but harboured the idea that she was carrying twins. Her premonition proved correct. According to the record book kept by Dr William Robert Hunt, at 4 a.m. that morning Gladys gave birth to a stillborn son, whom she named Jessie Garon Presley. At 4.35 she delivered the second child and he was named Elvis Aron Presley. According to the doctor's records, Vernon and Gladys were unable to afford the $15.00 fee that he charged, and he was forced to recoup his money from the local welfare bureau. Jessie Garon Presley was buried in an unmarked grave in Priceville Cemetery.

According to all written accounts, Gladys Presley was very protective of her young son Elvis. Perhaps the fact that she had lost the stillborn Jessie Garon made her doubly concerned for little Elvis. Gladys would speak to Elvis of Jessie Garon as an angel hovering over him, looking out for his well-being. In time, Elvis was to claim that his dead twin brother spoke to him in a way that only he could hear.

Gladys, who had been such an effervescent person experienced a growing feeling of loss in the early 1930s. She had buried – in unmarked pauper's graves – both her father and her stillborn twin son Jessie Garon, and then two years later, her mother was deathly ill with tuberculosis. After her mother died, Gladys didn't think things could get much worse. She was wrong.

Still struggling to make ends meet, Gladys's brother Travis Smith, Vernon, and a friend named Luther Gable were charged with forgery. It seems that Vernon and his friends were issued with cheques for sharecropping on Orville S. Bean's property, and the trio added numerals to the cheques in an attempt to receive greater amounts of money. This turned out to be a big mistake, compounded by the fact that the three of them claimed that they were innocent of the charges, although the evidence of the forged cheques was in the possession of the court. The following May, at the 11th hour, Vernon and his cronies changed their plea to 'guilty as charged' in the hope that the court would be lenient. Instead they all headed off to prison to serve three year sentences. To complete the picture, Orville Bean threw Gladys and three-year-old Elvis out of the legendary shotgun cabin, and they moved in with Gladys's in-laws.

Supposedly, Gladys was so over-protective of Elvis that she actually walked him to school and back again in the afternoon – right up to high school. There was a strong and unbreakable bond between Gladys and her son which bordered on the obsessive.

With her family dropping dead at early ages all around her, and her husband in jail, she began to drink heavily. An overweight drunk, she always seemed to have raccoon-like dark circles around her eyes. Elvis grew up attached to Gladys with almost incestuous overtones. Because of this, he was to grow up with a totally warped sensibility when it came to the opposite sex.

While Vernon was doing time behind bars, Gladys all but crushed young Elvis with attention. She used to sleep in the same bed with him because he had bad recurring nightmares. He would have bizarre dreams, and he would tear the covers off the bed and claw at the mattress. In hindsight it seems almost as if Elvis knew when he was a kid that he was going to have an incredible and extensive success in his life, and he proceeded as if all of his dreams – both good and bad – were going to come true.

Vernon spent much of his prison term at Parchman Prison picking and bailing cotton and farming and picking corn for the state. He served most of his sentence and on 4 January 1941 he was released five months early for good behaviour. He continued to do farm work until 1946 when he moved his family into Tupelo and landed a job as a truck driver for a grocery wholesaler.

According to legend, Elvis was first exposed to music in church services which he attended with his parents. He sang songs and hymns in church with Vernon and Gladys and became fascinated with singing. He made his first public performance at the age of 11 singing *Old Shep*, which is a sentimental song about the loss of a beloved pet dog. He sang it in a competition and took the first prize.

Although they were 'dirt poor', Vernon and Gladys did their best to spoil little Elvis. Two of his prized possessions were his bicycle and his guitar. How could they have known at the time what an influential gift that guitar was to have been?

When Elvis was growing up in Tupelo there was a local country singer by the name of Mississippi Slim and he had a younger brother named James, who just happened to be in Elvis's class at Milham Junior High School. On Saturdays, Mississippi Slim would broadcast his singing show on local radio station WELO in front of a tiny studio audience. Elvis attended several of these shows since the station was just across the alley from where the Presleys lived.

In September 1948, Vernon, Elvis and Gladys packed up all of their belongings in a 1939 Plymouth and headed for Memphis, where there were more job opportunities. They spent a cruel winter in a cockroach-infested house and on 1 May 1949 they moved into a welfare housing project known as Lauderdale Courts. They had no sooner moved into their two-bedroom first floor apartment when Vernon's mother Minnie Mae moved in.

In Memphis, Vernon drove a truck for a while, then took a job with the United Paint Company. His job was packing paint cans in wooden crates, a position he was to hold for five years.

As a young teenager, Elvis attended L.C. Humes High School. His first steady girlfriend was Betty McMann, who lived on the third floor of the same project building complex. Occasionally on summer nights, Elvis would get his guitar out and sing country songs he had learned from listening to the radio.

In September 1950 Elvis was a sophomore in high school and had landed his first job as an usher at Loew's State Theater on Main Street. Worried about the late nights interfering with Elvis's schoolwork, Gladys convinced him to quit. At the annual Christmas high school variety show his teacher, Miss Elsie Schivener, persuaded him to enter. He repeated his rendition of *Old Shep*, and again he won the first prize.

Around this time, the look of tough street punks was personified by sideburns, and greased back 'D.A.' haircuts, which ended up at the back with a 'ducktail' flip. Elvis started sporting such a haircut and began wearing flashy clothes. Once a quiet young boy who blended into the crowd, Elvis was starting to develop a look and a reputation for being the flashy would-be singer.

With his greased-up hairstyle, Elvis tried out for the high school football team in August 1951. The football coach wouldn't let Elvis on the team with that hairstyle. He ridiculed him so much that after the tryout a group of high school 'jocks' were going to pin him down and shear his hair when one of his buddies, Red West, intervened and broke up the scuffle. Elvis was to remain close friends with Red West for the rest of his life and I would come to know him as the oldest and most devoted of Elvis's core group of friends, who later became known as the 'Memphis Mafia'.

That fall, Elvis began hanging out in the local clubs in Memphis, exposing himself to all kinds of music, from blues, to country, to gospel. In 1953, during his senior year in high school, he continued to distinguish himself from his classmates with his upswept hairdo. In addition to Red, Elvis also became chummy with Marty Lacker, whose family had just moved to Memphis from New York. Marty was another of Elvis's friends whom I came to know in the Memphis Mafia.

With Vernon working, Elvis picking up a part-time job at Marl Metal as a metal fabricator and Gladys beginning to work as a nurses' aid, the family's income exceeded $3,000 for the very first time and they had to move out of welfare housing. They moved from house to house, finally settling at an apartment at 462 Alabama Street. On 3 June 1953 Elvis graduated from high school. The following day, he began a new job at Parker Machinists Shop.

On 18 July of that year, something very monumental happened. Elvis decided that as a birthday present to his mother he would go to Sam Phillips's Memphis Recording Studio, to cut a two-sided 'acetate' recording of himself singing and playing his guitar. This pair of historic recordings can be heard on compact disc today and are known for having begun the most successful solo recording career in history. At the recording studio that afternoon while Elvis was waiting to record, the office manager, Marion Keisker, chatted with Elvis and she was convinced that he was someone very unique with an overwhelming amount of raw talent. She had a feeling he would be back.

Elvis floated from one job to another that year, landing a job at Precision Tool, working on the assembly line. He then began working at Crown Electric, where he drove a truck around town, from construction site to construction site, delivering electrical supplies.

During his time off, he frequented the music clubs around town and began to emulate some of the outlandish clothing styles of the blues performers he saw. At a local revival meeting, Elvis was exposed to the gospel stylings of several famed vocal performers and groups, including J.D. Sumner.

Marion Keisker was right, and on 4 January 1954, Elvis parked his Crown Electric truck in front of Memphis Recording Studio, and recorded two more 'sides' that day. This time Sam Phillips paid closer attention to Elvis. After he had recorded *Casual Love Affair* and *I'll Never Stand In Your Way*, and had left, Phillips commented to Keisker that in his opinion, Elvis needed some more work before he had any commercial potential.

On 26 June of that year, Sam was set to record a song that he really felt would become a hit. It was called *Without You*, and Sam had another singer lined up, who cancelled the session at the last minute. In a pinch, he phoned Elvis and asked him to come down to the studio immediately. Sam wasn't entirely happy with Elvis's recording, so he had a guitar-playing friend, Scotty Moore, get in touch with Presley, and work on his singing style. On 5 July Scotty, Elvis, and bass player Bill Black went into Sun Recording Studios and recorded his first professional session. What they produced that afternoon was to become Elvis's first hit recording, *That's All Right (Mama)*.

Sam Phillips had a friend by the name of Lamar Fike who was interested in becoming a disc jockey. He would often come into the studios to see how the music business worked and to discover the ins and outs of a recording studio. Sam had played one of Elvis's first demos for him, to see what he thought. Lamar told him that he really liked the recording, so Sam invited him to attend the 5 July session. From that point on, Lamar was to be part of Elvis's inner circle.

The song was released to the public later that month, and on 30 July Elvis Presley performed his first billed concert date, as the first of two opening acts for the *Slim Whitman Show* at the Overton Park Shell in Memphis. Throughout the following month Elvis went out on tour with Scotty Moore and Bill Black backing him. His pal Red West accompanied them out of town for several dates in Texas. This was the beginning of Elvis's insistence that he always travel with a group of one or more of his friends accompanying him wherever he went.

In September, accompanied by Sam, Marion, Scotty and Bill, Elvis went to Nashville to make his debut on the *Grand Ole Opry* radio show. Although he had become a huge hit on the Memphis club circuit, at country capital Nashville they turned up their noses at his music and his rhythm and blues-based rock sound. The following week, Elvis was back in the recording studio recording three new sides, including *Good Rockin' Tonight*.

He continued to hold court at Memphis nightclubs, primarily at the Eagle's Nest. On 16 October 1954 he made his debut on the famed country music radio programme *Louisiana Hayride* and suddenly things started to click. His version of *Blue Moon Of Kentucky* hit the Top Ten charts in Nashville and Louisiana, and by November Elvis signed a contract to appear on *Louisiana Hayride* every week for the remainder of the year.

That was the first month that he received a royalty cheque from Sun Records and he immediately went out and bought himself his first brand new car – a pink Cadillac.

As a headliner on *Louisiana Hayride*'s Saturday night weekly broadcasts, Elvis's popularity just continued to grow in leaps and bounds. In January, drummer D.J. Fontana joined Scotty and Bill in Elvis's band, the Blue Moon Boys. At the same time, Elvis signed with Bob Neal as his personal manager. By May, the success of his recordings and personal appearances had kept him so busy that he was forced to buy his way out of his weekly contract to free himself for the growing demand for concert performances. He agreed to make occasional appearances on the programme through 1955 as part of the deal.

Throughout his time at Sun Records, Elvis was marketed as a rockabilly/country performer. However, with songs like Bill Haley and the Comets' *Rock Around The Clock* in the charts, rock and roll was beginning to gain popularity and it was obvious that Elvis was destined for bigger things than just the country market. His songs from this era included *Milkcow Boogie Blues*, *Baby Let's Play House*, and *I Forgot To Remember To Forget*.

Booked on Hank Snow's Jamboree tour in May, Elvis caused a sensation wherever he went. With his wild on-stage gyrations, and his smooth rockabilly songs, Elvis put Sun Records on the map. Unfortunately, they were unable to keep up with the demand for his records and Sam Phillips was sinking in debts. By the end of the year, Hank Snow's manager, Colonel Tom Parker, had managed to squeeze Bob Neal out of the picture as he stepped into the seat of personal manager for Elvis. One of his first business deals for Elvis was to negotiate a new recording contract with a major label, so that Sam Phillips could make back his investment, plus a healthy profit, and so that Elvis would be with a label that had more power and clout. RCA Victor won the bidding war, paying Sam Phillips $35,000, as well as paying Elvis a $5,000 bonus for royalties owed to him.

The year 1956 virtually belonged to Elvis. There wasn't a top-rated network television variety show in America that didn't turn cartwheels to have an appearance from him by the time it was over. In turn, the exposure he received from television catapulted his career into the stratosphere. Starting with his first Number One single, *Heartbreak Hotel*, RCA began pumping out hit after hit. Four more times during the year he hit Number One – with *I Want You, I Need You, I Love You, Don't Be Cruel, Hound Dog* and with *Love Me Tender*. Elvis occupied the Number One slot on America's record charts for 26 weeks out of that year.

Part of the reason for the huge success was the total multi-media approach that was employed that year in launching the career of Elvis. People often criticise the efforts of Colonel Tom Parker for the way he managed Elvis's career in the later years, but it is impossible to criticise the launch that Elvis received in 1956. Not only was he all over the radio airwaves, but he was also one of the hottest draws on American network television and he made his movie debut that same year.

While all of this was happening, RCA Records was able to release 17 Elvis Presley hit singles that year. So hot was he, that he also racked up six Top 20 hits in Great Britain as well.

There is no question that controversy fanned the flames of Elvis's initial popularity. No one had ever seen anything like him. He virtually mesmerised teenage girls with his overtly sexual bumping and grinding in the middle of a song. Television didn't know what to do with him and because he was so offensively sexual they did everything they could to tame him but to no avail.

In 1956, as millions of parents of teenage girls in homes across America caught Elvis's act in their living rooms, they were instantly appalled. Almost unanimously they perceived Presley as being every bit as threatening to their daughters' safety as the black-leather jacketed motorcycle maniac portrayed by Marlon Brando in the '50s cult film *The Wild One*. That same year, John Crosby wrote a scalding editorial in *The New York Herald* which asked, 'Where do you go from Elvis Presley – short of obscenity, which is against the law!?!?'

America in 1956 was ripe and ready for excitement. The post-McCarthy era viewers needed some shaking up, and some fun – and Elvis arrived at just the right time to deliver just that. What few people realise is that Elvis had been totally rejected by television only one year before. He had auditioned for *Arthur Godfrey and His Friends* in 1955, and he was crushed when the show flatly turned him down as a potential guest. As it turned out, he made his network debut on an unlikely low-rated show called *Stage Show*, which starred 1940s big band leaders Tommy and Jimmy Dorsey.

To fit into the 'big band' format of the staid variety programme, Elvis and his rock combo were accompanied by the show's full orchestra. The first song that he sang on the show was *Blue Suede Shoes*. The tune was coming out so tamely that at one point in the song, Elvis shouted to the musicians, 'Rock it! Go, man go!' to get the tempo cranked up. For his second number, Elvis sang the newly-recorded *Heartbreak Hotel*, which ended up losing much of its rocking fire in this fully orchestrated version. However, he made quite an impressive impact.

The telephone switchboard at CBS-TV virtually lit up from calls around America asking 'What the hell was that on *Stage Show*?' Jackie Gleason, who 'presented' the Dorsey show on the air, remarked with disbelief, 'The kid has no right behaving like a sex maniac on a national show!'

He was able to turn each of his television performances into rock and roll showcases. Suddenly all eyes were on this ball of energy and his outrageously suggestive musical performances. Meanwhile, RCA released the Elvis Presley album in April 1956, and it immediately became the fastest selling LP in the company's history.

On 23 April 1956 Elvis opened at the New Frontier Hotel, for his first Las Vegas engagement. Although he was originally booked to perform for four weeks, the ticket sales for the engagement were so disappointing that it was cut short after two weeks. Las Vegas was such a staid environment at that time, that a teenage idol was a totally foreign creature to them. Thirteen years later, Elvis would change their tune when he became the city's biggest draw. Instead, Colonel Parker had other things up his sleeve for Elvis. He was going to become a movie star.

On 6 April 1956 Elvis signed his first film contract, a seven-year deal with Paramount Pictures. Hal B. Wallis was part of the production deal, specifying that Elvis would be doing three films on an upwardly sliding pay scale, beginning with $100,000 for the first one, and $200,000 for the third. Principal photography on *Love Me Tender* was set to commence on 23 August in Hollywood.

On the personal side of things, Elvis was becoming so rich that he was able to buy his parents a new house. On 11 May 1956, he purchased it with $40,000 cash, and they moved into 1034 Audobon Drive in Memphis. They had come a long way from the $180 shotgun cabin they once lived in on the poor side of Tupelo. In the Presley family, his wealth was unprecedented, and paying cash for a $40,000 house was unheard of. The neighbourhood was reportedly very unhappy that this 'hillbilly' rock star had moved into this exclusive area, especially since it became a Mecca to teenage sightseers who loved to drive by and gawp.

With *Heartbreak Hotel* lodged at Number One, and the demand for Elvis's first album outrageously strong, other television variety programmes were chomping at the bit to book Elvis. Unfortunately, many of them were very poorly handled. He found himself trapped in silly comedy skits on the *Milton Berle Show*, and dressed uncomfortably in a tuxedo and tails on the *Steve Allen Show*. However, the sex appeal showed through.

As the grand finale to his appearance on Steve Allen's show, Elvis was forced to sing *Hound Dog* to a real live dog – a basset hound. The following day, groups of irate teenagers picketed the NBC-TV studios carrying protest signs that read, 'We Want the REAL Elvis!' Regardless of any repercussions, the mission was accomplished, as Steve Allen had finally beaten his strongest competition on the airwaves, the *Ed Sullivan Show*.

Elvis's appearances on the *Ed Sullivan Show* are nothing short of legendary. When Sullivan was originally approached by the William Morris Agency about booking Elvis for one appearance for the fee of $5,000 Ed reportedly replied, 'I wouldn't touch him with a ten-foot pole.' However, after being trounced in the ratings by Presley's appearance on the competing *Steve Allen Show*, he was forced to change his tune.

Sullivan cut a deal that would entail three Presley guest appearances over a six-month span for a total fee of $50,000. The first time he performed on the Sullivan show was on 9 September 1956. It was telecast as a 'live remote' from Hollywood. On the show that night, Elvis sang three songs: *Don't Be Cruel, Ready Teddy* and *Hound Dog*. The number of viewers was reported as being an incredible 54 million people across America. That particular programme set an all-time ratings record for the Sullivan show, garnering 82.6 per cent of the viewers!

On 28 October 1956 Elvis hade his second appearance on the programme, singing *Love Me Tender*, *Love Me*, *Don't Be Cruel* and *Hound Dog*. It was on that show that he announced that his debut film, *Love Me Tender*, co-starring Richard Egan and Debra Paget, was scheduled to open in theatres by Thanksgiving.

During this era, one would assume that Elvis would be a natural for an appearance on Dick Clark's *American Bandstand* television show. This was the top-rated teenage rock and roll dance party programme but his manager Colonel Parker wouldn't allow Elvis to appear for the 'scale' amount of money that Clark was offering.

On Halloween, 31 October 1956, Hollywood stars Natalie Wood and Nick Adams arrived in Memphis to see Elvis and to hang out with him. The trio rode Harley Davidson motorcycles, went out on the town, and cruised around Memphis for fun. The hot rumour was that Elvis and Natalie were having an affair and when the newspapers got hold of the story, they called it Elvis's 'Motorcycle Romance'.

When Natalie and Nick went with Elvis to his newly-purchased house, Natalie was reportedly appalled by what she saw there. The driveway was littered with autograph-seeking fans, awaiting the arrival of the stars. It wasn't just a handful of teenage girls – there were hundreds of people, and even vendors selling popcorn and hot dogs. She was even more taken aback when Elvis insisted that Natalie, Nick and he go out to chat with the fans for half an hour, commenting that these people were the reason that they were stars, and that they had to be catered to. A native of Beverly Hills, Natalie was shocked by the lack of privacy that Elvis accepted as normal.

According to several people, Elvis had a strange bond with his mother, Gladys. She was very possessive of him, and oddly jealous of the young girls who showed an interest in her son. Lana Wood, Natalie's sister recalls Natalie calling home to California after only two days with Elvis and Nick and complaining, 'Gladys has wrecked everything. I don't have a chance [with Elvis]. Get me out of this, and fast.'

On 15 November *Love Me Tender* opened at the Paramount Theater in New York City. On top of the marquee in Times Square, they erected a huge 40 feet tall poster of guitar-wielding Elvis. The crowds were so huge that people had to be turned away from the theatre. On 21 November, the film went into national distribution, and it was an instant hit. In the original version of the film, the character that Elvis portrayed died at the end of the film. Preview audiences who saw it in September reacted so violently that a new ending had to be filmed so that Elvis could live on forever.

On 4 December Elvis dropped by Sun Records for old times' sake and he ran into Carl Perkins recording a song with Jerry Lee Lewis playing piano. When Johnny Cash showed up, the foursome began fooling around with songs in the studio. Sam Phillips wisely turned on the tape recorder, and captured what was to become known as the *Million Dollar Quartet*. The sessions by Perkins, Lewis, Presley and Cash remained in the can until 1977, when they were finally brought out of the vaults.

That Christmas, Elvis celebrated the holiday with his parents and several of his friends. Red West, who had joined the Marines, was on leave and was present to play touch football with Elvis and his pals.

In October of the busiest year of his life Elvis heard from the local draft board about his induction into the army. On 4 January he reported to Kennedy Veterans' hospital for a pre-induction physical. He passed, and was subsequently classified as being '1-A' – or perfect draft material. No efforts were made to dissuade the army into re-classifying him. Popular singer Eddie Fisher had nearly ruined his own career when he had wriggled out of being drafted. This could not happen to Elvis, for fear that it might have an adverse effect on the controversial yet strangely 'all-American' image he was projecting.

His third and last visit to the *Ed Sullivan Show* came on 6 January 1957. He sang a total of five songs and this was the programme on which Elvis was filmed 'from the waist only' to avoid any shots of him humping the microphone stand mid-song, or offending anyone in any way. After Elvis had finished performing, Ed Sullivan made a public statement announcing what a moral, decent and mature young man Elvis had been to work with – even though he gyrated while singing.

On 21 January 1957, Elvis began principal photography for his second film, *Loving You*, co-starring Lizabeth Scott and Delores Hart. He was able to get his parents in the movie as well, using them as extras in the audience in one of the concert scenes. In March, right after the movie was wrapped, Elvis returned to Memphis, where he purchased his palatial mansion, Graceland.

So much of the Elvis legend is wrapped up in that magical house. He purchased it for $100,000, which at the time seemed like a fortune. One reason for this purchase was to give his family a home that was large enough to accommodate everyone and the other reason was because it was secure enough for safety reasons. It was to become a monument to the legacy of Elvis. Vernon and Gladys moved into Graceland on 10 April and Elvis stayed there for a month-long rest in between concert tours and movie schedules. By 1 May Elvis was back in Los Angeles to begin pre-production on his third film *Jailhouse Rock*.

While he was filming it, he heard from Sam Phillips's aspiring disc jockey friend, Lamar Fike. He had been working at a radio station in rural Jacksonville, Texas, when he phoned Elvis in Hollywood. When he told Elvis that he hated the job and was bored in Texas, Elvis told him to get in his car and drive on out to stay with him. Lamar Fike was with Elvis from then until 1977. He became the first non-family member who lived at Graceland with the Presleys. Elvis had gathered another member who would be part of his Memphis Mafia.

Throughout this era, eligible bachelor Elvis was linked romantically with every young starlet under the sun. For a short while he was dating an actress by the name of Yvonne Lime, who had been one of his co-stars in the film *Loving You*.

In July 1957 he began going out with a pretty young Memphis girl by the name of Anita Wood (no relation of Natalie). In Memphis, Elvis and Anita went on a double date with his parents, Vernon and Gladys. They went to a local theatre to see his new film, *Loving You*. It was a special screening not open to the public, but rented out by Elvis for his guests.

Elvis seemed quite serious about his relationship with Anita. While she was in Memphis with him, he presented her with a sapphire and diamond ring.

After spending a month of dates with Anita in Memphis, Elvis left for the American Northwest for a series of concerts in Spokane, Vancouver, Seattle and Portland. The opening Spokane date was a huge success and Elvis sang 18 of his hit songs to the screaming crowd. However, days later, near pandemonium broke out in Portland and Elvis was forced to leave the stage after performing for only 15 minutes so that the security guards could restore order.

The next day, Elvis boarded a train and headed down the west coast for Los Angeles, where he had a rendezvous with Anita Wood, and began work on his forthcoming Christmas album. She had recently won a beauty contest in New Orleans, and was given a screen test.

On 28 and 29 October, Elvis performed two highly-touted concerts at the Pan-American Auditorium. Amongst the Hollywood stars who showed up to witness the King of Rock and Roll in action were Ricky Nelson, Russ Tamblyn, Carol Channing, Rita Moreno, Tommy Sands, Nick Adams, Sammy Davis Jr. and Vince Edwards. There was so much controversy about Elvis's sexual pelvis thrusting on-stage gyrations, that the first show was actually taped by the Los Angeles Police Department, just so that they had evidence if there was any lewd behaviour on stage amid the show.

After he sang his first song that evening, Elvis announced from the stage, 'I'm sorry this came up, but we're not gonna let it stop us from puttin' on the best show we can for you people. If they think it's obscene, that's their problem, not mine!' He then put his two thumbs and forefingers together, and hovering the circle they made over his head like a halo, proclaimed, 'I'm gonna be an angel tonight!'

During this year, Elvis kept pumping out the hit records with hot succession, including: *Too Much*, *All Shook Up*, *Teddy Bear*, and the international hit, *Jailhouse Rock*. Everything that he touched seemed to turn instantly to gold. It was this same year that the Hollywood designer, Nudie, created a gold lamé suit for Elvis as a publicity stunt. The suit cost an outrageous $10,000 and was made with real gold threads.

On 17 October Elvis' third film *Jailhouse Rock* had its debut in Memphis. When RCA released the soundtrack album it became an instant million seller. It seemed as if nothing could stop the incredible momentum of Elvis's career – except perhaps the army.

4

Tempted by the Fruit of Another

In November of 1957, Elvis returned to Graceland to spend the Thanksgiving and Christmas holidays with Vernon and Gladys. On the 19th of that month Elvis received his draft notice. It stated that he was to report to the Memphis Draft board on 20 January 1958. However, since he was scheduled to begin filming *King Creole* on 13 January in Hollywood, a two month extension was requested. It was granted. He ended 1957 with a sold-out New Year's Eve concert in St Louis.

Filming for *King Creole* began on the 20th, a week late. That was wedged in between recording dates on 15, 16, 23 January and 1 February at Radio Recorders Studio in Los Angeles. These sessions yielded 17 songs, including those for the movie soundtrack.

On 6 February accompanied by Nick Adams and an entourage, Elvis and the rest of the cast and crew of *King Creole* headed for New Orleans for location filming. Filming ended on the 10th and he returned to Memphis, to catch his breath and get ready to report to the military.

Every night in Memphis, from 14 March until he left town, he rented out the Rainbow Rollerdome, where he had parties for his family and friends. It was at one of these roller skating parties that Red West introduced Elvis to his cousin, burly Sonny West. Sonny was eventually to become a member of Elvis's Memphis Mafia when he returned from Germany. On 15 March he performed his final pre-induction concert at Russwood Park in Memphis, and ended the last roller skating party early that morning.

At 6.30 a.m. on 24 March 1958, Elvis arrived at the local draft board. His entourage, who all pulled up in late model Cadillacs and Continentals, included Gladys, Vernon, Lamar Fike, Colonel Parker, his uncle Vester Presley, Anita Wood and several others. As he was taken in a bus with the other recruits to Kennedy Veterans' Hospital for his final physical and processing, a whole procession of these high profile cars followed him there and then back to the draft board that afternoon. He was sworn in as soldier 55310761, and into the army he went. That evening he was on a bus headed for Fort Chaffee, Arkansas.

At 5.30 a.m. the next morning, when Private Elvis Presley awoke, Colonel Parker and a team of press photographers were there to capture his every historic move. Never before in history had a peacetime soldier received so much publicity simply for having been drafted.

The press circus atmosphere continued through all of his military activities, so that the newspapers and magazines could run photos of Elvis being issued a uniform, being weighed, receiving his first $7.00 military paycheck, and getting a military haircut.

On 1 June after completing his basic training, Elvis was met at Ft. Hood by Anita Wood, who drove him to Memphis for two weeks of leave time. He continued the all-night roller skating parties with his family and friends, and he and Vernon and Gladys got a chance to screen the final version of *King Creole*.

When he reported back to Ft. Hood, Elvis received his orders to spend the next eight weeks in Armour Crewman's school. He was allowed to live off the base, and he rented a large house in Killeen, Texas. Vernon, Gladys, Grandma Minnie Mae, and Lamar Fike all lived in the house with him, and for a while life went on just like normal. That was until August, when Gladys suddenly became ill.

Gladys looked 20 years older than her age of 46. She was grossly overweight and had been taking diet pills in hope of shedding the weight. She also drank alcohol to excess and chewed tobacco. Her diet consisted mainly of bacon, pork and heavy gravies. In other words, she did not take very good care of herself and slowly her health had gone downhill.

She was treated by a local doctor but when she was clearly not improving, she was taken to Methodist Hospital in Memphis. Jaundiced, she was diagnosed as having acute hepatitis. On 11 August Elvis went to Memphis on leave to spend the evening by her side. At 3.15 a.m. on 14 August she passed away. The doctors were rather mystified by her sudden death but Elvis would not permit an autopsy to be performed on her.

A friend of the family was later to explain, 'She wanted to be what she thought Elvis wanted her to be. She wanted to look good for Elvis, to be thin and attractive. But she was not supposed to be thin and she stayed heavy, and began to put on more weight. She began to take pills, diet pills. I guess they became a habit with her. And then she switched to alcohol. All she wanted was to make Elvis proud. She just wanted him to be proud of her, and, of course he *was* proud of her. But she kept on taking those pills and drinking . . . and finally her big ol' heart gave out.'

Her body was brought back to Graceland to lay in state, and on 15 August she was laid to rest at Forest Lawn Cemetery. That same week Red West's father died, and on 16 August Elvis, Lamar and the growing Memphis Mafia attended the funeral. With Red's father's death, he was suddenly adopted into the Presley family.

On 12 September 1958 Elvis completed his training and received orders sending him to West Germany as a tank gunner. He received a grand send-off the following week, when Anita, Lamar, Red, Vernon, and Grandma Minnie Mae all came down to the train station to wave goodbye.

Never one to travel alone, Elvis's musician friend, Charlie Hodge was on the same train and shared that same military assignment for West Germany. After he boarded the USS *General Randall*, Elvis gave his final press conference, just prior to leaving for Germany.

'One of the last things Mom said was that Dad and I should always be together,' Elvis said to the press that day. 'Where ever they send me, Dad will go too . . . Mom and Dad and I often talked about going to Europe. I guess that's where we'll go now – the two of us.'

The USS *General Randall* arrived at Bremerhaven on 1 October and the dock was teaming with screaming rock and roll fans. Four days later, Vernon, Minnie, Red and Lamar arrived in Germany, and together with Elvis and his secretary Elizabeth, they all lived together the whole time that he was in the army. The troupe started out with rooms at the sedate Hotel Gruenwald and finally moved to larger quarters at 14 Goethestrasse.

While in Germany, Elvis was part of the Third Armoured Division. By November, Elvis was promoted to Private First Class, and just before Christmas, he bought himself a flashy new BMW sports car. Vernon, on the other hand, chose for himself a hot little black Mercedez Benz. Because of the loss of his mother, Elvis and the family spent a relatively quiet Christmas together that year.

The public image of Elvis was press release perfect during his stay in Germany. It was totally believeable to think of him as the serious young soldier boy stationed on a foreign shore, pining for his hometown sweetheart, Anita Wood, thinking about her while going on manoeuvres, and marching his way through his structured military duties. In reality, he had the pick of any of the available young girls in the area and he 'held court' at the house that he and his family rented at Goethestrasse 14.

In addition to the traditional German cuisine which was abundant, Elvis insisted that all of his favourite foods were generously served – doughy flour biscuits, fried eggs, burnt bacon, jelly, syrup, butter and white gravy made from the grease of the freshly-fried bacon. Before going off to his daily military duties, Elvis would finish it all off with chilled canned yellow cling peaches. His favourite night-time snack was also in abundance: mashed bananas and peanut butter made into sandwiches. A second favourite was fried potato sandwiches, made of quarter-inch slices of fried potatoes, burnt bacon and gobs of mustard. It seemed that no one had a clue that it was this same fat-laden hillbilly cuisine that had just put poor Gladys into an early grave.

The three-ring circus atmosphere continued in Germany as well. There was a hand-painted sign posted outside the house in German, which read '*Autogramme Von 19:30-20:00*' – in other words, '*Autographs between 7.30-8.00 p.m.*' Just as he had done at the first house in Memphis, at the appointed hour, Elvis would go out of the front door to sign pictures and albums and to greet his fans. In many ways it was business as usual for Elvis.

While he was in Germany, Elvis picked up a couple of new recruits for his famed 'Memphis Mafia.' The new army pals he acquired while stationed in Germany included Joe Esposito and Charlie Hodge. Both of them were to remain devoted friends, staying close to Elvis for the rest of his life.

During 1959, while Elvis was busy in the army in Germany, Colonel Parker kept his career alive in America. RCA Records had cleverly got enough songs in the can to release hit singles in his absence. On 8 January, Elvis's 24th birthday, Dick Clark interviewed him via a transatlantic hook up, and by 10 March RCA had over a million orders for his latest single (*Now and Then*) *There's a Fool Such as I* backed with *I Need Your Love Tonight*. That summer, Elvis released his 14th million-selling 'Gold' single, *A Big Hunk O'Love*, and Paramount Pictures announced that his first post-army movie was to be *G.I. Blues*.

In 1959 something unique happened to Elvis and Vernon Presley while they were in Germany. Elvis met a 14-year-old girl named Priscilla Beaulieu and fell in love, and Vernon met my mother, Dee Stanley, and he too fell in love. This is where the story all gets very complicated.

A controversial, overtly sexual, 24-year-old rock star falls in love with a 14-year-old girl – it could be very messy in the press, especially falling right on the heels of Jerry Lee Lewis who had virtually ruined his career by marrying his 13-year-old cousin only months before, in December 1957. Such hillbilly behaviour was publicly condemned by the church, and the general public boycotted Jerry Lee Lewis concerts in droves. When Lewis had arrived in England in early 1958 for a series of 37 concerts, hot on the tail of the negative press he received, 34 of the concert dates had to be cancelled. When he returned to America, he found that Sam Phillips and Sun Records had not serviced his latest single, *High School Confidential* to radio D.J.s, for fear that it would only tip off negative publicity. The very concept of grown men having sex with underage girls was not to be tolerated on any level. However, nothing could stop Elvis from getting his own way, no matter what the odds.

And then there was the case of Vernon and my mother. Here he was, recently widowed, and plotting to have an affair with the wife of a burly, hot-tempered soldier, right under the soldier's nose. Potentially, it could be very bad for his son's public image. Now that Vernon was retired from any real job – except for that of 'father of the star' – his fate relied on Elvis's very public career.

Thanks to Elvis's money and celebrity status, both father and son were going to have their way, regardless of public opinion. They could each rest assured that in both cases money would conquer all.

It was in 1959, while my Dad was stationed in Germany, that my mother heard that Elvis was in the same town. The fact of the matter was that the whole area was abuzz with the news that the singer was stationed there.

One evening at a local night club where the soldiers frequently gathered while off-duty, a distinguished looking gentleman with curly chestnut hair sat down at the table next to my parents. He was flanked by two burly guys who seemed to act as bodyguards. As they talked amongst themselves, Dad overheard them mention Elvis several times.

Curious, Dad turned to them and asked if they knew the star, and the curly-haired gentleman told him that Elvis Presley was his son. He introduced the two men with him as Red West and Lamar Fike.

According to my mother, she was instantly attracted to Vernon the minute she saw him. Recalling her first meeting with Vernon, she was later to proclaim, 'I was completely aghast at how handsome he was! I just didn't expect him to look like that. I felt very vulnerable, and I was afraid of saying something foolish, but I must say, it was an immediate attraction. The same way it was with Bill.'

Dad remembered the conversation that night, and it seemed like one big happy family reunion. 'Vernon talked about Elvis, and I could see he was indeed proud of his famous son. He talked about his early life – of being poor and working hard. I could relate to both readily, thinking of my own humble beginnings. I could feel a bond of friendship developing between us. Red and Lamar were from Memphis and Dee was from Clarksville, so we found all of us had something in common.'

They continued to drink and chat until the early hours, and when it came time to leave the nightclub, the five friends weren't ready for the party to end. So, Dad invited everyone over to our place for a nightcap, and they accepted. At the time I was just three years old, and my brothers and I had long been in bed when Mom, Dad, Vernon, Lamar and Red came in for more drinks.

According to my father, Red and Lamar were hesitant to take Vernon home, claiming that he had had too much to drink, so he offered all of them the guest room. When he woke up the next morning, Red and Lamar were gone but Vernon was still there. My brothers and I were awake by this point and this was the first time we all met Vernon.

I was much too young to have a clue about the strange triangular relationship that was unfolding between these three adults. Mom stayed at home with us and Dad drove Vernon back to his home, at Goethestrasse 14. While there was a strange flame of sexual attraction burning between Mom and Vernon, Dad and Vernon were striking up a strong friendship.

Dad was later to recount, 'We drove up to a fine German home and Vernon asked me in to meet Elvis. He introduced me to his son and Elvis and I shook hands. My first meeting with the King: idol of teenagers, controversial among parents. What I saw was a neat, courteous, good-looking G.I. I had to appreciate a young man who, at a rising time in his career, would join the army to serve his country because it was expected of him.' Unfortunately, Dad didn't have a clue how totally these people were about to screw up his marriage and his life.

He spent a couple of hours that morning with Vernon, Red and Lamar. They gave him a tour of their house, which my Dad found to be 'luxuriously furnished'. When Dad returned home, and told Mom about his visit and meeting Elvis, she began plotting how to get to know them better. She tried to persuade my father to call Vernon and ask him over for a home-cooked dinner that evening. Dad recalled, 'She believed they would accept. I tried to explain that I felt the Presleys were far out of our class. I refused to call.'

Much to his surprise, at about 4.00 that afternoon the telephone rang and it was Vernon on the other end, inquiring about their plans for that coming evening. When Dad told him that they had none, Vernon asked if he could come over. Dad mentioned how ironic that was, because Dee had wanted to invite him over for dinner. When he inquired if Vernon would have preferred to go out to eat, he said that he would be delighted to have dinner at home with my parents.

Apparently, Vernon went straight to work ingratiating himself with the entire family. Dad was to recall, 'He arrived about 6.30 p.m. Dee had prepared a very nice dinner and while she was busy in the kitchen, Vernon made friends with my sons by getting down on the floor and playing with them. They liked him right away.'

Throughout dinner, apparently, Mom kept asking Vernon, 'When am I going to meet Elvis?' He told her that it would happen all in good time.

After we had all finished dinner, Vernon asked my parents if they would like to go out for a drive in his new black Mercedes Benz. Dad explained that this wouldn't be possible, because there was no one who could babysit. Vernon replied that this was not a problem and said that Billy, Ricky and I were welcome to come along. So the three of us boys piled into the back seat of the car. Dad asked if he could drive, and Vernon was more than happy to give him the keys. Mom sat in the front seat in between Dad and Vernon. The triangular relationship was well underway.

It had been Vernon's intention that Dad would drive us over to the Presley house, and we could all meet this famous Elvis person. At the age of three I had not a clue what was unfolding, or who Elvis was. As it turned out, when we arrived at the house, the entrance was surrounded by fans and once they spotted Vernon's familiar automobile, the car was engulfed by fans. I remember staring out of the car windows with amused fascination.

Vernon instructed Dad to proceed slowly and eventually the crowd subsided enough to let him pass. Free of the mob, it was decided that we should just wend our way home and that we could meet Elvis another time.

When we got home, there was also a group of people gathered outside our house. Word had spread that Elvis Presley's father was a family friend who was visiting us, and now, by association we were semi-celebrities too. After several drinks Vernon left and we all went to bed. About 45 minutes later, the phone rang, and my mother answered. After she had spoken for several minutes, she handed the phone over to Dad – it was Vernon. He had called to tell them how much fun he had had that evening, and that he hoped it was the beginning of many more.

When Dad got home the next night, he found Mom on the phone with Vernon. Dad recalled, 'She asked me if he could come over. I repeated my invitation of the night before. He arrived a short time later. We arranged for a babysitter and went to the NCO club for dinner and drinks. While we were having dinner, my fellow non-commissioned officers kept coming over and introducing themselves and their wives to Vernon. It was amazing how many close friends I suddenly had.'

Like the serpent offering Eve an apple in the Garden of Eden, it was apparently all becoming too intoxicating for Mom to resist. Not only did Vernon have unlimited money, thanks to Elvis, but he was very sharp looking back in those days. He looked dashing with his thin moustache and that Clark Gable look, his son was a superstar, and he was actively looking for a new wife. Gladys, who had been dead for less than a year, had been uneducated and unsophisticated, from the South, overweight, and consistently had dark circles around her eyes. In comparison, Dee was a knockout. She was 115 pounds, with stylish blonde hair and blue eyes. Mom knew exactly what Vernon was up to. A major league flirtation was underway. It was only a matter of time before my mother and Vernon were to become lovers.

She was dissatisfied with her marriage to my father, and her frustrations drove him to drink. Something had to give.

Within a month of having met him, Dee and Vernon had consummated their love affair. As impossible as their personal situations seemed, they managed to carry on this affair behind everyone's back, including my Dad's. Vernon was so openly nice to him that Dad accepted his friendship at face value. Little did he know that Vernon was on a mission, and Mom was the target.

Vernon had no job, except to drink and party all night, and play the role of father-to-the-star. Mom was a housewife, and although she had to look after my brothers and me, she had all day to recharge her batteries. However, Dad would stay out partying with them all night, and then report to the military first thing in the morning for a full day's duty. It began to take its toll on him: 'Night after night going out, all the excitement, the drinking and carrying on associated with our evenings on the town began to pull me down. I was fatigued and was having difficulties keeping the pace,' he later confessed.

Vernon gave the appearance of having a genuine attraction towards both of my parents: my father as a friend, and my mother as his lover. He used every manipulative trick in his bag by offering Dad his Mercedes Benz when he departed Germany the following year, and even offered him a lucrative job with Elvis – as a bodyguard – when Elvis was discharged from the army in 1960. Looking back at everyone's different side of the story, it is now very clear to me that Vernon made false promises to Dad, simply so that he could sleep with Mom. Dad wanted to believe that Vernon was his friend and bought his story – hook, line and sinker.

I once sat down with Red and Sonny West and the subject of the affair of Dee and Vernon came up. They both said to me, 'Don't judge your mother,' and I haven't. It was simply the case that she wanted one thing, Vernon wanted one thing, and Bill became the victim.

At this same time, Elvis knew all about what Vernon was up to. After all, two of his buddies – Red and Lamar – were babysitting for the three of us boys while Vernon and Dee were busy doing their thing while Dad was out on manoeuvres. Their relationship developed more and more, much to Elvis's dislike. Elvis's mother had only been dead a matter of months but Vernon was determined to do what he damn well pleased.

While my brothers and I were oblivious to any of the goings-on between these three adults around us, the plot was clearly thickening. Dad seriously considered Vernon's offer, and looked at employment with Elvis as a viable way to pay off all of the excessive bills that Mom had racked up since moving to Europe.

Then, things started to become a bit bizarre. One afternoon, Dad came home at the usual time, and there was Vernon on our living room floor playing with Billy, Ricky and me. Dad asked him what he was doing there with Mom and us kids, while he was away. Vernon offered some story of how he was in the area and would have been coming over in the evening for one of his regular visits anyway. Dad insisted that Vernon leave immediately, and told him not to come over unchaperoned, otherwise the neighbours would start talking. Vernon left, and Mom and Dad had a huge argument.

For a week, Vernon did not come over, but every night Mom spoke to him on the phone. She begged Dad to talk to Vernon, but for several days he refused. 'She reminded me of the job offer and the promise of the Mercedes,' claimed Dad. 'I forbade her calling him anymore. As usual though, Dee had her way and by the end of the week she talked me into calling him.' Finally, she managed to get the two men on the phone together, and Vernon apologised for the big misunderstanding. Once again, Dad had been deceived.

Then they were back on again, the three of them out doing the town together. Until, one day when Dad arrived home just in time to see Vernon's car disappearing down the street ahead of him. When he confronted Dee, she claimed that he must have been visiting one of the neighbours. Dad believed her because he wanted to believe that this was the truth. When Vernon came over that evening like nothing was wrong, Dad accepted the story as the truth.

What he was also not aware of was the fact that Vernon had already presented Dee to Elvis, announcing his intention of marrying her. Elvis was in Frankfurt in the hospital at the time, having just had his tonsils removed in a routine operation. Elvis said to my mother that day, 'Mrs Stanley, I want my Daddy to be happy. He was a wonderful husband and father, and I've always wanted a brother. Now I guess I'll have three. We can just add another room onto Graceland.' From that point on, my mother was on a clear-cut agenda. She, Billy, Ricky, and I were going to Graceland.

In late November, on Thanksgiving night, Mom and Dad and Vernon went out to Freiberg for dinner and dancing. Late in the evening, Vernon asked Dad if he minded if he and Mom danced – he didn't – however when they got out on the dance floor, he felt that they were embracing each other much too tightly and intimately, and protested. When it continued, Dad had had enough of their public displays and he went out onto the dance floor and physically dragged the two of them apart. Another huge fight ensued, and again there was several days of silence. However, Mom continued to speak to Vernon many times during the week.

Not knowing who or what to believe, Dad turned to the bottle to numb all of the swirling thoughts in his head. According to him,

'I was confused about their relationship. I tried to think things through, but would come to dead ends. Between Thanksgiving and Christmas, my drinking increased. My heart couldn't accept what my mind was saying.'

Around this time, even Mom was wondering what the hell she was doing. When she tried to break off her affair with Vernon, he said to her, 'This isn't what you're saying it is, Dee. This is not cheap, because I want to marry you. I know you're not going to stay with Bill forever. I want you to fly back to the States and begin divorce proceedings. I'll be there, Dee. I love you, baby.'

Confused and obviously lied to by Mom and Vernon, Dad made the big mistake of showing up for duty under the influence of alcohol one day. His life was falling apart, his new so-called best friend was stealing his wife, and he didn't know where to turn. 'Within a few days (I) was relieved of my duties as first sergeant. I couldn't disagree with them. A week later I reported for duty as regimental CQ, and was again relieved of those duties due to drinking. I was restricted to my quarters on the post, pending court martial,' he wrote in his memoirs.

One day on the base, his first sergeant came to find him and to tell him that Dee and Vernon were waiting in their car to talk to him. When he went to see them, Mom informed him that she was going to return to the United States, and that she and Billy, Ricky and I were going to move in with her sister. Dad asked how that was possible, since her sister lived in a two-room trailer, and she told him not to worry about it. With that, Dee and Vernon drove off.

Two days later, Dad was fined $100, given a summary court martial, and was released. When he arrived home, he saw all the packing cases and realised that Mom and the three of us boys were truly going to leave.

That afternoon, Vernon called to ask where to deliver some Christmas presents which he had promised to Ricky, Billy and me. Dad agreed to meet him, pick up the presents, and return home.

As Christmas 1959 arrived, Elvis threw a big Christmas party, and the triad of Bill Stanley/Dee Stanley/Vernon Presley were in attendance. Somehow everyone got through the holiday without any major problems.

From the perspective of my brothers and me, none of what was going on really affected our day-to-day life. We never did meet Elvis in Germany, and the arrival of Vernon in our lives only meant more Christmas toys for us boys.

To envelop everything in further subterfuge, a couple of days later Mom asked Dad if Vernon and his mother, Minnie Mae, could come over for dinner. According to Dad, 'I told her it really didn't make any difference to me anymore.'

When they came over, Dad asked Vernon to go with him to the NCO club for a man-to-man talk. When Dad asked him if he had anything to do with Dee's announcement that she was leaving, Vernon replied, 'I think Dee is letting this thing go to her head. I have no intentions of making plans with your wife or anybody else's. You and I are friends, and it seems to me Dee is taking this too seriously. As far as our relationship is concerned, the job offer when you and Elvis get out of the army, the Mercedes when I leave Germany, stands. Don't let Dee upset you with her carrying on. I have met a lot of people since coming to Germany, and in my life, since Elvis has become famous. Everyone thinks we are millionaires. You, Bill, are the only one who has never asked me for anything.'

According to Dad, 'I wanted to believe him. Oh God, how I wanted to.'

Not long afterwards, Dad's unit was shipped out of town for manoeuvres. While he was stationed away, stories began leaking out from the other enlisted men, about how they had run into Dee and Vernon out on the town while he was working.

When Dad finally got home he confronted my mother and a huge argument ensued. Dad started slamming down beer after beer in his anger. To break up the loud argument that continued, the military police were called by the neighbours.

Now that the military was involved in the disturbance, Dad was ordered to be confined to his quarters on the base. His commanding officer called him into the office the next morning and told Dad to cool it with the drinking, and to try to work out his marital problems in a more logical fashion.

A couple of days later Vernon showed up on base and repeated the same lie that he had told Dad at the NCO club. He ended their conversation by telling Dad that it was best to just let her go back to America, and to let everything blow over.

The very next day, Dad's commanding officer came to him and instructed him to go and pick up his wife and children, and to take them to the airport. All of the necessary arrangements had been made. Dad had only been home a few minutes when Vernon arrived. It was a done deal at this point, and Dad walked through the rest of the day emotionless.

It was Vernon who drove us to the Rhinemein Airport, right outside Frankfurt. According to Dad, 'We waited for the boarding call. Dee was making light conversation to Vernon, the boys were fussing about. I found my attention turning to the boys, ignoring Vernon and Dee. The boys were so small. Billy and David had my colouring, Ricky was blond. I tried to talk to them, but no words would come. I couldn't even bear the thought of parting with them, having no idea when I would see them again. They were curious and inattentive to me, so it was just as well. I walked around the airport terminal alone, thinking and trying to determine just what was happening. The only conclusion I could come up with was there was absolutely nothing I could do. I knew I couldn't fight the Army, because of publicity, nor with Vernon, because of his fortune. My sole problem was losing my boys. Their flight was paged, and I assisted my family to the boarding area. I hugged each one tight, and was so sad I couldn't help crying. Dee and Vernon tried to comfort me. I turned from them and walked away.'

We boarded the aircraft as scheduled and Mom and my brothers and I returned to America. That was the last time we saw Dad for several months.

What makes me saddest is the way Mom and Vernon treated my Dad. They were planning their life together and not really caring what happened to my father; they did hurt him so badly. After we got on the plane for America, Bill looked over at Vernon, and Bill knew that this was the man to whom he had lost everything. Not only did he know that he had lost his wife and family but he knew that he was about to get totally screwed-over by Vernon and the Presley family.

Poor Dad. He pulled himself through an exceptionally rough childhood and made something of his life. He was a decorated war hero who had so valiantly fought the Nazis in World War II, and the Communist North Koreans in Asia. In spite of his heroic deeds, he was finally up against an adversary he was unable to beat: the Presleys and all of their money.

5

'I'm Going to Graceland'

As a direct result of Elvis having been stationed in Germany several lives had been permanently changed. My mother had spotted the goose that laid the golden egg, and she was about to stake her claim on it. My brothers and I were finally going to have a stable atmosphere amidst wealth beyond our wildest dreams. Vernon had found himself a new mate. And, unfortunately, Bill Stanley was going to lose everything that he held dear to him.

Meanwhile, while all of this intrigue between Vernon and my parents was brewing, there was Elvis's love affair with ninth-grader Priscilla Beaulieu. With all of the sophisticated Hollywood starlets such as Yvonne Lime, Debra Paget and Natalie Wood, and devoted home-town beauties like Anita Wood who Elvis could have fallen in love with, what was it about this 14-year-old girl that she should cast a spell on him?

Ever since Elvis had become the king of the rock idols, with young girls literally swooning at his feet, he had also been beseiged by eligible women who wanted to have sex with him. In spite of all the beautiful women Elvis could have pursued and won, he perferred them young and, as time went on, it became apparent to everyone the younger the better.

In spite of his 'clean cut' and 'all-American boy-next-door' public image that was being promoted in the press, Elvis had the sexual appetite of a stud horse. Speaking of the sea of girls that Elvis was having sex with, Red West was later to recall, 'Elvis then started to relax a lot more when there were gals around. Like everything, when Elvis did something, he went all the way. Once he discovered how easy he could get girls, we were routing them through his bedroom two and sometimes three a day. That boy sure had a constitution in those early days.'

Priscilla Beaulieu was also to become a major player in our lives at Graceland. Through a most unlikely turn of events, the King of Rock and Roll had at last found his queen. All she had to do now was grow up to an age where they could marry.

Priscilla was a typical 'Air Force brat', shuffled along with her family from one United States military base to another. In 1956, her father, Captain Joseph Paul Beaulieu, was based in Austin, Texas, at Bergstrom Air Force Base.

One day Captain Beaulieu came home from the Air Force Base's 'PX' store for enlisted men. In his hands was the debut album by the new singing sensation, Elvis Presley, which he presented to his young daughter. At the age of 11, how could Priscilla have ever known that this was the man she was going to grow up to marry?

A pretty young girl with brown hair, blue eyes and a close circle of friends, Priscilla was voted the 'Queen of Del Valley Junior High' in a school contest.

When her father announced to her that he had been transferred to Wiesbaden, West Germany, she thought that her entire world had suddenly ended. Little did she know, but it was just about to begin.

In Wiesbaden, there was a family-oriented place called the Eagle's Club, where enlisted families could have dinner and mingle. There was also a jukebox there, and a snack bar. Often after school, Priscilla would be there listening to the latest American hit records on the jukebox and writing letters to the friends she had left behind in Texas.

One afternoon in the summer of 1959, Priscilla noticed that a young man in his 20s was staring at her. It wasn't long before he came over and introduced himself as Currie Grant. He engaged her in some small talk, and asked her if she liked this popular American singer, Elvis Presley.

When she replied, 'Of course, who doesn't?' he said to her, 'I'm a good friend of his. My wife and I go to his house quite often. How would you like to join us one evening?'

Priscilla cleared this with her parents, and it was arranged for her to accompany Currie and Carole Grant to the rented house of Elvis Presley. Bad Neuheim, where Elvis lived, was a 45-minute drive away from Wiesbaden. Priscilla sat quietly in the car as they pulled up to the modest house with that 'Autographs between 7.00 and 8.00 p.m. only' sign on it.

She was escorted into the house and greeted by Vernon. He led Priscilla and the Grants into the plain-looking living room. There, in the middle of the room sat Elvis Presley, listening to a recording of Brenda Lee's *Sweet Nothin's*. They chatted politely, and Elvis informed Priscilla that he was surprised to discover that she was only a student in the ninth grade, as she looked very sophisticated and mature for a 14 year old.

Announcing that he was hungry, he took Priscilla into the kitchen to meet his grandmother, Minnie Mae. She was standing at the stove frying up a pan full of bacon, searing it nearly black, just the way Elvis liked it.

From that one awkward meeting that night, Priscilla quickly found herself in an environment that was very warm and comfortable. As the evening came to a close, Elvis invited Priscilla to come back and visit again.

On her second visit, Priscilla was more relaxed, and was now admittedly infatuated with this 24-year-old singing star. When he whispered in her ear that he wanted to be alone with her in his bedroom, she imagined what was about to transpire. Although nervous, she said 'yes', and went up to his bedroom to wait for him. He arrived 20 minutes later, and the two of them chatted. Elvis poured out stories about his dear departed mother, Gladys, and how his father was involved with a married woman named Dee Stanley. With his arm around Priscilla, he poured his heart out about his life and his family. He said that he had never seen his father act so silly over a woman.

According to Priscilla, Elvis said to her, 'What's Dee trying to do? Make him into some dude he's not? Why can't she just accept him the way he is? I've never seen him so lovesick. She meets him at some restaurant and exchanges love notes all day.'

Before they got up to return to the party downstairs, Elvis kissed her on the mouth. That sealed it right then and there, Priscilla was infatuated with Elvis and he became the only thing she could concentrate on. This second date took place in October 1959.

By the time Priscilla had returned to the Presley house for the fourth time, her parents put their foot down: either they met this rock and roll singer, or their daughter was forbidden to see him again. When Priscilla announced to him, 'I can't come to see you anymore unless you come and meet my parents,' Elvis immediately agreed.

Arrangements were made and on the appointed evening Elvis arrived at the apartment of the Beaulieu family, dressed in his military uniform, and accompanied by Vernon. Elvis was nothing but polite, and Priscilla's parents were quite impressed by this perfect gentleman. So began the romance of Elvis and Priscilla.

Captain Beaulieu laid down the ground rules to Elvis – if he agreed to comply then he could continue to see Priscilla. First of all, he personally had to pick up Priscilla and at the end of the evening he had to bring her back home. He agreed, and from that moment on Priscilla and Elvis saw each other constantly.

Although young Priscilla might have been susceptible to Elvis's sexual advances, according to her he made none. He explained to her, 'We have plenty of time, Little One.' Over the next months, Elvis and Priscilla became inseparable. Only the Army and school kept them apart. Although they became quite physical with each other – lying in Elvis's bed with their arms around each other – Priscilla maintains that they did not have sex.

Living nearly an hour away from the Presley home and having to attend school every day, this schedule began to take its toll on Priscilla. When she fell asleep in Elvis's bed one evening, he inquired as to how many hours of sleep she was averaging. When she told him 'four to five,' he went into the bathroom and returned with a handful of little white pills. He instructed her to take one of these whenever she was exhausted, and they would solve everything. They were amphetamines. In Elvis's hectic life, even at this early point, drugs were to become the instant solution to being either asleep or awake. Elvis's drug use had begun as innocently as that. Whenever anyone he liked to spend time with became sleepy he simply gave them a hit of speed, and the fun continued unabated.

Elvis was due to return to the United States to be discharged from the Army on 1 March 1960. With the photographers from *Life* magazine and dozens of other press representatives present, on that date Elvis bid Germany, and a teary-eyed Priscilla Beaulieu goodbye. Potentially, this could have been the end of their relationship, but this was to be just the beginning. Although the Atlantic Ocean now separated them, neither could seem to forget the other one.

Years later, in a press interview, Elvis looked back on his romance with the 14-year-old girl he had met in Germany, and recalled, 'Priscilla was just a kid – more than ten years younger than me. But she wasn't like so many of the other girls. I guess most of them were a little overawed by me, by what I'm supposd to be. Dunno why, because I'm shy myself and do my best to make other people feel at ease. But with this chick, it was different. She didn't give the impresssion that in any way she was tongue tied.'

For Priscilla and Elvis, and for Vernon and Dee, life had somehow become magical again. Love seemed to heal everything. However, for my father, Bill Stanley, life had become a living hell. He found himself on a downward spiral that just wouldn't quit.

That day in Germany, when my mother, brothers and I boarded the plane and headed off to the United States, my Dad was so depressed that he and Vernon headed for the first tavern they encountered. Dad still wanted desperately to believe that Vernon had no part in his wife's decision to leave Europe. Once there, they proceeded to drink the night away, Dad slipping deeper and deeper into a melancholy mood.

They got so loaded that night that they pulled their car off on the side of the autobahn to sleep for a couple of hours. They were awakened by the police, and continued their journey back toward the base. When they got there Dad was late for the time he was expected to be on duty. Hungover and ill, he was reprimanded by his commanding officer, and confined to his quarters pending court martial.

He was later to recall, 'My apartment was the last place I wanted to go anyway. My family was gone now, the army was all I had left, and I was very unsure where I stood there. It really didn't matter anymore. It didn't make a great deal of difference what the Army would do to me.'

Out of his mind in emotional pain, Dad retired to his quarters. Feeling sorry for him, one of his buddies came to the door and handed him a brown paper bag and immediately departed. It contained two fifths of German potato schnapps. The last thing he recalled was the first long drink. Two days later he woke up in a hospital bed, unaware of what had happened.

His attempt at drinking himself numb had ended up with him getting his stomach pumped and being committed to the psychiatric ward at the army hospital located in Frankfurt. Three days later, having regained his strength, Dad was taken to a psychiatrist's office, where he explained how Elvis and Vernon Presley were ruining his life. The psychiatrist listened to the story and when he was finished, he had him repeat the whole story in front of two of his collegues.

The three psychiatrists concurred that Dad had a major drinking problem, and his inability to handle alcohol had caused him to become delusional about all of this Elvis nonsense.

Several days later he was asked to tell his story to still another psychiatrist. He again told my father that it was his drinking that was the root of all of his problems, and that he had blown this Presley story totally out of proportion. The psychiatrist questioned whether he had in fact ever met Vernon and Elvis Presley at all.

Resigned to the fact that his life was a shambles anyway, Dad decided that there was no use fighting it. His calm behaviour afforded him certain limited privileges on the base, including visiting the base store, the Exchange. Roaming around the Exchange one day, he ran into his friend Jack Washburn and his wife. They had been at Bill and Dee's wedding and in the last few weeks had lost touch with Dad.

The three of them sat down for coffee and Dad poured out his whole long, sad story. Jack not only believed Dad's version of the story as fact, but he revealed that several weeks before he had run into Dee and Vernon at the Exchange in Frankfurt, some 60 miles away from where they lived. When he had asked Dee what she was doing there with Vernon, she told him that she had convinced Vernon to take her there so she could find several items that were hard to locate at the local Exchange.

Jack was incensed over the fact that no one seemed to believe my father. He even went so far as to have suspected that Vernon and Dee were having an affair, and reminded my father that he had warned him about it months ago when he ran into the three of them out for a night on the town.

Jack and his wife vowed to go and see Dad's doctor to set him straight. When Dad ran into Mrs Washburn a few days later, she informed him that she and Jack had been told by the doctor to keep their mouths shut, and to mind their own business.

Now Dad was pissed off. He devised a plan to lure Vernon to the hospital, which would convince everyone that he did indeed know the Presleys. He got in contact with Vernon and told him that he was in ill health, and begged his 'friend' to come see him.

Vernon came the very next day, and as they were walking down a hallway in the hospital, Dad told him that he wanted him to meet someone. He steered him into his doctor's office and introduced him. The doctor told Dad that he wanted to speak to Vernon alone, so he left the room and shut the door.

When the door opened again, Vernon said a hurried 'goodbye' and left. With that, the doctor had Dad come in and speak with him. He concurred that obviously Dad did know Mr Presley, however, he totally denied anything about an affair with his wife.

He was then escorted out of the office by two burly attendants, and was promptly locked up for the next two weeks – all privileges denied.

One day several attendants came in for him, put him in a straitjacket, tied him down to a stretcher, and placed him in an ambulance. He was then loaded onto an Air Force Medivac plane, and was given an injection to put him to sleep. He recalled waking up on the jet, and showing just enough signs of consciousness to merit another injection.

When he fully regained consciousness, he was in a ward in Walter Reed Medical Hospital. For the next few weeks he was confined to the ward he was in, where it was explained to him that he was being treated for alcoholism. They put him on medication – which he secretly flushed down the toilet, for fear that he would be drugged. Although he could never convince the psychiatrists, Dad was to go to his grave knowing that Vernon Presley, with all of his money and clout had somehow pulled some strings to convince the army doctors that this Bill Stanley character was some sort of nutcase. Finally, new orders arrived for him, and he was assigned to Fort Jackson in South Carolina. It was his duty there to qualify new recruits for the firing range.

While there, Dad began to plot how he was going to find his family. He realised that his marriage was over – but he had to see me and my brothers, and make certain that we were fine and happy.

With both Bill and her responsibilities to us kids taken care of, Dee returned to Germany to resume her affair with Vernon. Anxious to get us out of the way as well, Vernon paid to have Dee put Billy, Ricky and me in a boarding home called Breezy Point Farms, at Newport News, Virginia. It was a place for rich kids whose parents had better things to do.

Breezy Point Farms was a dark, dingy, dirty boarding home, run by an old, fat lady wearing a knee-high smock, hose and a black uniform.

If you ever did anything bad, or against the rules, they would deliberately take you out in the hall and put tabasco pepper sauce on your tongue as punishment.

When you first arrived there, they rode you around in a motorboat, because it was on a peninsula. But, when everyone left, the chamber was shut off from the outside world.

To me, at the age of four, Breezy Point Farms seemed like a nightmare come true. I used to cry myself to sleep at night, because I couldn't understand what was happening to me.

When I was born, I was badly crippled. I had a clubbed foot on my right leg. I had 21 operations to correct this condition. By the time I was in the boarding home, I was wearing heavy corrective shoes and braces. This whole experience with Mom and Dad suddenly gone, and the three of us boys in Breezy Point boarding school, was very frightening and disconcerting.

The reason that I want to emphasise this particular episode, is to illustrate the vindictiveness of Vernon and his ability to eliminate anything and anyone who came between him and anything that he wanted. This really shows the Presley mentality at this time. Five years previously, they were powerless and dirt poor. They had nothing, and their past history had shown them that they had no earthly reason to expect to ever have anything in life.

However, since Elvis became a millionaire, they began exerting their power and their money to get anything that they wanted. Vernon was the first to use his new-found wealth to have his own way. He came from nothing and if it wasn't for the total fluke of Elvis's wide-spread fame, he would still have had nothing.

Both Dee and Vernon returned to America ahead of Elvis. Vernon went immediately to Graceland and Mom came to retrieve us boys from Breezy Point Farms. Vernon had provided Dee with enough money to rent a small house near the ocean in Newport News, Virginia. It was there that Dad was to track us down.

That spring, not long after arriving at Fort Jackson in South Carolina, Dad went to his commanding officer and poured out his story one more time. When he came to the end of it, he requested a ten day leave, so that he could locate my brothers and me. His request was granted, and with $20 he borrowed from the Red Cross, he hitchhiked to Newport News, Virginia.

He went right to the trailer park where Mom's sister, Margaret, lived with her husband. He found their trailer and knocked on the door, explaining that he wanted to find Dee so that he could see his boys. They wouldn't open the door to let him in but after Margaret's husband persuaded her to call Dee, they told him where we were staying at an apartment near the beach.

According to Dad's memoirs, 'I found the apartment with no trouble. I knocked on the door. Before Dee opened the door, she asked if I had been released from the hospital and if I was all right. I said "Yes" to both questions. I wanted only to see the boys. Slowly she opened the door. I walked in without looking at her, my eyes searching the room for my boys. The boys recognised me and came running to me, exclaiming, "Daddy!

Daddy! Daddy!" I gathered them to me, feeling a moment of pure joy. Being too young to understand what had transpired, they asked if I had come home to stay with them. I told them I had come to see them, and we would talk about it later. William Jr., was going on seven then. He started jumping up and down, begging me to stay. We sat down on the couch to talk, I asked him if he had gotten settled in school. His reply was they had not started school, but Mother had told them soon they would attend a nice school. Most of the time they were staying with Aunt Margaret. He soon grew tired of the question-and-answer game and wanted to go out and play. When they were outside, I asked Dee her plans. Her reply was, "I thought you knew by now."'Clearly he did not.

I don't want to insult my mother, but she was in control in this situation. She made clear-cut choices. She knew what she wanted, and she was going to have it at all costs. She knew that Vernon had unlimited cash at hand, and between the two of them they were going to either buy Dad out of his marriage and rights to his sons, or they were going to wreck him, and/or his military career – or all three if necessary. Obviously the wheels were already in motion to get him out of the picture.

Dee informed Bill that she was waiting that very evening for a phone call from Vernon that would confirm whether or not she and Vernon were to be married. Dad argued that she had no legal grounds for divorce, and that he would try to stop it for the sake of his boys. According to him, 'She asked why I would want to stop it, knowing she had a chance of marrying into millions and my sons would be raised like royalty. I told her I couldn't care less about royalty and I was only concerned about the boys. I told her I knew about her and Vernon, her reasons for coming back to the States, why [they] had me restricted to the post, and the only way she was going to get a divorce was by my saying "yes".'

At 8 that evening the phone rang. It was Vernon calling from Germany. Billy, Ricky, Dad and I went out on the front porch to sit, and Mom talked on the phone for about 45 minutes. Then, she came to the door and told Dad that Vernon wanted to talk to him.

Vernon asked Dad if he would give Mom a divorce or not. Dad told him that he couldn't care less about his marriage, but said he wouldn't allow the divorce to take place because of his sons. Dad also argued that Mom had run up quite a few bills during her courtship with Vernon, and if he wanted Mom, he inherited her debts too. He estimated the total at about $2000.

Dad got off of the phone with Vernon, and Mom resumed her conversation with Vernon. A few minutes later, Mom asked Dad where he intended to sleep that evening. When he told her that he wasn't sure, she got back on the phone with Vernon. She then relayed a message from Vernon: Dad could sleep on the sofa that night and, if he promised not to make advances towards Mom, Vernon would immediately wire him the $2000.

The conversation went around in circles, with Mom arguing with Dad. She informed him that if he didn't give her a divorce, Vernon was simply going to fly her to Mexico to establish legal residence there and legally divorce him in six weeks. The next morning, Western Union called to inform Dad that two separate $1000 cheques were waiting for him to retrieve.

Dad cashed one of the cheques, said goodbye to us, and took a taxi to see two of his buddies at nearby Fort Eustis. Apparently local gossip travelled fast there. According to Dad, 'They told me they had heard I was confined to a psychiatric unit at Walter Reed Hospital and that I would probably be confined to a mental institution for the remainder of my life. They asked me if I knew Dee was planning to marry Vernon. I told them I had just come from her apartment. They said she had voiced concern about my being confined to the psychiatric ward, which wasn't part of the plan, but she felt pretty sure the Presley money would overcome any difficulty.'

Dad was being railroaded into divorcing Mom and giving up any rights to see my brothers and me. If he didn't co-operate, they would simply buy the testimony of an influential doctor, and have him legally committed. When he returned to his post in South Carolina, he again found that no one would believe his elaborate stories of how Elvis Presley's family was trying to ruin him.

Meanwhile, it was time for the Presleys to return to the United States from Germany. Elvis returned to America from Germany in March 1960, and when he came back to Memphis, the press was everywhere. In his military uniform, he was welcomed back as if he was a conquering war hero – which was ridiculous because this was peace time! Elvis had dressed up in a military uniform, and had been given all of these 'good conduct' medals, when in fact he had never seen a real battle. On the other hand, my Dad had risked his life in two wars and no one really cared.

Even Elvis knew what a joke this was. He would later say to me, 'My military career was nothing compared to your Dad's. He was a combat veteran.' I really have to hand it to Elvis, he had the utmost respect for my father. If only Mom and Vernon had a fraction of this respect for Dad, I wouldn't feel so bad today. To the press you would have thought that Elvis had single-handedly won a war.

That day in Memphis the press was everywhere and there were dozens of photographers capturing the fact that this blonde woman – Dee – was suddenly living with Vernon at Graceland, and they were *not married*.

Elvis barely had time to put down his suitcases and re-pack, as Colonel Parker had seen to it that his schedule was back in full tilt, just like it was before he had left for Germany. Elvis immediately flew down to Miami to tape a Frank Sinatra TV special. Also on the show was Nancy Sinatra, Frank's daughter. She was destined to not only become one of his many lovers, but she was to become one of his most famous movie co-stars as well.

Elvis returned to Graceland after taping the Frank Sinatra television special to find his father living with my Mom. It was a little hard on Elvis at first even to accept her into the household, but not long afterwards Billy, Ricky and I were suddenly transported to Graceland and Elvis was presented with the three of us. I'll never forget meeting him for the first time, because my life was never quite the same after that.

One day we were in a boarding home, and the next day we were at Graceland and there was Elvis Presley, standing there saying, 'Hi, I'm your new big brother. Welcome to my house. I've always wanted a little brother, now I have three.'

I was four years old at the time, Ricky was six and Billy was seven. Although he was a little cool towards Dee suddenly replacing his mother in his father's life, he welcomed the three of us boys with a sincere and warm hug. He knew that we were victims of circumstance and that we hadn't the power to leave. We had no choice in the matter, and the very look of awe, apprehension, fear and uncertainty on the faces of Billy, Ricky and me must have melted his heart. Because of this situation, I think that he was very sympathetic towards our feelings and our emotional needs. Basically, from that point on, Elvis took the three of us boys under his wing and competed with Dee to raise us.

As far as Mom was concerned, I can understand why Elvis was reluctant to accept the arrangement. He knew how and what had happened with the triangle of Vernon, Dee and Bill. He must have been harbouring plenty of doubts about this new situation. At the time, Elvis was thinking, 'Hey, is this girl going to come in here and say that she is my new mother and try to dictate actions in the house that I live in?' Elvis had the right to have been paranoid about this strange scenario. I know I would have been.

To Elvis the ultimate way that he could express his feelings was to spend money on us. He, Red, Lamar and Sonny went out that evening and purchased the contents of an entire Memphis toy store. Bicycles, stuffed animals, trucks, games, everything little boys like to play with were laid at our feet the next morning.

That was my first introduction to Elvis. While some would say, 'God, what generosity!' – and it was great generosity – I now look at it as a replacement for the father we had lost. It was more of a monetary thing than a psychological thing. We had lost our natural father in the shuffle, but this act of generosity was meant to lessen our loss.

The same situation was about to happen when Bill Stanley came to Graceland to sign the divorce settlement papers. The Presley mentality was: 'We have to buy everything that we want.'

Over a month had gone by when Dad was summoned to his company headquarters, where one of the officers informed him that he had a phone call from Vernon Presley. Again, Vernon asked Dad if he would grant Dee a divorce. Dad told him that he could have Dee, but not his kids. The conversation ended abruptly with nothing resolved. Dad had his commanding officer listen in on the call, just so someone on the base would believe him and his stories of how the Presleys were trying to ruin his life.

A couple of days later, Dad received another call from Vernon. Again he had his commanding officer listen in on the call. Vernon offered Dad round-trip airline tickets to come to Memphis to resolve this matter once and for all. With the officer's encouragement, Dad agreed to the meeting.

'When I arrived at the Memphis airport,' Dad was to recall, 'I was met by Vernon and two or three uniformed Presley guards. We went to Elvis's mansion, Graceland. During the drive there was no conversation between us. As we entered the foyer, I couldn't help notice three children's bicycles. Knowing there were no children in the Presley household, I felt the boys must have been there, but I never saw them. I was introduced to several people, three being Presley attorneys. I was ushered into the living room. Besides Vernon, I knew no one present. I was asked to sit down. Papers were put before me, informing me of the options of the divorce.'

Fearing that if he didn't sign them he would never see his sons again, he put his signature on them, without even reading them. He knew that he was defeated. In an attempt to ease his own guilt, Vernon took Dad to the local Cadillac dealership and bought him a blue 1956 Cadillac. Vernon paid for the car with cash. Vernon then handed Dad an envelope and told Dad to put it in his pocket. Dad began driving south towards his army base. After six hours on the road, he stopped to get something to eat. While there he opened the envelope. It contained ten $100 bills.

In Dad's words: 'I drove out of Memphis in a Cadillac paid for with Presley money, without a wife I didn't want anyway, and without three boys I wanted more than anything in the world.'

Obviously, with regard to my father, Vernon's whole attitude was: 'Screw this military guy.' Knowing what my Dad was like, it is a miracle that Bill didn't go absolutely wild and kick the shit out of all of them. In retrospect, I might not have been so forgiving.

In later years, Red West said to me many, many times, 'This guy could have easily killed us all with his bare hands for screwing up his life. He could have ripped our lungs out of our chests with absolutely no problem. Elvis had no fear for any human being, except Bill Stanley and his temper.'

I really have to hand it to my Dad. Here was this wealthy family who decided that they wanted his wife and kids as their own and he was forced to step back and allow it to happen. The fact that he didn't get physical reflects his sense of military discipline.

Through this whole ordeal he remained a true gentlemen, in spite of what it did to him inside. There were several offers and compromises along the way, but ultimately he lost his boys, and as a result of his loss, Bill was the fall guy. Bill was the politician who took the punches, and sustained all of the losses.

The beneficiaries in all of this intrigue and double-dealing were Billy, Ricky and me. We were the ones who got to grow up in a mansion with every luxury we could have asked for at Graceland.

Finally, when the divorce papers were official, our mother and Elvis's father went down to Huntsville, Alabama, while my brothers and I stayed in Memphis. Vernon and Dee got married there on 3 July 1960. We had been living at Graceland from February to July, before they were married. They took a lot of flak about that.

Elvis's manager, Colonel Parker, was influential in making sure that everything went smoothly and that Dee and Vernon were legally married as soon as possible, or the situation could have potentially blown up in everyone's face and ruined Elvis's career. He essentially said, 'Hey, you've got my boy here. His mother has just died, and his father is living with a woman who is married to someone else.'

When Mom and Vernon came back to Graceland they were radiantly happy. My brothers and I were very excited and enjoying our new lives at a mansion with unlimited toys. Everyone was happy – everyone but Dad that is.

Little did we know it at the time but his life was spiralling quickly downward into the depths of depression. When he had returned to the base with his shiny new Cadillac, the non-stop heckling that he received was endless. People constantly tormented him about having traded his wife and kids for a new car.

'I was literally driven from camp in my off-duty hours to escape the harassment. In my own company, the harassment was constant – asking me to get autographed pictures of Elvis, some even wanting my autograph,' Dad was later to explain. 'I started going into town, where I could maintain some sense of anonymity. I began to drink again, heavily, to relieve my memory for at least a few hours. Again I was in trouble with the Army.'

One day in late June Dad reported for duty very hungover, and was confined to the stockade. After a week the commanding officer of the post came to get Dad. In the CO's office, Dad again reeled out his story of how the Presleys had ruined his life. The officer produced a newspaper, and on the front page of it was a photo of Vernon and Dee, announcing their marriage.

Finally, someone believed Dad's story and all the charges that had been brought against him for disorderly conduct were dropped. By mutual consent, Dad was discharged from the army. Nineteen years and six months he had been in the military, and at 20 years he would have been eligible for a full pension. Instead – to add insult to injury – this whole situation with Vernon and Dee had robbed him of even that. Defeated and broken, he moved to Jacksonville, Florida, where he took a job at a local hospital, lived with his sister Pearl and her family, and for a while continued to drown his sorrows. From there he began to attempt to put what was left of his life back together.

Not long after Dee and Vernon's wedding, Dad came to Memphis for a nursing seminar that the hospital was paying for him to attend. Dad tried out his visitation rights on this trip and was allowed to visit us at Graceland. He was later to recall, 'The boys seemed distant. They were so wrapped up in their toys and games, they gave me their attention for only a little while. They were excited at first and called me "Daddy" hesitantly. My heart was heavy.'

Before he left Graceland, Dad picked up Billy and gathered the three of us boys together and said, 'Always love your mother, boys. Mr Presley is going to be your new father. I won't be here anymore. I want you to say, "yes, sir," and "no, sir" to him and remember to always take care of your mother.' That was the last we saw of Dad for quite some time.

From my vantage point, I certainly had no idea what had happened between Dee and Vernon. Any conclusions that I now have on the triangular relationship of Dee, Vernon and Bill only came to me in the 1990s when I was able to read my father's memoirs. For 30 years, I had only been brought up with one side of the story of what really happened. Dee only told us, 'Your father had a drinking problem, and I had to divorce him.' We were taught to believe that everything wrong in the relationship was Bill's fault. I always somehow suspected that there was something wrong with the story, like a puzzle with a missing piece. In this way, I too was being brought up not to know what reality was, but to accept the facts as they were presented to me.

While this was taking place, my brothers and I were enjoying our new surroundings. Life at Graceland was 'a trip' to say the least. The existence that we were suddenly living couldn't have been more bizarre if we had been transported to Mars. In terms of material possessions we were given everything we could possibly want, and more. However, all of this wealth completely obliterated any form of normality. I now lived in the world of Elvis, a world where money and power could change all of the rules for us. This took some adjustment on our part. Along with all of this wealth came a lot of fun and – as we were later to find out – several inherent problems.

I very clearly remember being driven to school in that huge pink Cadillac. It was the car that Elvis had originally purchased as a gift for his mother when he first hit it big. My brothers and I certainly made a grand entrance when we arrived every morning at Graceland Elementary School.

That kind of arrival made an instant impression on the other kids in school. We were teased constantly. I remember being called 'Hound Dog' and 'Sideburns' by my classmates. We were often threatened just because we were Elvis Presley's little brothers. This had a profound effect on me personally. I had a deep fear of rejection due to peer pressure living under the shadow of Elvis, and the boarding school. As a result, I became very rebellious and was thrown out of three schools by the time I was in the seventh grade.

I became a 'problem child', who was always in trouble with the teachers. This came about because I didn't know who liked me because I was David Stanley, and who liked me because I was Elvis Presley's brother.

I went to a private school after that. My mother was very religious when I was growing up and she put me into a Christian school. That still didn't work out, so they finally put me in a military academy.

At the time I was really hostile and I had a lot of fight in me. I think I realised that I was living in the shadow of Elvis and it upset me. I needed to have my own sense of achievement. My Mom was beside herself with me at the time because I was so hostile and she sent me to a psychologist who put me on Lithium to calm me down. I had a tremendous amount of energy at the ages of six, seven and eight.

My Mom was especially concerned because she lived with the guilt of dumping Bill Stanley to be with Vernon. I'm not saying that she didn't love us unconditionally – because she did – but her own guilt certainly came into play.

I distinctly remember going to the psychiatrist's office. I was given a test where you are shown ink blots that have no set form and you have to explain what the shape suggests to you. When the doctor asked me what they meant to me, I asked myself, 'What have I done wrong?'

My brothers and I would discuss this strange new world we found ourselves in. We really weren't sure what it was that Elvis did to obtain all of this attention and adulation. We used to say to each other, 'Oh, he makes movies.'

We all three had our own ways of dealing with it. I began to realise that if I got a piece of yellow writing paper and went home and signed it 20 times or, better still, got Elvis to sign it, I could go back to school and sell the autograph.

That was the beneficial side of things. Everyone you knew at school wanted to come to your house for dinner. Teachers would put you on a special grading curve, and say, 'I'd like Elvis's autograph, and instead of giving you a "C" on that paper, I could give you a "B".' That was amongst the earliest benefits of having Elvis as my older brother.

Elvis would come to watch our football practice and everyone made us feel like we were playing in the Superbowl. Simply because he was there, there would be a huge crowd. He would do that when I was in the fourth and fifth grades.

Elvis wasn't really involved with us boys on a day-to-day basis but he would come to football practice, or he'd take me out in the backyard at Graceland, and we would play football and he taught us the basics of the game.

When it came to encouraging us into musical careers, he gave us musical instruments one Christmas. He gave me an SG Gibson guitar, Billy received a bass guitar and Ricky was given a drum set.

Every year, Elvis's manager, Colonel Parker would give us presents for Christmas and on our birthdays, as would Elvis. He really developed that pattern for giving. Whenever Elvis did something, we three boys were involved. He made us feel that he always wanted us involved in everything he did. That part of my growing up was very 'family oriented'.

You have to remember that Elvis was born in a 12 x 20 feet house in the middle of nowhere and suddenly he went from a guy who was in a field in blue jeans picking cotton to an international star. For that reason, Elvis would never be seen in blue jeans. To him, wearing jeans represented being poor white trash, and he was never to be seen in them ever again. He became so rich so quickly in the 1950s that he kept that little boy mentality about him. He always wanted to play with everything, and suddenly he had these little brothers with that same sense of adventure and wide-eyed enthusiasm. Because he never had anything himself when he was growing up he wanted us to share that excitement with him.

That was the kind of relationship that I developed with Elvis. His thinking at the time was, 'I'm going to give these little guys everything that they will never experience anywhere else in their lives.' Everything was done with that type of feeling, a feeling of total inclusion – always.

He was constantly going to my mother and saying, 'Dee, let me have them for the day,' 'Dee, let me take them to . . . wherever,' 'Dee, I want them to go with me to . . . whatever.' At first she was apprehensive about letting him take us off galavanting across the countryside with his entourage of adult buddies and their girlfriends.

Then, eventually, Elvis and Dee had a relationship where she trusted him to look after us and to return us home safely. I remember at the age of six, Elvis rented out the fairgrounds so that we could ride the rides all night long. I recall my mother saying, 'You can't take those boys, they'll fall asleep. They can't keep up with you.' To make sure we boys *could* stay up with him, he gave each of us Dexadrine!

There were also the underlying tones of my mother's guilt for deserting her first husband, which led her to grasp religion. My brothers and I were forced to attend church. I recall Elvis saying to me, 'Always listen to your mother, you can't get enough church.'

That was about the last thing I wanted to hear. Ricky, Billy and I had to attend Sunday School, Vacation Bible School, singing in the choir, serving 'The Lord's Supper'. I remember at the age of 12, making the decision to be baptised at the Church of Christ and my impressions of their religion. They believed that you must be physically immersed in water, or you would go directly to hell.

When it came to Christmas, Elvis never grew up. The holiday season made him unashamedly sentimental, and no eight year old looked forward to 25 December with more excitement and anticipation than the King of Rock and Roll. During that whole holiday season, he was the biggest kid of all!

The opulence of Graceland gave him the opportunity to celebrate the holiday in style. The driveways and the main house were lined with blue lights, and in front were six eight-feet tall Christmas trees decorated with multicoloured lights.

Inside, the mansion was also completely decked out for the season, with the focus on a huge Christmas tree in the dining room. After dinner, everyone would gather around the piano to sing Christmas carols.

Although Elvis loved to receive gifts, his favourite Christmas activity was giving gifts. In addition, his friends normally got big cash bonuses. The presents for family members ranged from jewellery to new cars. Elvis loved their reactions to his extravagances. For Billy, Ricky and me, it was like having Santa Claus as your older brother!

I was always a very creative kid, and I was always a 'why' person, always questioning everything. I was very impressed with Elvis. I thought he had an incredible presence. He could walk into a room of 100 people, and everyone would instantly know it. He just had that gift, and that magnetic personality.

Everything that you've ever read about or heard about Elvis's personality is true, especially as far as having magnetism and charisma. He could give you a look that could change your life. With one glance he could knock you down or he could lift you up completely. Elvis was an unusual individual. He definitely had the gift of making you feel good about yourself, but he was as good as he was evil.

Analysing it now, nearly 40 years later, I realise that I was living in a very synthetic, disposable world. After the experiences that they had had, Elvis and Vernon both believed that everything and everyone had its price and that everything could be bought.

There are no two ways about it: Vernon bought Dee at the expense of Bill. Elvis bought our affection at the very beginning. Obviously, at the age of four, I didn't know then what I know now, but I can look back with clarity. It has even spilled over into my own life. If I have a strained situation with someone I care about I have a tendency to say or think, 'What can I give them?' as opposed to dealing with the actual issue.

After Elvis became famous, he learned very quickly that if he wanted something in life, a simple display of cold hard cash would give him anything he wanted or let him do anything he wanted. Any situation in life that proved in the least bit 'uncomfortable' and he handed out some cash and everything was suddenly comfortable and loving.

From time to time Elvis would lose his temper and insult or attack someone and come back with regret. In these instances, his temporary remedy was a monetary or material gift rather than dealing with what had happened. That was the way he was with everything he did.

In that way, everything was easily justifiable. When it came to drugs, his rationalisation would be: 'I need them.' When he had done a bad show, it would be: 'I'm tired,' and never 'Maybe it's the drugs.' He had a completely off-kilter perspective on life, and even during my first days at Graceland, I could see and recognise this to a degree.

People still come up to me and ask, 'How did Elvis lose touch with reality towards the end of his life?' Well, I can honestly say that his touch with reality was totally gone by 1960 when I arrived on the scene. Evidently, he was not living in the real world from as far back as 1956. I didn't know it at the time, but in retrospect I can see that the pace was already set. Once he became Elvis Presley the singing star, all sense of reality was gone.

6

Inside the Gates

As a kid, growing up with Elvis as my older brother was almost like being sucked into a strange and surreal atmosphere, like being beamed up to a vortex in outer space. Even as a kid, we had very specialised rules of conduct that applied to anyone who lived inside of the gates of Graceland. The words 'You don't do this . . .' and 'You don't do that . . .' usually prefaced everything. Going to school was no escape from the bizarre life that we lived at Graceland either. First of all, everybody wanted to come over to your house after school and everybody wanted you to talk about your brother. These were both strictly forbidden activities. As a general rule, my brothers and I were kept out of the media as much as possible. However, we were still obviously living in a huge fishbowl.

It was a good thing that we had the 14 acres of land at Graceland to play on, and the three of us to play with each other. We weren't really allowed to socialise with 'the public'. The kids at school all acted so strangely towards us that we really didn't have any burning desire to hang out with them. For me, the key to survival at Graceland was Ricky and Billy.

Feeling isolated from the rest of the world, at Graceland I always had my brothers to lean on and depend upon. There is no doubt about it, we were very protective towards each other. It was totally necessary for my survival there. The three of us were always very tight, and that whole boarding home episode was a real test of emotional survival. But we somehow all made it through, because we had each other.

When we got to Graceland, we still bonded tightly together. We could really talk to each other about what was going on around us. Obviously that sense of bonding, as time went on, got us through every situation.

I was making slow adjustments to my new life at Graceland. Even Mom, who had orchestrated this dramatic scenario, felt a bit odd. According to her, 'I really felt like an outsider when I first came there. Gladys's clothes stayed in the closet of our bedroom, and her picture was everywhere. I felt as if she was hovering over me.'

My new step-father was a funny man. He had a very strong sense of humour. A simple man with only a fifth grade education, Vernon was very tight with his money, and very distrusting. Every morning at 7.00 a.m., when I was going to school, I had to go into his room, wake him up, and ask him for that day's lunch money. He was the kind of guy who refused to give me the $5 or $10 it might be for that week, he would only dole it out to me one day at a time.

He personally dispensed our 25 cent pieces to each of us individually. He grew up dirt poor, and he was going to teach us not to take money for granted. This was in direct contrast to Elvis who was so generous. It was as if he went through life aware of the fact that his twin brother Jesse had died and he had been allowed to live, and he proceeded through life as if he was genuinely thankful for his existence. Elvis had a very generous and trusting nature, and he had a need to share what he had with those people in his life whom he genuinely cared about. Vernon didn't have that characteristic in his personality at all.

Of course, Elvis himself was the most influential man in my life. With Dad out of the picture, and our new 'Daddy' – Vernon – suddenly in the picture, it was a bit confusing, especially for me at the ages of four to seven. While the cast of characters seemed to be changing, Elvis became a constant force in my life. How could I not want to grow up and be just like him? He had all his friends living with him, he had the coolest toys, and his life seemed like one big non-stop party.

Although Graceland was the home that he always came back to, much of his time in the years 1960 to 1968 was spent making his famous string of movies in Hollywood.

Once he was back in America, Elvis's entire career was wrapped up in making one movie after another. In a way, all 31 of his acting feature films were the same script recycled over and over again. No matter what the setting, he was always the romantic renegade, battling against the odds, singing a dozen or so songs, and winning the heart of the pretty girl at the end.

Elvis didn't do any more concert touring, and from the Frank Sinatra TV special at the beginning of 1960 up until 1968, he wasn't seen on television either. This is because his manager, Colonel Tom Parker, had jacked the price of an Elvis appearance right out of the ballpark. Elvis's six minutes of camera time on the Sinatra special had earned him $125,000. Right after the show, the Colonel announced that a TV appearance by Elvis would now cost $150,000. Between 1960 and 1968 Elvis starred in an astonishing 23 movies, but he didn't make a single network television appearance.

If the public wanted to see Elvis Presley, they had to go to their local theatres. At his peak, Paramount Pictures paid him $1 million for his appearance in the 1964 film *Roustabout* with Barbara Stanwyck. The following year, MGM had to match that figure, paying him another cool million for *Girl Happy*.

Right after he had settled in from his Army stint in Germany, Elvis was back in front of the cameras in *G.I. Blues* (1960) with Juliet Prowse, and *Flaming Star* (1960) with Barbara Eden and Dolores Del Rio. He was to follow these up with *Wild in the Country* (1961), *Blue Hawaii* (1961), *Follow that Dream* (1962), *Kid Galahad* (1962), *Girls! Girls! Girls!* (1962), *It Happened at the World's Fair* (1963), *Fun in Acapulco* (1963), *Kissin' Cousins* (1964), and *Viva Las Vegas* with Ann-Margret (1964).

Elvis could never go anywhere alone, and he didn't want to. When Elvis went anywhere, the entourage always included at least a handful of people – bodyguards, valets and friends – very much like a presidential motorcade.

Wherever he went, so went the 'Memphis Mafia'. It was like Robin Hood and his Merry Men. Lamar Fike, Red West, Sonny West, Charlie Hodge, Joe Esposito, Jerry Schilling, and the whole gang, were all included in all of his activities. Elvis never had a second to feel alone, lost, or lonely as long as he was in a crowd at all times; thanks to the Memphis Mafia he was always in a crowd.

Dee was amazed to see all of this unfold. She viewed them all as a bunch of free-loaders. She was later to recall seeing 'Elvis's guys sitting around the television set with their wives or girlfriends, waiting for Elvis to get up and come down. And when he did, everyone jumped at the same time to be the first one to him.'

At this point, up until Lisa Marie was born in 1968, none of the guys had children of their own, so Billy and Ricky and I had the spotlight for quite a while in the troupe. I was treated with even more special attenion, as I was literally the youngest kid on the block at Graceland. It was funny for me to see Joe or Lamar pout and be upset because they couldn't ride with Elvis in his car.

Vernon didn't really care for any of the guys, he felt that they were all taking advantage of Elvis. But Elvis wanted them there, and there they were. He would complain from time to time, but the only reason they were there with him was because he wanted them there. Elvis was very loyal to all of these people, but he expected the loyalty to be reciprocated.

There was a strong sense of loyalty that was developed at Graceland. From the minute I first passed through those gates, a bond of loyalty began to grow which only intensified with time. It was the written rule for all of Elvis's close circle that discussing him with any outsider was strictly forbidden.

Throughout that entire year, Priscilla continued to write love letters to Elvis. Dee was later to recall that Elvis showed her one of Priscilla's snapshots, which was included in one of her many letters from Germany, and said to her, 'Check this out Dee. You know, Dee, I've been to bed with no less than 1,000 women in my life. This is the one – right here!'

In December 1960, Elvis convinced Dee and Vernon to start a campaign to get Priscilla's parents to allow her to come to America to spend Christmas at Graceland. Elvis usually got his own way, and with Priscilla exerting pressure on her mom and dad, she was allowed to spend the holidays with us.

Growing up at Graceland was nothing short of fantastic. Christmas dinners there at the massive round table have given me many warm memories, with Priscilla, Lisa, Elvis, Vernon, Dee, Grandma Minnie Mae, Aunt Delta, my brothers and me. It continued very idyllically like this from 1960 to 1971. Reluctantly, Priscilla returned to Germany in January 1961.

For a while, Elvis's musical career continued quite successfully. In 1960 and 1961 he produced more Top Ten hit singles, including *Stuck On You*, *It's Now Or Never*, *Are You Lonesome Tonight?*, *Flaming Star*, *Little Sister*, *Surrender*, *His Latest Flame* and *Can't Help Falling In Love With You*. In August 1961, Billy, Ricky, Dee, Vernon and I went down to Florida to watch Elvis on location for his film *Follow That Dream*.

That same year, at the age of five, I got to see Elvis on stage for the first time. He was giving a benefit concert at Ellis Auditorium in Memphis, and Mom took my brothers and me to see it.

However, instead of being excited, I was horrified. When Elvis hit the spotlights, the crowd started screaming and rushing towards the stage. Unprepared for this sight, I thought they were trying to attack him. I screamed and cried so loud that Mom had to take me out of the auditorium immediately.

In 1962, Vernon and Dee and the three of us boys moved out of Graceland and into a house on Hermatage Street, because Dee wanted her own house. It was a nice suburban house, with two stories, located about a mile from Graceland. We were only there for a short time while we were building a house on Dolan Street that was adjacent to Graceland. The two houses were situated so that you could go through a gate right into the backyard of Graceland. We moved to 1266 Dolan Street in 1965 and Elvis would walk through the back gates of Graceland and across the pasture to our house. We would do likewise and go to Graceland.

Priscilla came over to live in America in 1962 and part of the deal that her parents made with Elvis and the Presley family to allow her to do that was that she was going to live with us at our house and Dee was going to be the chaperone.

When Priscilla came over she hung out a lot with my brothers and me. She was only 17 and still in school. I remember her riding in the car with Vernon, who was taking her to the Catholic high school that she attended in Memphis.

Priscilla was introduced to me as a friend of Elvis's. Everyone has to have their first crush on someone, and ironically, when I first saw Priscilla as a kid, I instantly had an extreme crush on her. She lived with us and she would stay over at Graceland a lot.

Although Priscilla's parents thought that Dee was chaperoning Priscilla, she in fact had free reign to go anywhere on the estate that she wanted – including Elvis's bedroom. Priscilla was later to confess that Elvis never had sex with her until they were married, although she admitted that she would have gladly had sex with him – and often made advances – but he always refused.

There was a weird angle to their entire relationship. He bought her expensive and flashy clothes – far more sophisticated in fact than anyone her own age should have been wearing. She was like a little living doll to him. He would dress her up and insist that she transform herself into his own vision of what she should be. He made her dye her medium brown hair jet black – just as he did with his. She wore her hair teased up in huge elaborate beehives, which was the fashion of the day.

He liked her to wear heavy Cleopatra-like eye make-up. She was his little virgin goddess – and he successfully kept her that way for nearly five years – until they finally made it to the altar.

Although they were nearly inseparable when Elvis was home in Memphis, he spent much of his time in Hollywood working on his movies. She was rarely ever invited to accompany him there. Instead, he took the Memphis Mafia guys along for months at a time, where they would all behave like they were at a never-ending stag party and where the wives and serious girlfriends were forbidden.

In that way, Priscilla was treated like a delicate china doll and kept safely at home like a possession. During those times at Graceland, when Elvis was in Hollywood and Priscilla was in Memphis with us, she was many different things to us: part playmate, part sister, part exchange student, and the object of my first real infatuation. It all made as much and as little sense as anything else that happened at Graceland – the mansion where all rules of convention were somehow left at the gate.

For the most part, Priscilla behaved like a big sister to me. I remember on one birthday she came and picked me up in the little Corvair that Elvis had given her and she took me out. She bought me a toy helicopter, a parrot and a skateboard.

I have great memories of Priscilla. Lots of them. I remember that when Priscilla moved into Graceland, before they were married, we'd go over there a lot, especially when Elvis was in Hollywood filming. Without him in town, it was a somewhat lonely house. Priscilla used to dress up as a vampire – with that black hair and dark eyes, she made a very convincing vampire. Then she'd turn off all the lights and chase us around the dark house. Those were the good times.

One thing that Elvis always did at Graceland before doing a concert and major show was to lie in the sun to get some colour. I can remember many a time when he and Priscilla would go to the pool. Knowing how much I liked being around them, they would often call me after school and say, 'We're going swimming, get your suit on and come on over.' This was always a thrill when I was a kid. After all, at the ages of ten, 11, and 12, I was a hormone with feet, and I thought Priscilla looked great in a bikini.

The cool thing about growing up with Elvis, and being at Graceland, was the fact that Elvis was just a big kid at heart. He would go off on different tangents from time to time, and it might be riding, or motorcycles, or any number of toys and games.

One Christmas in the early '60s, Priscilla gave Elvis his own miniature slot car race track. That was all the rage at the time and those little miniature cars were the latest thing. A variation on a model railroad, these little cars had powerful but tiny engines in them and their speed was individually regulated by hand controls. The equipment was very sophisticated and pricey and those little cars could certainly whizz around those twisting looping tracks! Billy, Ricky and I were fascinated by them, and Elvis – big kid that he was – totally got into it as a hobby as well.

The original slot car set was just big enough to set up on the top of the pool table, down in the billiard room at Graceland. The slot car craze was really on in 1964 and 1965 and Elvis and my brothers and I used to go into town to a place called Robert E. Lee's, which was in a shopping centre strip where they had 35 feet racetracks for racing your slot cars.

At the time, Elvis was remodelling Graceland and redoing the interior of the house. In the back, they were adding an extra room to the house and he decided that he was going to put the track in it. This was a perfect example of his obsessive behaviour in full swing. He couldn't have a two-track race course – he had to have 12 separate tracks, so that all the guys could have their own cars, their own controls, the whole thing. It was obsession all the way.

Later, Elvis gave the track away to the local boy's club. He had got totally burned out on it, and he was on to some new and different obsession to throw himself into.

Another thing that he liked was those little 'You Control' airplanes with the gasoline-powered engines. He got into that very heavily. And, if Elvis did it, everybody did it – Lamar, Red, Sonny, Charlie, Vernon, Billy, Ricky, myself – we all became involved in his latest crazes.

If it wasn't one thing it was something else. It was an outrageous way to grow up. From time to time a new obsession would replace the previous one. We all had our own slot cars, we all had our own horses, then we got our own motorcycles.

When motorcycles were the latest craze I started out on a mini-bike. I was so small and just a runt at the time but I had my own little mini-bike, while the guys cruised around on their Triumphs and Hondas. Eventually I had my own full-sized motorcycle as well. Cars and motorcycles were two constant passions for Elvis amidst all of the constant change.

These were all toys to Elvis. If you were going to have a hobby, you had to have a team of buddies to share it with. Since money was no object, Elvis just bought everyone their own toys so that they could play with him. Excess was best!

During the initial horse phase at Graceland, I remember on one occassion in the middle of winter when we were riding around on a John Deere tractor with a trailer on the back equipped with hammers and nails, fixing the broken fences on the property. When we were finished we'd have big campfires and throw a big old party. Elvis really fancied himself a cowboy and he loved doing things like that.

You can certainly say that Elvis lived out his childhood dreams. Other toys included 'go-karts' that he would race around the front of Graceland in, some of them capable of doing 60 to 70 miles per hour. In the winter it was snow mobiles that would hit 70 or 80 miles an hour, for cruising the 14 acres of land at Graceland.

As time went on, his toys became more and more expensive. At first, Elvis wasn't too keen on flying. He had tour buses to go out to Los Angeles to film his movies. He hired George Barris, the famous car customiser who created the 'Batmobile' for TV's Batman and a great customised Pontiac G.T.O. for the Monkees – known as 'The Monkeemobile'. Elvis got George to customise motorcycles for himself and Priscilla. She had her own pink Honda 300 done by Barris and Elvis had a black one. That was at the height of the 'Elvis and Priscilla' days. They were like a family unit, and one by one the guys in the Memphis Mafia were getting married, and then their wives would be part of the troupe as well.

Meanwhile, Billy and Ricky and I were still kids, and we got to come along on many of their excursions. We were included in everything that Elvis did.

When Elvis changed his mode of coast-to-coast travel from buses to airplanes, they too became one of his passions. It all began with Elvis getting his first one, and really getting into flying. Then he bought another one, and another, and soon he had a whole fleet of private planes which he owned. He really did it up big: he had an 880 Convair, he had a couple of Learjets and Falcons. That was where he spent his big money. So, it was always the next high, always the next kick. It was as if he was thinking, 'What's the next thing that can preoccupy my mind?'

Renting out the local movie theatre and having all-night screening parties was a constant passion for him. This was years before home video players and wide-screen television. Elvis would simply take over a Memphis movie house, and use their facilities for his private guests.

It was never a pre-arranged thing. He would just call at night and announce 'We're coming,' and the whole place was his, right after the public left the last show. A guy named Paul Shafer was the local big movie theatre manager in Memphis. Paul and his wife and family were friends of the Presleys, as were local jewellers, the mayor and all of the most influential people in town.

Then there was racketball. Suddenly he was into racketball, and he had to have a whole racketball court built.

My brothers and I would go over to Graceland. Elvis would get up at about four or five in the afternoon, and we would ride motorcycles, or hang around the house, or ride horses, or watch TV. Then we would go to the movies at midnight or about one in the morning.

Elvis loved to go out on New Year's Eve or the Fourth of July and buy fireworks. He would spend thousands of dollars buying them by the truckload. His idea of having fun was to split up into teams and have a fireworks war. We would don flight suits, helmets and goggles and shoot bottle rockets, aerial displays, and Roman candles at each other. I know this sounds dangerous but nothing could have been more fun. A couple of people ended up with singed hair, and the backyard was filled with burnt divots where Roman Candles fried the grass, but that was – miraculously – the most damage that was done.

Sometimes one of Elvis's hobbies would veer out of control. The horses fell into this category. All the horses started to overrun Graceland and Elvis bought the Circle G ranch near Tupelo where there was room on the property to stable them. All of us, including the Memphis Mafia guys and their families, would join Elvis at the ranch to ride and hold rodeos. We spent so much time at the place that Elvis began buying pick-up trucks and installing mobile homes on the grounds so that everybody could stay overnight. Everybody had to have their own Ford pick-up truck in their favourite colour. Everybody had to have their own saddles. Elvis rarely bought something just for himself – he bought one for everybody. Eventually, interest in the ranch waned and Elvis sold it. Some of the favourite horses were brought back to Graceland. Unfortunately, the new owners defaulted on payments and the Circle G Ranch eventually reverted back to Elvis and Vernon.

During this period, Elvis was coping with the 'British Invasion', where the Beatles took over the airwaves. Elvis had been on top for nearly ten years, when 'the changing of the guard' in rock and roll music occurred.

I liked Elvis's music, but to me the Beatles, The Who and the Rolling Stones were rock and roll. One thing that I will never forget is my mother turning the Beatles away from our front door. I also remember her breaking my Beatles albums.

In 1964 we were living on Dolan Street, and I was in elementary school. The Beatles had just played in Memphis and they had gone by Graceland but Elvis wasn't at home. He was out in Los Angeles working on one of his movies at the time. Uncle Vester, who manned the front gate at Graceland, said to them, 'Go around the block and go and see Vernon, his father. He'll want to meet you.'

My brother and my Mom were at home that particular day. Dee wasn't a particularly big Beatles fan – it was as though she felt she had to choose between either Elvis or the Beatles. The tension of the Beatles/Elvis relationship was always there, because those four guys had taken over the entire American music charts and everybody knew it. The press took great delight in pointing out that the Beatles were now breaking album sales, ticket sales and popularity records that had been set by Elvis a decade before.

Even the Beatles' appearance on the *Ed Sullivan Show* had broken Elvis's record for the number of viewers who tuned in to see their prime-time American network television debut. As a Beatles fan, I had to suffer the consequences of the whole Elvis versus the Beatles competition.

On that particular evening our front doorbell rang and I opened it. There stood John Lennon and Brian Epstein asking me, 'Little boy, is Elvis at home?' I nearly fell over.

Vernon came up from behind me and said, 'No, he is out in Los Angeles making a movie at the moment.'

While Lennon was speaking to Vernon, I looked out to the long black Cadillac limousine that was parked out in the driveway. The windows were rolled down and I could see Ringo Starr, Paul McCartney and George Harrison perched inside to see if 'The King' was there or not.

Imagine how I felt at the time: the Beatles were sitting in a car in my driveway – I was in total awe. I certainly didn't feel that way towards Elvis at that time – he was just my big brother the entertainer. These were *the Beatles*, and much more important in my mind at the time, because I still didn't quite grasp the fan mentality towards Elvis. I said to my mother, 'I'm going to go outside and say "Hi" to the rest of the guys.'

She told me bluntly, 'No.' She didn't like the Beatles because, like Elvis, she felt threatened by them. She had an intense dislike for the

Beatles that progressed throughout the '60s. It was taken to an even further degree when in 1966 John Lennon made the flippant remark about the Beatles being more popular than Jesus Christ. His statement so offended Dee's conservative Southern Christian background that she felt compelled to destroy my Beatles LPs. Needless to say, I was very upset.

As you can see, the atmosphere that I grew up in was very conservative and in it Elvis was regarded by everyone as this wonderful super-patriot.

After that episode, the Beatles went out to Los Angeles and they met Elvis in August 1965. They played pool, and Elvis and McCartney played bass. The effect of the Beatles' success hung over Elvis like the Sword of Damocles. He had been the undisputed King at the top of the charts, and here, seemingly from nowhere, the Beatles were everywhere. Suddenly his impact on the music charts dwindled substantially. From 1963 to 1969, Elvis only managed to place one single in the Top Ten – 1965's *Crying in the Chapel*, which he had actually recorded in 1960.

When they first came out with *I Want To Hold Your Hand* in 1964, he was great with it. Then they started to eclipse his career. In later years Elvis was finally able to put his battle against the Beatles to rest, and he recorded several of their songs including *Hey Jude*, *Something* and *Lady Madonna*. For a long time, however, the Beatles seemed to him to be a threatening force from across the Atlantic.

Even though we had moved to the house on Dolan, I still spent most of my time at Graceland. I would go to school, then come home and go over to Graceland and go swimming in the pool with Priscilla and Elvis. This was in the springs and summers of 1964 and 1965.

We all went out to Los Angeles in July 1965 and spent the whole summer there. We got to visit Elvis on the backlots when he was filming *Frankie and Johnny* and *Paradise Hawaiian Style*. When we were out there we took up residence at the Beverly Hilton Hotel, and Elvis had a house up on Perugia Way at Bel Aire Estates.

It was a very family type thing. There were always people around to chaperone us, and nothing that alluded to any mischief in any way between Elvis and Priscilla.

In 1965, our Dad, Bill Stanley Sr., came to visit Graceland with his second wife. He had moved from one job to another over the past couple of years, doing everything from hospital work to being captain of a tug boat in the Caribbean Sea. The last time I had seen him I had been four years old. At best, he was but a distant memory to me at this point. In retrospect it was sad.

Dad was later to recount the reunion by stating, 'We arrived in Memphis about noon on a Saturday, visiting for several hours. Vernon and Dee were cordial to us. We spent most of the time visiting the boys. I noticed they hesitantly called me "Bill" now, and referred to Vernon as "Daddy". The transfer of affection was complete. Somehow I felt like a stranger. It seemed Dee had accomplished her dream.'

One of my favourite Elvis memories comes from that year. It is a cold November evening at Graceland in 1965. It was quiet in the house that night. I was walking through the living room, where it leads to the dining room, and at the end of a long hallway is a pearly white piano in a room with white couches and all white furniture. In the middle of this setting I came upon Elvis, all alone at the piano, playing music.

There was an arch that led into this piano room, and the arch was festooned with long draperies. I was just nine years old, and I stood quietly behind those drapes and listened to big brother Elvis playing the piano and singing just for the sheer joy of it. It was a wonderful sight, and an exciting musical experience that was witnessed by no one but me. That scene is etched into my memory.

Everyone who ever met Elvis Presley can recall their meetings with him and their distinct impressions. This little scenario is my favourite memory of Elvis. He was in incredible voice and he wasn't singing to impress anyone, he was singing because that is what he loved to do. In terms of true, raw talent, that was the real Elvis.

I had gone through a problem child phase and finally in the seventh grade I was sent to military school, and I really hated it. Everyone finally realised that a disciplinary military school wasn't going to work for me, and I got out of there, and went to Whitehaven Junior High School, which is the name of the suburb where Graceland was located.

I remember one instance in 1967, when Elvis was out of town, and Dee and Vernon were in Las Vegas. I got up and got dressed like any other day and that afternoon I was picked up by Mrs Wilma Spartman, the housekeeper who took care of my brothers and me when Dee and Vernon weren't around. As we prepared to drive home from Whitehaven Junior High, Mrs Spartman said to me, 'Have you heard that your brother has gotten married?'

'No,' I said.

'Well, he got married today,' she said.

Later that night, when we were at home, Dee and Elvis called and we talked to them and Priscilla, and that's how we found out that Elvis and Priscilla were married on 1 May 1967.

The official reception was in Memphis later that week because they had such a small service in Las Vegas. The wedding, the reception and the press releases were handled within just four or five days. A lot of people still ask me, 'Well, David, how could you know that?' Well, it's because I was living there and eventually heard everything that was going on.

We were in Los Angeles when Elvis was filming *Speedway* with Nancy Sinatra, Bill Bixby and Teri Garr. What none of us knew at the time was that Elvis was having a relationship with Nancy, right after he married Priscilla. I didn't know it at the time, but years later I've heard all the stories, and then later witnessed first hand that the word 'loyalty' wasn't ever in Elvis's vocabulary – at any point in his life. His attitude was always, 'This is me, this is the way I am, this is how I live my life, and this is how I am going to remain.'

To the press, and to the world, announcements went out that The King of Rock and Roll had married his queen. Priscilla got what she wanted, she had finally married him. The whole Cinderella story was completely fabricated and he continued partying and womanising as he always had done. Elvis was not loyal to Priscilla when she first moved to Graceland and he was not loyal to her once he married her.

Elvis and Priscilla returned to Memphis after that. Dee and Vernon were at the wedding ceremony itself and Marty Lacker was there as the best man. Joe Esposito and his wife Joni, Michelle – Priscilla's sister – and Priscilla's mother, father and brother were also there. Basically, it was just a family affair because it was done so quickly. Not even Red and Sonny attended.

I think that the reason for the speed was because Colonel Parker was looking at the image of Elvis at that time. It wasn't cool to have Priscilla, as an unwed young girl, living at Graceland anymore. They had pulled it off up until this point but what if this scenario was discovered and ended up in the wrong hands? It threatened to capsize the good ship Elvis in one swift stroke.

It was a repeat of the Dee and Vernon situation all over again. Colonel Parker insisted that Elvis either make his situation with Priscilla legal or else that he dump her altogether. Colonel Parker made all of the arrangements, and made them very quickly.

When they came back to Memphis they had a reception for all of the hometown family people and friends. The entire crew that took care of the Presley business and the Presley estate were all there. The room at Graceland which is now on view as the trophy room was then called the Blue Room. That room had once contained Elvis's little model slot car track, and it was very big. The track had long since been given away, and now the room was the site of one of Graceland's most lavish events.

The whole family was in attendance that day: Billy and Ricky and I, Vernon, Dee, Grandma, Aunt Delta and Aunt Nash. Then there were all of the friends plus the attorneys, the bankers, the mayor, the local jewellers, the whole Memphis Mafia.

Right after the private Las Vegas wedding Elvis and Priscilla had gone to Palm Springs for several days, and then returned to Graceland for this event. It was an elaborate black tie affair with a formal receiving line, and everybody gave gifts as part of a traditional ceremony.

When Billy and Ricky and I walked up in our suits, everyone said, 'Stop right there, and let's get a photo of this.'

In between photos Elvis and I would horse around. I recently saw someone's home movies from the event, and there was Elvis putting his hands around my neck and shaking me and goofing around. He used to like to grab hold of me and pick me up by the neck, and I'd grab his hands. I was 12 at this point, so it was a little hard for him to do that, but he did horse around with me at the reception – just teasing his little brother like any normal big brother might do.

Elvis always referred to us as 'the boys'. We knew and felt that he loved us and we loved him back. We felt that he had welcomed us into his family when he didn't have to, and we were thrilled to be part of everything. We were just grateful to be there.

The older we got, the more we realised how élite our position in the whole household was. We weren't just employees, and when we went somewhere we could see the pettiness of some of the other people. A lot of the others were jealous of us boys because of our unique relationship with Elvis. They might have been with him longer but we were soundly ensconced in the inner circle and there was nothing the Memphis Mafia guys could do to eclipse us.

It got to the point where, if we were going to go somewhere, and we were travelling in two or three different cars and they didn't get to ride in Elvis's car with him then they would have 'pity parties'. We never really thought anything about it one way or another –

we'd just jump into any old car. We were happy to be along. But amongst the Memphis Mafia members there was a strong sense of competition to be riding with Elvis, and to have the attention and the ear of 'The King'. Most of the time there would always be someone with hurt feelings. But, since we three were his brothers, we would usually ride with him. This certainly tipped off some jealousies.

As kids, we didn't really think about this in those terms. We were just grateful to be along for the ride. And in a way, all of the guys were like our uncles; we felt as if we were being raised by them all. I was living amidst a pack of wolves. It was like being raised by 12 or 15 people all the time.

Generally, Elvis didn't take Priscilla out to Los Angeles when he made the movies. In the summer, it was a family time when we would stay behind at Graceland, and I would stay in Priscilla's room, like a slumber party – all of us young kids. Those were the really good times at Graceland. I always considered Priscilla somebody whom I liked and I thought she was really pretty.

It's not surprising that the marriage wasn't destined to last. For Elvis, the word commitment did not exist. He was certainly never faithful to her. Priscilla was on to it. She would mark the spots where her clothes were in the bureaus when she left. Then she'd leave and a new girl would come in, and Priscilla's clothes would be removed. But Elvis caught on about the marks, so he foiled Priscilla's trap by making sure that her clothes were all lined up when she came back.

Elvis was hard on Priscilla. There was never a quiet moment between the two of them because Elvis always had the guys around him. It was by no means a traditional marriage, which was what Priscilla wanted. She certainly had it tough – she must have felt she was married to the whole Memphis Mafia.

Exactly nine months after Elvis and Priscilla were married, on 1 February 1968, Lisa Marie Presley arrived on the scene. Elvis was so thrilled about the birth of his little daughter that he would spend hours with her, talking and playing with her. This marked the first time since I came to live at Graceland that I wasn't the youngest one there.

Poor Priscilla. She had waited for so long to consummate her relationship with Elvis. Following the birth of Lisa Marie, one would have thought that their sexual relationship would resume. What none of us knew at the time was the fact that after Lisa Marie was born, Elvis rarely, if ever made love to her. She was no longer his little virgin goddess. She was now his wife and he behaved differently towards her.

Instead of spending time together, just Priscilla, Elvis and Lisa Marie, the guys from the Memphis Mafia were all there too. And, now that Elvis had a family, the guys and their wives began to start families of their own. This didn't break up the tightness between Elvis and the Memphis Mafia. They continued business as usual, more likely than not leaving all of the wives in Memphis to take care of the kids, while Elvis and the guys continued to drink, party,and womanise in Los Angeles.

Christmas remained the one big exception, however. Following the birth of Lisa Marie, Elvis's excitement about Christmas only intensified. After most of the guests went to bed or went home, Elvis and a few of the guys would bring out Lisa Marie's presents and put them under the tree. The early morning hours of Christmas Day were very often the best times at Graceland. Elvis would talk about his mother and about the Christmases of his boyhood. He would often say something like, 'I wonder what all the poor folks are doing tonight. I wish I could feed all the poor kids and give them presents.' He would reflect on how grateful he was for his success. Then he would wait with the eagerness of a child for Lisa to awaken and find her presents under the tree.

In 1968 Elvis starred in his own television special, *Elvis*, which is also known as *Elvis: One Night With You*. Originally, the Elvis special was planned as a Christmas show, which was to be entitled *Elvis and the Wonderful World of Christmas*. The concept was Colonel Parker's idea – his reasoning being that it could be re-broadcast annually every December. NBC-TV loved the idea of landing Elvis, but the holiday theme turned them off. What ultimately happened was that he did the exciting back-to-basics rock and roll show that the network wanted, and he sang the song *Blue Christmas*.

The *Elvis* special was divided into two main segments: first with Elvis standing up on stage singing to a concert audience seated on bleachers and second, seated on a small platform singing with his musicians and surrounded by a small mostly-female audience. The show was taped in late June 1968 at NBC studios in Los Angeles. Four hours of Elvis singing, joking and playing music that made him a star, was edited down to 50 minutes, and broadcast for the first time on 3 December 1968.

This marked a turning point for Elvis. Throughout the 1960s, Elvis had continued to pump out one 'B' movie after another.

Although they had all made money, he was bored with it all, and was eager to get back to performing before a live audience.

He had done the TV special with Steve Binder as producer/director, and it was extremely successful. He had on this very cool-looking black leather suit, and it was as if he was showing the Beatles, the Rolling Stones and the rest of the rockers, that he was still around. After all of the poor movies he had made – many of them filmed in only three weeks, Elvis was finally on the comeback trail.

In the intervening years, Elvis's hit-making prowess on the record charts had subsided greatly. His last Number One hit had been *Good Luck Charm* in 1962. However, on 23 January 1969 he recorded *Suspicious Minds*. For some reason he felt that this was going to make up for his absence from the top of the charts. He was right. His first big single of 1969 was *In the Ghetto*, which hit the Top Ten. It was to pave the way back to the top.

At the time, the Beatles, the Stones, Led Zeppelin and Crosby, Stills, Nash and Young were all dominating the American music scene. I remember Elvis telling me the night he found out that *Suspicious Minds* had gone to Number One. He said, 'David, I've been wrong for so long, but I'm right tonight.'

At this point, he was more than anxious to get out of doing the movies. The way out was paved by the TV special, then when 1969 rolled around, he was ready for live performances again. He cut a deal with the International Hotel in Las Vegas to make several appearances there over the next couple of years.

He arrived in Las Vegas in July 1969 to rehearse and prepare for the show. At the same time, Priscilla and Lisa Marie, Priscilla's sister Michelle, Ricky, Billy and I all went to Hawaii, where we had a great time.

About a week or so after Elvis's historic opening at the International, Priscilla, my mother, my two older brothers and I flew back to Los Angeles to spend some time. Priscilla stayed at her and Elvis's home in Beverly Hills, while my mother and two brothers and I stayed at the Beverly Wilshire Hotel.

On the morning of 9 August, Billy, Ricky and I were watching the news on television when it was announced that Charles Manson had massacred Sharon Tate, Jay Sebring and all of their friends up in the Hollywood Hills, not all that far from our hotel on Sunset Boulevard.

It was no more than a few seconds later that the telephone rang. It was Vernon saying, 'Security's on their way up. Elvis says to pack your things now. We're leaving.'

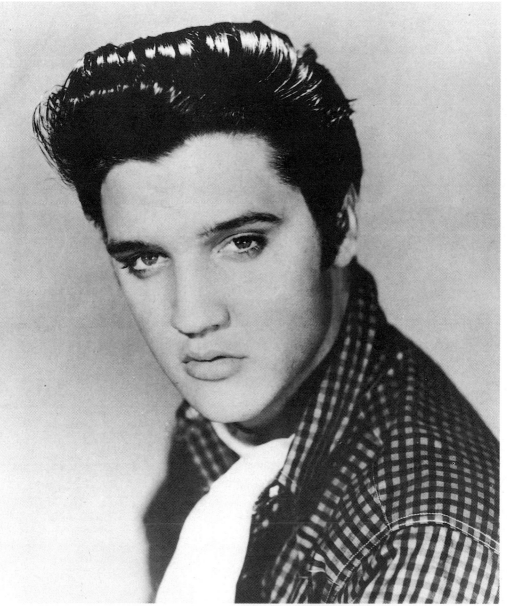

When my big brother, Elvis Presley, first became an international singing sensation in the 1950s, there was no one around like him. I was born the year that his career really took off, and had no idea how influential he would be in my life. *(Photo: RCA Records/MJB Archives)*

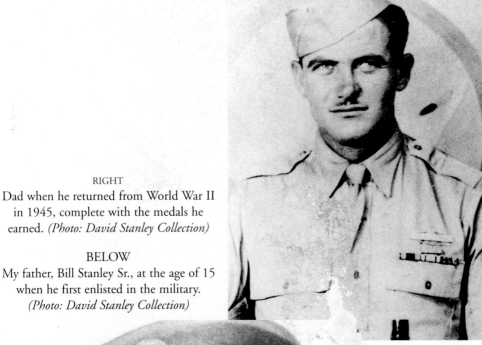

RIGHT
Dad when he returned from World War II
in 1945, complete with the medals he
earned. *(Photo: David Stanley Collection)*

BELOW
My father, Bill Stanley Sr., at the age of 15
when he first enlisted in the military.
(Photo: David Stanley Collection)

My mother, Dee Elliot Stanley Presley. This photo was taken during the era in which she met her first husband, Bill Stanley. *(Photo: David Stanley Collection)*

Elvis made the transition from singing
star to movie star in the 1956 western
*Love Me Tender. (Photo: Twentieth
Century Fox/MJB Archives)*

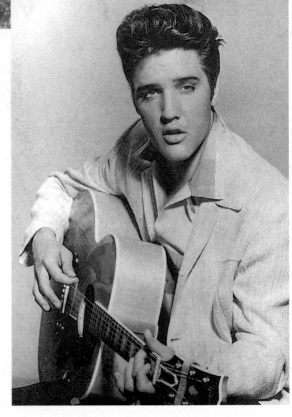

In the 1957 film *Jailhouse Rock*, Elvis
proved that he was a huge box–office
draw. *(Photo: MGM/MJB Archives)*

When Elvis was inducted into the
army in 1958, every move he made
was captured on film. *(Photo: courtesy
Baby Jane of Hollywood/Charles Moniz)*

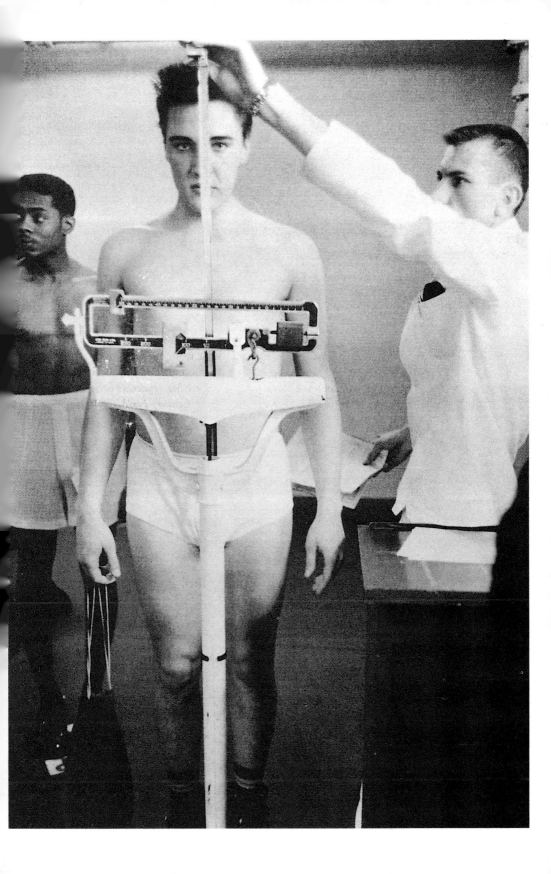

LEFT
Private Elvis Presley with his girlfriend
Anita Wood, his buddy Eddie Fadal,
and Eddie's wife, at Ft. Hood, Texas, in
1958. *(Photo: courtesy Eddie Fadal)*

RIGHT
My dad, Bill Stanley Sr., with my brothers Billy
(left), Ricky *(right)*, and me. He was destined to
lose everything he held dear . . . especially his
boys. *(Photo David Stanley Collection)*

BELOW
Graceland mansion in Memphis, Tennessee was
the house that Elvis was proud to purchase in
the late 1950s – it became my playground as a
child. *(Photo: David Stanley Collection)*

RIGHT
With my brother Billy *(centre)* and Vernon *(right)* at Elvis's Circle G Ranch in Mississippi in the 1960s. *(Photo: Jimmy Velvet/David Stanley Collection)*

BELOW
With Mom in the backyard of our first house in Memphis, in 1962. We lived here until our new house, which backed onto Graceland property, was completed. *(Photo: Lou Hediger/David Stanley Collection)*

Elvis made 33 films in all, including this one, *Fun in Acapulco* in 1963. *(Photo: Paramount Pictures/MJB Archives)*

We rushed out of that hotel and were driven under armed guard to the airport. There we were met by Priscilla and Lisa Marie and we all boarded the *Christina*, a DH125 jet owned by Frank Sinatra and we were immediately flown to Las Vegas.

We were all surprised at Elvis's reaction: I mean, what did Charles Manson have to do with us? Then we found out later that Elvis was on Manson's hit list, and we realised he was right.

This was happening just a couple of days before Elvis opened at the International. There was all sorts of activity going on – Woodstock, the Manson murders, and the first man on the moon.

The night before Elvis's opening, Barbara Streisand was closing her engagement. We all went that night – Elvis, Priscilla, Michelle, Dee, Vernon, Billy, Ricky and me. At the time I was 13 years old and the idea of going to a Barbara Streisand concert sounded like the squarest thing that one could possibly do. I was totally into Crosby, Stills and Nash's first album, and I was deeply committed to Led Zeppelin. All of a sudden, we were in Las Vegas – not exactly counter-culture territory – getting ready for Elvis's big comeback and about to face what I thought would be the ultimate bore: a Barbara Streisand concert at the International Hotel. This is something I would never have done on my own at that time in my life. Elvis made me go, he said I needed to be 'cultured'. Two songs into her performance, I was star-struck. She was wonderful. I thank Elvis for exposing me to that beautiful voice.

The following evening, the family and I all got dressed up for this special engagement.It wasn't like going to a concert today, where you wear your jeans and a casual shirt. Back then we would *really* get dressed up. We were part of Elvis's family and we were swept up into the glamour and the excitement of it all. That night I was dressed in a really sharp suit that was purchased at Lansky Brothers in Memphis, which is the store where Elvis bought most of his clothes.

You could feel that it was going to be a major event, it was like going to the Superbowl. There was a sense that Elvis was really going to do something significant that night. Gregory Peck was there, George Hamilton, Minnie Pearl, Earl Scruggs, Fats Domino, and countless other celebrities were in attendance. There was an electric atmosphere in the room that night.

Since the previous time that Elvis had played Las Vegas, back in 1958, his act and his stage persona had changed greatly. He was no longer regarded as the teen idol maniac who rolled around on stage or dry-humped the mike stand while he sang. The change in the entertainment world's perception of him partially had do with all of the movies that he had made since then. They were no longer thin-plotted teenage rock and roll films like *Jailhouse Rock*. He had worked hard to become a matinée idol who could hold his own on the screen with some of the most famous and respected actors in Hollywood. He was also known as the charismatic leading man who had caused sparks on film with his glamorous co-stars.

This performance showed that Elvis was truly back on the scene. He just had a killer band that night. When drummer Ronnie Tutt started into his break and Elvis came out, you knew that it was something special. He had James Burton who played on the rock TV shows *Shindig* and *Hullabaloo*, and had played with Ricky Nelson. He had a great solid rhythm section, and he broke out with *That's Alright Mama*. He hadn't done anything like this since he left for Germany, and the 1960s were recognised as the weakest era in Elvis's career. What had made his career hot to begin with were his exciting live performances. He had coasted by with all of those movies for the last nine years, and now he was officially back.

In that performance he really proved himself. Everyone who was a veteran, seasoned Elvis fan was really blown away. For someone who had experienced the Elvis phenomenon from a 1969 show, as opposed to a 1957 or 1958 show, it was apparent to me that he had never lost his ability to entertain a crowd. I could see right then and there, that this was why Elvis was called The King of Rock and Roll.

He came out at the opening wearing a black suit and he had his guitar and his band, and he just levelled that crowd. He just put us under! There was no doubt about it that evening: Elvis Presley really rocked. He was *dangerous*, and the people just went nuts.

I had seen Elvis at the Ellis Auditorium in 1961, and I had seen him on the backlot of the movie studios, I had even seen him play his pearly-white piano at Graceland mansion when he was at his best which nobody but I saw. But, when he came out on the stage that night, he re-established the fact that he was the creator of rock and roll.

I never considered Elvis a rock and roll star. He was my big brother. Man, I didn't even care too much for his movies, so I went to his opening concert that night with less than high expectations and less than an open mind. It was the second time I'd seen him perform. The first time when I was five didn't count!

With the Barbara Streisand performance the night before, that marked the second time in two nights that I was totally laid out. What a double header: Streisand one night, Elvis the next!

Afterwards I went backstage and my eyes were as big as pizza platters. I said to him, 'God almighty, Elvis, that was unbelievable.' And he looked at me and said, 'David, that's why they call me the King of Rock and Roll.' That became a monumental turning point in my life. After that show when I went back to school I was able to say proudly, 'I'm Elvis's brother,' and have an idea what they all saw in him – and I felt it myself.

He was a huge hit, and he proceeded to do two shows a night for 30 consecutive nights there. He also had a contract with the hotel to do two shows a night, for 30 days, for the next seven years, every February.

He went back to the International Hotel in 1970 and did the concert film, *Elvis: That's The Way It Is*. Suddenly my brothers and I would find ourselves in Las Vegas with Dee and Vernon, to attend another of Elvis's opening engagements. Every time Elvis appeared in Vegas we were right there. We would also attend his Lake Tahoe engagements.

Throughout this period, I had an even stronger bond with Elvis, because he was spending more time in Memphis. This was mainly due to the fact that he was no longer flying to Los Angeles to act in the movies.

In 1969, I was still a big Beatles fan, and Elvis still wasn't. He felt their music tried to promote an anti-establishment generation and, as we all know, it did. So when he recorded *Hey Jude* in the winter of 1969 it was a complete surprise to me. I guess he was feeling a litle mistreated by the Beatles' massive success and thought if *Hey Jude* worked for them, then maybe it would work for him. In this case, he was wrong. I've never heard a worse rendition of a Paul McCartney song. Hey, nobody's perfect!

In February 1970 my brother Rick went to work for Elvis as his personal aide. Meanwhile, I had my introduction to liquor and recreational drugs. After Rick came back home from the first tour, he bragged to me about what he saw – the sex, drugs and partying that went along with rock and roll. I listened intently to his wild stories of life on the road with Elvis, and longed for the day when I graduated from high school so that I could do the same thing, and 'get into the family business' so to speak.

On 27 and 28 February 1970, Elvis sold out the Houston Astrodome playing two nights, two shows a night. Mom, Vernon,

Billy, Ricky and I spent the weekend in Houston and attended all
the concerts at the Astrodome. It was one thing to see Elvis
perform in a 2,000-seat showroom in Vegas, but now here he was
in front of 44,000 screaming fans. I was in school at the time, and
I got time off to fly from Memphis to Houston to see this event. It
was during this weekend that I actually realised that Elvis was the
biggest entertainer in the world.

Looking back on this era, I think Elvis must have been happiest
when he was on stage. He was in his element. He knew he was good,
knew he could control an audience. He loved to make people happy.
Elvis was very genuine about his love for people. That must sound
strange, because he was practically a recluse. Maybe because he had
such trouble forming close relationships with individuals, he
transferred his natural affection for people to groups of people,
where he knew he could communicate, knew he could make contact.

Elvis wasn't a great conversationalist with strangers, or even his
peers. He didn't know a lot of stars, but a lot of stars knew him.
That sounds strange, but it's true. In the 1960s Elvis and Tom
Jones became friends. Tom would come over and they'd sing. Elvis
loved the way he sang, he thought he was the best of the best, and
vice versa. That was the basis of the relationship. They both had a
healthy respect for each other.

He was also friends with Ann-Margret. Their friendship
developed during the filming of *Viva Las Vegas* in 1964 and lasted
up until Elvis's untimely death. But as far as hanging out with his
peers, it just didn't happen. Do you know why he didn't associate
with others in the business? He was intimidated by his inability to
make conversation. He wasn't one to sit around and just talk to
anybody. He had to know you, trust you, so he isolated himself.
There were times when Elvis made Howard Hughes look like a
public persona!

Things also started becoming more bizarre in the 1970s when
Elvis was getting into what I call his 'Super Cop' era. He got into
this frame of mind where he was going to be 'Super Elvis'.

It was also in this era that Elvis came up with the idea of having
a symbol created for his whole 'Super Elvis' club. He hit upon the
idea of having the initials 'TCB' (Taking Care of Business)
emblazoned on everything from gold and diamond-encrusted rings
and necklaces to his personal jet. That whole 'TCB' insignia, with
the lightning bolt through it, came right out of 'Captain America',
who had the insignia of a lightning bolt on his chest. Elvis took
that symbol directly from that character.

It had all started back in Memphis. He had the habit of hanging out with policemen which was actually a great public relations connection for him to have made. Wherever he went he needed bodyguards and protection, so it helped him to get chummy with the local police.

Elvis was always a big weapon and gun collector but at this point he began purchasing a lot of police paraphernalia. There was a place downtown called the Polk Building where you could buy handcuffs and nightsticks and surplus law enforcement equipment. Elvis had also become friends with the Deputy Sheriff in Memphis.

Suddenly, he got it into his head that he wanted to be Deputy Sheriff. This can be an honorary title bestowed upon a citizen pressed into law enforcement service but it also allows you to wear a gun.

The next thing we knew, Elvis was on a crusade against the misuse of drugs. He was taking prescription drugs at this point but for him they were still more recreational than addiction-oriented.

I didn't have a clue then that Elvis was taking drugs at all. He was still really good at keeping it in control and at that time the drugs weren't running his life. It all really began when he started out with a sleeping pill to assure a good night's rest, and then maybe an amphetimine to get going in the morning so that he wasn't groggy from the sleeping pill. The body gets used to them and it becomes two sleeping pills, and then two hits of speed, and it all just snowballs.

Due to his well-publicised return to the top of the music charts, and his Las Vegas triumph, Elvis was back in full form. Somehow, in his 'Super Elvis' mode, he became obsessed with the idea of meeting the President of The United States. In his mind it was going to be as if Batman and Superman were suddenly joining forces to defend 'truth, justice and the American way'. Somehow, because of all his police and government associations, Elvis was sworn in as a Department of Justice Deputy by President Richard Nixon at the White House on 21 December 1970. I will never forget this day as long as I live.

My brother Billy and I were out on the town and just cruising around in Memphis. This was the first time that I smoked pot. We were rolling down the street listening to *4-Way Street* by Crosby, Stills, Nash and Young, Grand Funk Railroad and Black Sabbath. We were just out on the town for a good time.

Billy and I got stoned that evening, and finally I said to him, 'Let's go back to Graceland.'

When we got back to Graceland, Lamar was sitting on the couch when we walked in. I said, 'Is Elvis back?'

'Yes,' he said, 'Elvis just got back in tonight from D.C.'

There was an intercom in the room, and the next thing I knew, it was ringing. I picked up the receiver, and it was Elvis on the phone from upstairs saying, 'Get your ass up here right now.'

I stood there, stoned out of my mind for the first time. Billy and I acted as if nothing was wrong, and we went up to Elvis's room and sat down. The next thing we knew he had whipped out a law enforcement officer's badge. Flashing it in our faces, he asked very seriously, 'Do you know what this is?'

'No,' I replied.

'Well, it's a Federal Narcotics Officer's badge,' he said with pompous authority.

'Yeah, well did you buy it?' I said with a laugh, like the little smartass brother I could be at times.

'That's not funny!' he snapped at me. 'I am the ears and the eyes of President Richard Nixon. What I want you two to do is to be my ears and eyes at Hillcrest High School. We're gonna clean up the streets. No more Jane Fonda-types, no more John Lennon-types, no more druggies.' By the look in his eyes I could see that he was deadly serious.

Over the previous few months I had seen him building up his police equipment, and now to see this during my first marijuana high was just too surreal for words. I looked over at Billy and shot him a glance as if to say, 'Oh my God, what are we gonna do?'

I was so stoned that I instantly became paranoid about this scene playing out in front of me. My first thought was, 'Oh, Christ – we're gonna be busted by Elvis!'

Much to our relief, he was so wrapped up in delivering his 'Super Elvis' speech that he didn't have a clue that we were both buzzed out of our minds at the time.

After he had finished his speech, Billy and I sensed our opportunity to escape, and we got up and said, 'Sure Elvis, anything you say.'

At the time Elvis was wearing a black pair of pants and a white shirt with a high collar and a black jacket and carrying a cane – the same outfit that millions of people have seen him wearing in that now-famous photo of Elvis with Nixon. He looked like something out of Marvel Comics, right down to the Elvis 'TCB' lightning bolt insignia necklace. It was big and gold, and diamond-encrusted like some ostentatious piece of Mafia 'Don's' jewellery.

Billy and I finally excused ourselves and left his room, and as we were going down the steps, we were rolling with laughter at the scene we had just seen played out before us. With that, we went downstairs and raided the refrigerator, and just cracked up over Elvis's latest trip, and the fact that we were stoned out of our minds.

The next thing we knew, we were startled back to reality by the sound of machine-gun fire. We knew that this was Elvis – Mr Extreme himself – out in the backyard playing with his Thompson submachine gun. You couldn't even think about putting a Thompson submachine gun in Elvis's hands and not expect him to see if it worked.

In the backyard of Graceland, we had a full rifle-range set up behind the house, complete with John Dillinger silhouettes. There was a big concrete door that went into a storage room and 20 yards to the right of it was a 500 gallon gasoline tank although not many people knew about it. It was a miracle that Elvis never hit it with his guns. The cops used to show up at the house when they'd get the calls because it sounded like a war zone in Elvis's backyard with all these machine guns going off.

Still high on grass, Billy and I walked out and there was 'Captain Elvis' in his black suit with his huge Superfly sunglasses on and the bullets flying. We watched as he emptied out a full magazine of ammunition into the rifle range. Finally, when he was done, I turned to Billy and said, 'I think that he's serious about this narc stuff!' Then we broke up and started laughing at this insane sight.

But he was Elvis Presley, idol to millions, so no one ever questioned what he was up to. Even the Memphis Police Department – his buddies in blue – turned their heads while this 35-year-old man in a black suit stood in the backyard of his suburban home in a residential part of Memphis, emptying a Thompson submachine gun into a gang of imaginary drug lords.

He was just playing his 'cops and robbers' game to the hilt, and now that he was so rich he could play with real guns and equipment. He was living out this whole 'Elvis Saves America' mission not only in his mind but with his actions.

And, what superhero does it all alone? If he was really going to bring this fantasy hero to life he had to have his band of supporting heroes. Batman had Robin, Sherlock Holmes had Dr Watson, and Elvis had the Memphis Mafia. To bring everyone into this adult 'cops and robbers' game, Elvis had 'the boys' deputised as well. Next to the snapshot of Elvis and Richard Nixon, the second most bizarre photo from this era was the one of the whole gang with their police badges, like some secret militia.

They had been deputised as a troupe by local Sheriff Roy Nixon of Shelby County, Tennessee, and were all presented with badges. The photo of them that afternoon depicted Elvis sitting dressed in black velvet pants with a white tie and white braces, like a gangster. Standing or kneeling around him were Vernon, Charlie Hodge, Sonny West, his boyhood friend George Klein, Marty Lacker, Dr Nick and Red.

It was a while before we began to realise that he was even more serious than we thought at first. All of a sudden, John O'Grady, Elvis's personal private investigator and crime expert, flew into town. When he arrived at Graceland, Elvis told him, 'John, I want you to make sure that Billy and Ricky and David are covered, I don't want anything to happen to them.' We realised O'Grady was supposed to be our protection while we were ferreting out drug villains at Hillcrest High.

I told John, 'This ain't gonna happen. We ain't doing it.' And John just nodded his head, and we all played along in front of Elvis. But he stayed serious about our undercover work for a good long time. Every day we'd come home from school and over the intercom would come: 'To the house. Report to me.' So we'd troop into his office. 'You see anything?' he'd ask.

'Not today, Elvis,' we'd say.

'Well, keep at it.'

Elvis was serious!

One aspect of Elvis that is rarely discussed is his own political agenda. When Elvis met President Nixon in 1970, he had a genuine concern for America and its youth. He was a true conservative who loved his country. He didn't care too much for the Jane Fondas, the Angela Davises, or the John Lennon types. He was wholeheartedly concerned about the influence these kind of people had on the American public. As a former Army sergeant he loved and respected all veterans and was always thankful for their sacrifice. Any music that degraded our country, he disliked immensely. He never tried to project in his music or his films anything that would be a disgrace to the country or its fundamental moral standards. As controversial as Elvis was, his beliefs were simple and traditional.

In the later part of the '60s, Elvis had a real problem with John Lennon and his politics. He was convinced that Lennon was the Number One reason for the decay in the morals of American society in that era: the flagrant use of illegal drugs, opposition to the Vietnam War and riots in the streets.

Meanwhile, life at Graceland was business as usual. From 1969 to 1971, there was a real family atmosphere prevailing at Graceland. Elvis had just won a 'Ten Outstanding Young Men Award' from the National Association of Jaycee's, and he was really at a peak in his career as far as establishing who he was in society. Lisa Marie and Priscilla were at Graceland, and Lisa had a full-time nanny living there.

My routine at that time was to go to school in the morning, and immediately come home to Graceland. My weekends were all spent at Graceland as well. All of the Memphis Mafia families were there too, Larry Geller, Joe Esposito, Lamar Fike, Billy Smith, Richard Davis, G.G. Gamble, Sonny West and Jerry Schilling. All of these guys had their families in tow, and they were all included in everything that was going on.

That was where it began to become tough for Priscilla. It was never just her and Elvis. It was Elvis and his buddies and their friends, and they were there every waking hour. I feel that this spills over into my own life today. Elvis liked to be surrounded by people all the time, and I have grown up the same way.

7

How Fast Will This Thing Go?

The year 1972 was one of major changes in the Elvis universe, and in my life as well. First, and of foremost concern in my life, was the fact that Elvis invited me to join him out on the road as his personal bodyguard. And, the second truly major aspect came with Priscilla announcing to Elvis that their marriage was over, taking Lisa Marie and walking out on him. Both events carried major consequences.

Elvis's marriage was doomed to crumble. Priscilla was later to reveal that Elvis almost never made love to her after the birth of Lisa Marie in 1968 – and if he did, she had to initiate it. He had it in his mind that if a woman was a mother, she was no longer a sex object, and of no interest to him in bed. Furthermore, she almost never had a moment alone with Elvis. The Memphis Mafia guys and their wives were always there, hanging around and Priscilla finally had enough of it.

She was also becoming very concerned for my niece, Lisa Marie, and her well-being. Lisa Marie, at the age of four, was growing up to be a very willful little girl. Whenever a member of the house staff reprimanded her, she had taken to blackmailing them by saying, 'I gonna tell my daddy, and you're going to get fired.' It began to prey on Priscilla's mind that she was going to have to get Lisa Marie away from Graceland, if she was ever going to have a normal upbringing.

In August 1971 Elvis had again appeared in Las Vegas at the International Hotel. One night, backstage after the show, a well-known record producer showed up, with his bodyguard. The bodyguard was a karate expert named Mike Stone. Elvis and

Priscilla enjoyed meeting Mike Stone and recalled having seen him in a karate competition a couple of years before in Hawaii.

Elvis suggested that Priscilla study karate with Mike Stone in Los Angeles, saying that she'd love the sport and the fitness aspect. She decided to do just that. Back in Los Angeles, she not only studied karate with him but with his friend, Chuck Norris, as well.

Through her martial arts training, Priscilla took a good long hard look at herself. According to her, 'A transformation had begun in which fear and indifference had no place. Along with this new confidence, off came my false eyelashes, heavy make-up, the jewels and flashy clothes. All devices that I'd depended upon for security I now shed. I was seeing myself for the first time, and it was going to take a while for me to get used to the image. I had a chance to observe marriages outside our immediate circle, where a woman had just as much say as a man in everyday decisions and long-term goals. I was confronted with the harsh realisation that living the way I had for so long was very unnatural and detrimental to my well-being. My relationship with Mike had now developed into an affair.'

In February 1972 Elvis was back in Las Vegas for his annual month-long engagement at the International Hotel. It was there that Priscilla announced to him that she was leaving him. He was totally in shock. No one had ever walked out on him – he walked out on them. Someone had finally stood up to him. The way he had treated her at the end of their marriage was very poor and the only thing in Priscilla's favour was that she could call herself Mrs Elvis Presley. I did my best to keep out of the break up.

Priscilla stayed at their house in Los Angeles, while he was at Graceland. They were living such separate lives anyway at this point that Elvis and Priscilla not being under the same roof didn't seem all that strange to me at the time.

Ricky had been touring with Elvis for a year and a half as his personal aide. Ricky would always come back from Vegas and the tours with all of these amazing stories. You can imagine how I was chomping at the bit to go along on one of these rock and roll tours. It sounded like the ultimate party job to me, and I bugged him about it constantly!

By the time I was 16, I had filled out to where I had a burly, football player's physique, not unlike that of my father. In me, Elvis could see my Dad's image. He was still highly impressed with the fact that Dad had once been the personal bodyguard to General George C. Patton. He got it in his head at the time that having the son of Bill Stanley Sr. protecting him elevated him to the level of importance of Patton. In that way, it was a bit of an ego trip. For me, the prospect of accompanying Elvis on his forthcoming concert tours sounded like a brilliant opportunity to have the summer of my life.

School was finishing at the beginning of June, just as Elvis was about to embark on his 1972 summer tour. I continually pestered him about taking me along. Elvis was at home at Graceland getting ready to open at Madison Square Garden on 8 June, and I had met his new girlfriend Lisa. I could always talk to Elvis's girlfriends. His newest flame was no exception. Lisa and I were talking and I said, 'Lisa, I've got to go on this tour,' and she just started laughing. I told her to tell Elvis that I was willing to perform any task on the tour just to be part of it.

Finally, on 6 or 7 June, Elvis asked me if I wanted to go to work for him as one of his personal bodyguards. 'Hell, yes!' was my immediate answer. With that, he put one of the solid gold 'TCB' emblem necklaces around my neck. It was as if I had been officially knighted by 'The King.'

I thought I had an idea of what to expect on the road, having popped in for several dates during the previous couple of years. However, nothing could have prepared me for some of the wild times I was about to jump off onto.

The first concert was in Madison Square Garden, New York City. Talk about starting out at the top rung of the ladder! We boarded a private jet which was owned by the Hilton. As soon as we got on the jet all of the wedding rings came off everyone's fingers and disappeared into their pockets. Everyone had left their wives at home and they all had girlfriends that they were going to meet in New York City. Even Vernon, my step-father, took his wedding ring off.

On these tours, either the girlfriends were going to be met, or all of the wives went. This was a tour on which none of the wives were invited. On our plane, it was just the inner circle: Red West, Sonny West, Joe Esposito, Jerry Schilling, Charlie Hodge, Vernon and Elvis.

I remember looking out of the window when the Manhattan skyline came into view. I was in total amazement to see New York City in all its glory, having never been there – except as a baby when the family left for Germany.

We landed, got out of the plane and we loaded into cars that were there to meet us. In the car I was in were Elvis, Joe and a guy named James Collie with Red in the front seat. We were driving in to the hotel and James Collie, an old Southern boy who was a friend of Elvis's and who had been with him for a couple of years, looked out of the window and pointed up to the Empire State Building. He said, 'Hey look Elvis, there's the *Entire* State Building!' We just cracked up over this.

We got to the hotel: the Hilton on Avenue of The Americas. We went in through the back way and up the service elevators for security reasons. All of the rooms were pre-assigned and we had the entire top floor suite. I was quite impressed. I was used to staying in hotel rooms, but when I walked in and saw a winding staircase leading to an upstairs bedroom, I was absolutely amazed. The private jet was impressive in itself, but this suite was just too much. I had never seen anything like it in my entire life.

From that first engagement forward I was knocked out by the preparations that had been made in advance. You walked in and found the rooms totally immaculate, and containing everything you could possibly need. The food that you wanted in the suites had already been ordered and waiting for you. When you talk about carte blanche, it was right there with Elvis and his entire inner circle who took care of him. If there was a certain kind of wine or food anyone wanted, it was done without question and was waiting for them.

I stayed in a room on the top floor and Elvis had the inner room suite which was behind double French doors at one end of it. Even my room was a suite and was absolutely huge.

I went into my room and opened the blinds. I turned on my portable stereo played some Led Zeppelin and looked out on Manhattan for the first time in my life. I was smoking a joint because I had brought one with me. I knew this really was going to be fun. Obviously, so did Elvis.

Suddenly, the phone rang. It was Elvis. 'Get down here immediately,' he demanded.

As far as I was concerned, when Elvis barked, I jumped to attention. I arrived down in the hall in his suite, and there were five girls on the couch with Elvis. He was sitting there in the middle and then he stood up.

'David,' he said, 'this is indeed a solemn occasion. You are on the road for the first time.' He looked over at the girls and introduced each of them by their names, and said, 'This is David, our newest edition. Girls, I give you the boy, bring me back the man.'

All five of the girls stood up and escorted me back to my bedroom. Two hours later and my room was a clutter of champagne bottles, strewn clothing, and the five naked girls. Elvis was making sure I got initiated to life on the road and losing my 'virgin' status was obviously step Number One on the agenda. I remember looking over at the clock when all of the smoke cleared – it was three-thirty in the afternoon, and I had just attended my first orgy, courtesy of big brother Elvis. If this was what life on the road was all about, I was ready, willing and able.

At Madison Square Garden, the stars arrive and leave the venue through a special underground entrance. When Elvis and I pulled into the entrance for that very first date we got out of the limo and off in the distance I spotted this thin bearded guy leaning against a beam. As we got closer, I realised it was George Harrison!

Elvis wasn't really impressed and just kept going to his dressing-room, but I was bowled over. He was one of my heroes, so I went right over to him and said, 'Mr Harrison, I'm Elvis's step-brother, David Stanley.'

He was totally charming and I asked what he was doing. 'Well, I'm here to see the King,' he told me.

I went back to the dressing-room and told Elvis that George Harrison would love to come in and say 'Hi'. Now, Elvis knew who George Harrison was so there wasn't any of the usual, 'Who's that?' stuff. But all the other guys – Red and Sonny West, Joe Espositio – were horrified, saying, 'David, you don't come in here running your mouth and inviting folks in.' But Elvis came to my defence and said, 'No, wait a minute. This is an exception.' He told me to bring Harrison in and they exchanged some pleasantries. This was after the famous Concert for the Bangladesh, to give you an idea of the time frame, but that didn't stop Elvis from saying, 'I understand you boys broke up.'

George didn't bat an eyelid, and said that the boys had indeed broken up.

'Well,' Elvis said, 'I know you'll do well. You're definitely one of the most talented: you and Paul.'

Never mind John. When it came to John Lennon, Elvis just couldn't help himself. Elvis patted George on the back, escorted him to the door and told him he hoped he'd enjoy the show. Harrison smiled and said, 'You don't have to hope. I *know* I'll enjoy the show.'

The whole summer of 1972 was an absolute ball for me. I had been in high school one day, and three days later, I was at Madison

Square Garden. I knew the entire entourage, and I was familiar with Vegas. I also knew the evening after evening drill, and suddenly I was part of it. At first it was all a bit overwhelming for me, especially when I saw the response of the crowds.

Many people over the years have asked me why Elvis needed so many bodyguards. The answer is simple. When he performed in concert, more often than not 500 young ladies would rush the stage during a show. Two minutes later, 500 old ladies would rush the stage. What I'm trying to say is when you have that many fans trying to touch you at the same time, it can get scary. It wasn't that the fans were trying to hurt him. It was because they all wanted a piece of the same thing at the same time. Sure you had the jealous boyfriend or husband, and occasional death threats, but we were mostly there for crowd control – to make sure not only that Elvis was safe, but to protect the fans as well.

When we landed at an airport, we weren't expected to use the terminal or the public entrance. We were met by limousines and brought into the hotels in the back entrance for security reasons. It was like being with the President or Queen Elizabeth or the Pope.

One of the first things that really impressed me that first summer was Elvis's physical stamina on the road. If you've never been on the road you don't know how hard it is, day after day. The further down the road you get, the more tired you are, and there's no way to catch up, so you just keep going. To be fresh and up in every town you play takes a lot out of you. Elvis was like a machine and reminded me of that mechanical bunny in the TV commercials for batteries. He just kept on going.

Elvis's drug use wasn't always abusive. In the time I was there it went from casual use to massive abuse. But in the early '70s nobody knew the dangers involved. These were still the 'feel good' years, with doctors prescribing drugs far less discriminately than they do now. Remember that President Kennedy used to get shots and years later it emerged those were full of amphetamines. It was also before the Betty Ford Clinic, before it was acceptable for celebrities, even the President's wife, to admit that they had a substance abuse problem and to deal with it – and eventually to be praised for taking action. Elvis was living in an earlier era. He was ashamed and embarrassed about what he was doing and he felt that if it ever came out, he'd be ruined.

One of the golden rules on tour was never to allow Elvis to read a newspaper. Everyone lived in mortal fear that he would read a negative review about himself, and that he would go ballistic!

Ricky and I spent the most time with Elvis. Elvis would relate to us each differently because of our distinct personalities. Me, I was the rough-house kind of guy. Elvis could relate to me, having met my father, who was a big burly sort of man. Ricky was more of the laid-back, 'Hey, let's hang out and do drugs' kind of guy. Billy and Elvis got along fine, but Billy was more devoted to Mom. Although he did go on some tours in the early '70s, he mainly stayed by Mom's side when Ricky and I went out on the road.

Dee suddenly felt abandoned by everyone, and Billy kind of stuck it out, and stayed with her so that it didn't seem that the entire family had deserted her. Dee and Billy are more alike, and Ricky and I are very much alike. We are all extremely affected by the results of our background.

Meanwhile, the Elvis and Priscilla situation was intensifying and I was suddenly dragged into it. Later that year I was in Los Angeles with Elvis, and Priscilla called me up. She invited me over to Marina Del Rey where she was living. I was a little nervous about it, so I went over there with a girlfriend. Of course I hid the visit from Elvis. No way could I tell him about this. And Mike Stone, her boyfriend, was over there. Now Elvis was 'bad', but Mike Stone was lethal. Elvis did not want to mess with Mike Stone, who was a karate champion. It was one thing to break boards. It was a whole other thing to be a competitor.

And I looked at Priscilla and said, 'I know I'm young and you probably don't think I'm capable of understanding, but I know there have been a lot of lonely nights for you.'

'Well, David,' she said, 'can I ask you a question? I just want to ask you about what it was like on the road?'

I told her that I couldn't tell her anything about that and that if that was the reason she'd asked me over there then I had to go. If Elvis had found out about it, that would have been the end for me.

My relationship with Elvis, up until the bitter end, was very good. My older brothers didn't fare quite so well. Although I was a total party animal, who could drink and smoke pot with the best of them, it didn't get to life-threatening proportions. Ricky was another story.

Ricky was always a laid-back guy. He was the one who would have enough nerve to put the heroin needle in his arm – and eventually that is exactly what he did. While Elvis was busy doing his prescription drugs, Ricky was getting heavily into street drugs. This was all happening during this era.

Then there was Elvis's relationship with my brother Billy. Billy fell madly in love with a young girl named Ann Hill. Mom just about had a heart attack when she found out that he wanted to marry her immediately. When she threatened not to consent, Billy told her that he loved her so much that he was going to elope. Mom had little choice, but to comply. Billy was indeed in love with her – so in love in fact, that he didn't realise that Ann was infatuated with Elvis, and Billy was merely her stepping stone into the Presley inner circle. They were married at our house on Dolan Street.

Billy and Ann were nothing more than kids at that time and had no right to get married in the first place. They were simply too young to handle the responsibility.

We all thought that it was a bit odd the way Ann would always seem to flirt with Elvis whenever he was around. Womaniser that he was, Elvis didn't see the fact that she was his sister-in-law a problem, and he returned the attention. Billy was so obsessed with Ann that he didn't even think it odd that Elvis would call over to the house from Graceland, to see if Ann wanted to meet him at the pool, and in the same call, ask Billy to run an errand at the other side of town. Elvis and Ann were having a hot and heavy sexual affair for a month before it all erupted into a horrible scene.

Elvis had recently fixed up Billy with a girl named Eleanor whom Billy had slept with while married to Ann. So, Elvis felt that moving in on Billy's wife would somehow be acceptable. Billy was mad at Elvis – rightly so – for several years. Elvis was so guilt-ridden that he couldn't face Billy for a long time. Billy and Ann divorced shortly after. It wasn't to be until 1976 when Billy and Elvis were finally able to put the bad blood between them to rest.

The first summer tour was fantastic, as was Las Vegas in August, and then I had to go back home. It was intended that I was to return to school in the fall.

It was very easy to quickly become spoiled by the lifestyle. Life on the road was a whole different world for me. Being around Elvis that first year was lots of fun. I was able to get up every morning and catch some sun around the swimming pool. There was nothing to compare to that first year on the road for me. It was excellent fun for quite some time.

We did two tours that summer. One leg of it was on the East Coast, and the other leg was on the West Coast. It was an amazing experience for me. By September 1972 I was back in Memphis and, much to my disappointment, back in high school.

I lasted exactly ten days back in school. I looked at one of my high school friends, and I said, 'I've got to drop out of school.'

And he said, 'Why?'

I said, 'Because I have to go back to work for Elvis!'

I remember sitting in the high school cafeteria, staring at a reheated piece of Salisbury steak when three days before I had been dining at Benihana's Japanese restaurant at the Las Vegas Hilton as if I was visiting royalty. In my mind, there was no logical choice between being on tour with Elvis or being back in high school. There wasn't even a choice: 'screw high school!' was my attitude.

I called Elvis, and told him how much I hated it. 'Come back out on the road then,' he said.

I came up with every excuse in the book that I could think of with my mother. Using my vast imagination, I told Mom that someone had laced the food at school with LSD, and I did my best to convince her that back on the road was where I belonged.

My mother was less than thrilled with my decision, but when Elvis and I ganged up on her she didn't have much of a choice. I wanted to be on the tour, he wanted me on the tour, and Mom finally declined to even waste her energy trying to talk me out of it.

With that, I dropped out of school and for the next five years I worked for Elvis. I never looked back. First hand I was able to witness all of Elvis's late career highlights, achievements and his eventual demise.

I soon realised that Elvis really liked young girls. I was dating a girl named Debbie Watts whom I knew from school. It wasn't a serious thing, but we went out several times. She was a year younger than me, so she was 15 years old at the time. I took her to the Memphian Theater on one of the nights that Elvis hired it for one of his private screening parties. It was a nightly event for Elvis to get the whole gang together and privately screen movies and everybody in the immediate circle would attend – all of the guys who worked for Elvis and their wives or their girlfriends.

I invited Debbie to join me a couple of times and that's how Elvis met her. Elvis sat in one row and Debbie and I were one row behind him. He turned around and said, 'Hey, why don't the two of you sit up here with me?'

I was still innocent about what was going on, but as soon as we moved into his row I could see him make his move on her. It caught me off guard at the time – Elvis was 37 and here he was making advances on a 15-year-old girl.

Not long afterward he got up to go to the bathroom and it was customary for two of us bodyguards to accompany him, just in case anyone unauthorised had managed to get into the theatre. On the way to the bathroom, Elvis said to me, 'Are you having a good time?'

And I said, 'Yeah, it's cool.' That was obviously my chance to voice any protest about him hitting on my date.

He went into the bathroom and the other bodyguard and I stood outside the bathroom door. When Elvis came out of the bathroom and we walked back into the screening room, he went back into the row he had been sitting in with Debbie and me and I sat in the row behind them. That was just my nature – to hang back in a situation like this. If Elvis was on the move with this girl then, in this instance, I didn't care one way or another. If she was someone I really cared about, I certainly could have and would have spoken up and said so. However, it did open my eyes to the fact that he liked really young girls.

When the movie was over, which was about 20 minutes later, Debbie turned around and said to me, 'Come on back.' Although that movie had ended, we always stayed up late and watched a couple of feature films. So before the next film started rolling, she came back to my row and said, 'Why don't you come back up here with the white folks?'

I just said, 'Hey, fuck you Debbie.' I knew the girl well enough to say that, and by now I felt really pissed off, both with her and with Elvis.

This event took place in between the June leg of the tour that began in Madison Square Garden and our August bookings in Las Vegas. As a result of that evening, Elvis invited her to go to Vegas, and Dee came along as her 'chaperone'. Again Dee was the culprit in importing underage girls to Elvis, as she had done years before with Priscilla, although she promised this girl's parents that she would personally look out for the girl's well-being.

When Dee and Debbie arrived in Las Vegas and Elvis expressed an interest in Debbie spending some time alone with him in his room, Dee finally got wise to what was going on. Dee took Elvis aside, and said, 'Elvis, do you have any idea what you are up to, and the potential trouble you could be starting?'

With that, Dee severed the liaison that Elvis thought he was going to have with Debbie, before it got completely out of line. Although Dee came in and shut that down, I still think that Elvis and Debbie had a sexual relationship, because Elvis was kind of obsessed with her.

As time went by, I just learned to deal with situations like this. There was another girl in the late '70s, and her name was Risa

Smith. She was around 15 years old and I knew her from school.
Elvis became very obsessed with her as well.

When Elvis met her, he had me bring her over to Graceland. I
was downstairs in Charlie Hodge's bedroom and I was just sitting
on the bed talking to Risa when Elvis came in. He thought up some
excuse to make me leave the room and leave them alone. When I
got up and left the room, I knew exactly what he was pulling – he
was doing another Debbie Watts routine. This was the second time
that he had done this, and moved in on my girlfriend. There was
no question in my mind what he was up to – he wanted to get
naked with her and roll around.

He was so obsessed with this 15 year old that he went out and
bought her a brand new Pontiac Trans Am, and took it over to her
mom and dad's and began to schmooze up to her parents with
financial favours. He did this to gain the respect of the parents in
the hope that he could sleep with their underage daughter. This
was nothing new and was a pattern with him. I watched him do it
with Debbie and here he was doing it again. In that aspect, Elvis
had a tremendously warped perspective, and a perverse power over
some people.

I remember going with Elvis to pick up the Trans Am and in
the car I said to him, 'Elvis, what are you doing? Do you have a
clue? This is a kid here.' When he wouldn't listen, I was very
judgmental towards him. I didn't say anything further, I didn't
curse at him, I knew better. But he knew by my actions that I did
not approve, and felt that his conduct was totally out of line in
this instance. For him it was all sport – the challenge of enticing
all the women.

At the same time, Elvis was banging lots of chicks in addition to
Billy's wife. He would take one of the girls out for a ride on his
motorcycle, and the next thing you know, he'd have them in bed.

During the fall of 1972, the concert tour continued to be a really
exciting experience for me. We went out to Hawaii in November,
and had Thanksgiving over there.

Now that Ricky and I were old enough to go out on the road
with Elvis, our presence gave the travelling troupe some new
blood. However, to the members of the Memphis Mafia, Ricky and
I were threats to the security of their jobs.

Elvis would get tired of the Memphis Mafia guys sometimes, and
that is when our relationship with them changed very dramatically.
Even at that point, the guys were all very jealous and very petty. It
was like when we were kids, and they were jealous of the fact that

we would get to ride in Elvis's car and they had to ride in the car behind.

In November 1972, Elvis's last movie, *Elvis On Tour* was released. A documentary that was filmed earlier that year, it was released to mixed reviews. Naturally, Elvis's true fans ate it up, and it made it to Number 13 in *Variety* magazine's 'Top Grossing Films' list.

As close as I was to Elvis that first year, he was very good at keeping certain aspects of his life away from me. I personally didn't see Elvis do drugs until 1973. I witnessed the effects of the drugs before that, but as far as seeing the drug use in action – that came later. I knew that something was going on, because he was always so cranked up during the day.

At the beginning, when I realised that he was doing drugs, I didn't think that it was on the level that it was. It was in 1972 that Joe Esposito sat me down one day and told me to be very careful talking to the press. He said to me, 'Never talk to the press, and never talk about his "medication".'

After I started working as part of Elvis's inner circle I slowly began to see it. I'd go into his dressing-room and bring him his outfit and I would see him take a handful of pills. It wasn't long after then that Dr Nick was on the road, and before every show he was in Elvis's dressing-room.

I was 17 and this was an era in which I certainly knew all about street drugs, so I recognised what was happening. I had my own supply of marijuana which I was smoking in my off-duty time, so I knew all about getting high. In fact, I was a prime member of the 'anti-establishment' that Elvis preached against. I was the hell-raising, Vietnam protesting, pot smoking, hippy that the flag-waving Elvis abhorred. However, he was so absorbed in his own world, that in his eyes I was just his little brother.

This made for a completely ironic situation. There I was on one side of the fence: the left-wing liberal joint smoking 'fuck authority' Led Zeppelin fan. And on the exact opposite of the spectrum, was Elvis: the all-American, right-wing, God-fearing, honorary Deputy Sheriff. Yet the common thread was the drugs. I was the unacceptable, illegal-substance abusing hippy, menace to law-abiding society. Elvis was the conservative, medication-popping, 'Superman' defender of 'truth, justice and the American way.' And, both of us were stoned out of our minds from the minute we woke up every day!

I began to understand the total hypocrisy of his words. If he preached strongly enough against something, the chances were that he was the biggest offender. There existed this complete contradiction in Elvis: the louder he barked against something, the more he secretly did exactly that.

As I said, Elvis would go into the Polk Building police surplus store, and come out with belts, badge holders, hats, gloves or handcuffs. Then there were the weapons he would buy: he had the Thompson submachine gun as well as an M-16, an M-14, an M-15 – all military weapons from the Vietnam era. He had an M-1 carbine that was gorgeous . These were prize guns that he liked to shoot.

Meanwhile, problems were developing in Elvis's own life. From the late '60s to the early '70s, he really did not have a clear understanding of the drug problem he had. Although he carried around a copy of the *Physician's Desk Reference* book so that he could read all of the descriptions of each of the dozens of drugs he was taking, he still didn't think that he had a problem. The danger signs were beginning to appear with his inability to distinguish reality from a distorted view of it. In fact he wasn't able to see how hooked he really was until late 1976 and early 1977, when the signs became undeniable – even to himself.

In time, Elvis went through a great transformation. He went from being a gregarious outgoing person, to becoming something of a recluse. This could all be traced back to 1972, when his marriage to Priscilla ended. He couldn't believe that she had left him.

He had no one to blame but himself. He had totally blown his marriage. He lived with the guilt of his actions and what he had failed to put into the relationship. Carrying those 12 guys around, with their wives and girlfriends all over the place, treating Priscilla like a second-rate citizen is basically what he did.

Priscilla had a right to dump him. Anyone with any self-respect would. People don't treat people that way. Elvis had that disposable lifestyle, and when he had to deal with confrontation, he took a disposable way out.

Just like his obsessions with his toys, when he tired of his fascination with Priscilla he was done, and she became a 'disposable' commodity to him. When he lost her, it hurt. It is times like that when a person realises that they've done something wrong. When he lost Priscilla, he didn't have to go far to figure out why. All he had to do was to look in the mirror.

Her leaving him had all happened so quickly that he didn't realise how it would effect him. She made her decision, and she was out of there. Elvis thought he had it all under control. He told himself, 'It doesn't matter – I've got all these chicks on the road everywhere.'

He knew that he was the king of the castle, and he knew that he had this magnetism, and he knew that he was the one with the power to lead people along. He thought he had total control over her as well but in an instant she was gone. This totally blew his ego.

I came into his professional life at a time when Priscilla was officially backing out. I had known her as 'the girlfriend,' then she was 'the wife,' and now she was moving into her new role as 'the ex-wife'.

It was Elvis's ego that was the most lastingly damaged. The idea that she could walk out on him just blew him away. He had failed at his marriage, and he was stunned that this could happen. In retrospect I can clearly see that this was when he started going downhill.

Elvis's last real achievement and peak was the Aloha From Hawaii TV special – broadcast to a billion people live, via satellite. He shed 15 pounds in the weeks before the show, and it was to be the last time he was to ever look so good, or so in control. Hawaii was also when I started to see very clearly the growing cracks in the armour.

In all the years that I was with Elvis, I never saw him get nervous, up until the Hawaiian concert. But when you're about to step out to a combined TV audience of a billion people, as Elvis would say, 'This has a tendency to get your attention.' Elvis had certainly come a long way from the *Louisiana Hayride* days. He was about to take another step into history, and he was very concerned that he had to be at his very best – no matter how many drugs it took.

Right before the show he asked me to shoot him up with a dose of amphetamines. I said to him, 'Elvis, I can't do this.'

He looked me in the eye and said, 'You can and you will.'

I told him, 'I said "No" and I meant "No".' When I refused, James Collie did it for him.

It was then that I realised that he had a 'serious' drug problem. From that point on, I watched my brother's self-induced demise.

As it ended up, the television special was a huge triumph. The soundtrack album from the event was also a huge international hit. It became his first Number One album in nine years. Unfortunately, it was also to be his last.

Elvis's 1970s stage shows were varied according to where they were staged. In Hawaii, they had this huge stage set up with an elaborate backdrop. They had flashing 'Elvis' and 'Hound dog' images, and different song titles in different languages flashing against a mirrored backdrop, plus a full orchestra.

The usual Elvis stage set at the time was just a flat black backdrop, with no orchestra, and just a horn section and a rhythm section behind him, and the spotlights. I was always frustrated after we did that 1973 concert in Hawaii. I had said that day, 'Now, this is a truly major stadium concert performance.' But after that, we just went back to the basic flat black backdrop on the stage, and then relied on the spotlights for atmosphere.

Las Vegas was the best setting to see him in. He had the full orchestra, the perfect sound system, great acoustics, and an amphitheatre atmosphere.

Out on the road, in concert, Elvis's show was very simple. I kept suggesting things to make his stage shows more exciting, and time after time I was shot down. I was constantly saying, 'Tom Hewlett, why don't we . . . ?' or 'Colonel Parker, couldn't we . . . ?' or 'Elvis, would it be cool if we . . . ?' Their whole mentality was, 'Why pay for the frills of a Kiss concert, when you have "The King"?'

In Colonel Parker's defence, why not keep it simple? He stripped away all the frills. There were no frills with Elvis, and that was it. It wasn't a concert, it was viewed as a historical event. Elvis was the Pope of rock heroes, why upstage him with gimmicks?

In a way they were right. Even when Elvis was near the end and was fat, and couldn't talk between songs, and slurred the lyrics, whenever he walked out onto the stage the crowd still went nuts. They didn't care what he did: he generated so much excitement and the Colonel fanned the flames constantly.

One of the most tempestuous episodes came in 1973 when Priscilla refused to let Lisa Marie come and visit Elvis at Graceland. Elvis was dating a pretty young girl at the time named Linda Thompson. She was wonderful with Elvis, but Priscilla didn't want Lisa Marie to stay up until all hours of the night, and didn't think that the atmosphere at Graceland was good for her.

Elvis, in his drugged-out haze, went completely ballistic, swearing and raging about how this was all Mike Stone's fault. Elvis got it in his head that he was going to take a contract out on Mike's life, and have him killed. All of us in the Elvis inner circle did our best to placate him until this insane ranting and raving subsided.

Elvis's rage was just his overreaction to being hurt. Normally, he wouldn't hurt anyone, let alone talk about having them killed. This particular fit of rage required heavy sedation over the next few days before it blew over. He was insisting that the Memphis Mafia perform this 'hit' on Mike Stone. He went on and on about what kind of killing machines his bodyguards were. While it gave him a certain sense of invincibility, he didn't like it when they took their showing of force too far, though. Unfortunately, he was attempting to have it both ways. He had watched too many of Clint Eastwood's *Dirty Harry* movies and he adopted that vigilante mentality of taking the law into his own hands. He must have been high as a kite when he came up with this elaborate scheme of his to rub Mike Stone out.

Things were beginning to veer out of control in Elvis's life. I remember several cancelled and missed concert dates and Elvis constantly justifying his drug use. There was growing abuse in the amounts of drugs he took, and incidents of his jumping up and down on tables insisting that doctors give him drugs, playing with guns and throwing violent temper tantrums. I remember him holding a gun to his former bodyguards and insisting, 'Either you kill Stone, or I will.' I had to call a doctor to sedate him.

With all his police paraphernalia, and deputising badges, Elvis was starting to believe that he was truly above the law. He was having trouble distinguishing reality from fantasy. When Elvis watched a movie, that movie became his reality. He had begun to believe what he saw up on the screen and acted accordingly.

It was frightening to see him this far off the deep end. I have always said that it's lucky he wasn't around when the movie *Scarface* came out, or that would have been a really rough year!

For me, however, there were still a lot of high points. Being around Elvis, I got to meet all kinds of people, including Elton John, Led Zeppelin and Eric Clapton. I was in Las Vegas with Elvis on one occasion in 1973 and it was prior to one of his openings. While he was preparing for an engagement he would be in town for a week or so and there would always be someone having either an opening or closing party. It might be Johnny Mathis, Raquel Welch, Ann-Margret, Juliet Prowse, or someone else of that calibre.

One night we went to see Raquel Welch's act, and she was just gorgeous. She was at the Hilton doing her nightclub act the night before Elvis opened. It was customary for the next night's headlining act to be in attendance for the closing act's final performance.

Just as we had done with Streisand, we attended Raquel's show. She did a lot of dancing and her roller skating routine, having just filmed her roller derby movie *Kansas City Bomber*. She did a segment to lampoon her role in *10,000 B.C.*, and all of her skits revolved around her movies.

Afterwards, we went downstairs into the suite which Elvis was going to be taking over the next night. We had been in that suite many times already, and I sat down in a chair, and there was a chair to the right of me, a chair in front of me, and a chair to the left of me. Raquel Welch sat down to the right of me, and Elvis had sat down to the left of me, and between Elvis and me there was a vacant chair.

Raquel had on a silk robe and she put her legs up on the chair across from her. My eyes nearly popped out of my head, it was all pure raw legs – no hose, just the silky legs of Raquel Welch, right up to the thigh, just short of the crotch.

I was 18 years old and I was incredibly impressed with that sight. Talk about an arousing view! Raquel and Elvis were carrying on this flirtatious conversation, and all the while they knew exactly what I was looking at. Knowing that I was staring at her stunning body, Raquel took one of my hands and put it on her thigh and rubbed it on her. She laughed, and Elvis was ribbing me and kidding me about it.

Through Elvis, I was suddenly exposed to the Las Vegas acts of several established stars, whose acts I would never have normally attended. He made me go with him to see Tom Jones, Buddy Ebsen, Sammy Davis Jr., and several 'middle-of-the-road' performers I would have never sought out on my own. However, I was grateful to him for insisting on educating me by exposing me to all this great talent. Of all of them though, Raquel was the real hard-on!

I continued to tour with Elvis throughout 1973 but then I started to feel burned out. There were times I loved it, and times that I didn't. I was desperately looking to find my own identity apart from Elvis. I was offered a job at RCA Records in Nashville, in the music publishing department. I would hold this job on and off in between tours.

While I was at RCA I met a girl named Angie Lofton, and we hit it off. I had just turned 18, and Angie was a senior at Franklin High School. I met her at a football game and she was one of the cheerleaders.

At this point in my life I was torn in two different directions. I had been on the road with Elvis and had seen all of the wildness that went along with it. At the same time, Mom was still instilling that whole church upbringing in me. When I met Angie, I was convinced that marrying her would somehow ground me.

We got married in April 1974, and moved into an apartment in Memphis. Angie wanted me to settle down and mellow out. I loved her very much, and wanted this to work out.

Not long afterward, Elvis was leaving on another concert tour. Elvis had invited me to come out on this tour, but Angie talked me out of it. He was using the private *Playboy* magazine jet and when he was leaving Memphis, Angie and I accompanied him to the airport. When we got there I saw that all of the 'flight attendants' were Playboy bunnies. I had no intention of going on this tour, and was going to drive home with Angie.

However, when I walked up the ramp to the jet I suddenly found myself reaching out and making out with one of the bunnies. I looked down at my wife, looked at the bunny, and waved 'goodbye' to Angie. I hadn't packed so much as a toothbrush, but I got into the jet and away I went.

I used to come home from a tour, and Angie would beg me not to return to the road with Elvis. I would swear that I loved her – which I did – but Elvis always ended up winning out. Poor Angie, I ended up treating her the same way that all of the Memphis Mafia members treated their wives. The tone was set at the top. Elvis had Priscilla stashed at Graceland all those years, and then he'd go off on tour and cheat on her nightly. I ended up falling into the same pattern and Angie ended up the victim.

Throughout his life, Elvis was a control person, and he had an effect on everyone he came in contact with. He liked to control everything. He liked to fix things, break them, and fix things again. He was the same way with relationships. He always had to be the very centre of attention.

There were all of these formal hierarchies of cliques at Graceland. There was the family clique, and there was the employer clique. Everyone would be juggling for position on the totem pole, and all the while Elvis was manipulating everything and everyone simply to have his own way at all times.

I personally never bought into this game. Unlike everybody else, I didn't have a healthy respect for Elvis. I thought he was cool, I thought he was a great singer, and he certainly knew how to have a good time when he was in an 'up' mood. However, when he was off, or depressed, he was miserable to be around.

I can say that there were some great tours that were a blast to be on. But suddenly, somewhere along the line, those tours became an absolute nightmare. Then they really became a job and a chore. It was tough work anyway for us, but suddenly, this guy was losing his will to live. After the Hawaii TV special, that's when the tours started to become a real bitch to be on.

8

Just a Little Rain Must Fall

I can't help but believe that Elvis barely scratched the surface of his music potential. If he'd tried harder, worked harder on the music, and got into writing, he would have been massive. I think part of why he didn't was that he didn't have to, and was never asked to. As Colonel Parker always used to say, 'If it ain't broke, don't fix it.' So, there weren't a lot of influences around Elvis telling him to go for it and to try new things. Quite the opposite in fact; Elvis needed to be pushed, and it's a great shame he wasn't. Some of us tried to point him toward good songs. Lamar did, and Elvis would listen. I was constantly trying to push him to expose himself to some of the new music that was happening at the time. Finally, we got him to listen to Neil Diamond, James Taylor and Simon and Garfunkel, and he really got into some of their music.

I think if Elvis could have, he would have sung only gospel music. Elvis didn't sit around the house and sing *Hound Dog* – he was always humming gospel although he didn't record that much. He did record three gospel albums – and two of them won him Grammy Awards, two of the only three he ever won. Those albums were: *His Hand In Mine* (1961), *How Great Thou Art* (1967) (Grammy Award for Best Religious Recording) and *He Touched Me* (1972) (Grammy Award for Best Inspirational Performance).

From an evangelical point of view, Elvis was 'called' to sing gospel music. Everybody can remember his gospel music and it would just cut right through you. It just did something to you. I truly believe that Elvis had a God-given anointing on his life when he sang gospel music. Even if you weren't a believer, that music would affect you. And I think there was a struggle in his life between what the 'world' wanted to hear and the gospel music he loved. A classic struggle: God's calling, but the world was pulling him the other way.

On the other hand, Elvis began to seek out alternative religious beliefs in the 1970s. He was absolutely fascinated with numerology, and he began to look at different ways to explain life's fortunes and misfortunes. When he wasn't exploring the meaning of his life, he was attempting to escape from it.

When he wasn't on the road it wasn't particularly unusual for Elvis to lock himself up in his room and abuse his medication for several weeks at a time. But it never got public until late 1974. Looking back on that time now, it's as though he was acting as if his life was already over. Every day of his life at this point – especially towards the end – was misery. I'd say, 'Good morning, Elvis,' and he'd say, 'What's so good about it?' This was coming from a man who had everything, and somehow the toys, the houses, the cars, and the whole career all ceased to make him happy.

When it came to eating, Elvis's constitution remained incredibly strong. I've always maintained that Elvis had the stomach of a goat, because he could eat and drink anything at all and never feel it. So when he got sick, and had something like 'flu he really got sick and he hated it. It was hard to keep him quiet and in bed. But it was different with the pills which he took to shut himself off. Since he was in control of the pills he regarded that as all right. But he really couldn't stand missing shows and would go a long way not to have it happen. People just don't realise how tough he was, what a trooper he was.

Elvis was perpetually restless. He acted like a caged animal at that time, always pacing, always moving. We would just get in a car and go, it didn't matter much where we went, except it was never anywhere new and he was never alone. On nights like that, we would just go back and forth to places he was familiar with and it was as if he was looking for something he'd lost, and that if he could find it, he would be happy. I think he really missed Priscilla and Lisa Marie at this point in his life, and couldn't figure out how it had all gone wrong. They represented a certain sense of security to him, and he had driven them away with his chauvinistic ways, and his out-of-control lifestyle.

At just the right time, Elvis met a pretty young girl named Linda Thompson. She was to be with Elvis for several years. Linda was refreshing, bright, and quite devoted to him. She had been Miss Tennessee in the Miss Universe competition of 1972, and she had aspirations of getting into show business. She was to be with Elvis through some of the high points such as the Hawaiian concert and through some of the lowest points – like his traumatic 40th birthday. She was to accompany Elvis on several of his tours. When she complained that she wasn't spending enough time with her parents and siblings, Elvis simply dragged the whole Thompson family along for the ride.

On 14 May 1974, we flew to Lake Tahoe, California, where Elvis was to begin a ten day engagement at the Tahoe Sahara. Amid the concert dates, on the night of 20 May one of the most brutal displays of bodyguard force cast a shadow over the booking.

We were sitting in Elvis's suite, four or five of us, and suddenly the lights started going off and on. This was not long after the Symbionese Liberation Army/Patty Hearst kidnapping. Elvis was fascinated with the SLA thing. Fascinated and a little worried about it at the same time. He was afraid for Lisa Marie, who was there for that engagement. While the lights were going off and on we were watching the SLA house burning on television and Elvis was saying, 'What's going on?'

We were all a little skittish. So I went out to check that everything was all right. I went through the double doors and into the hall and I passed a locked emergency exit. Somebody was banging on it from the other side. I opened the door and there was this guy, a really big guy, dressed to the nines in Vegas style with lots of chains and jewellery – polyester to the max and with a couple of babes. The power circuits were right there on the wall and he had obviously been switching them on and off. 'What are you doing?' I said to him. I saw the hotel security people assigned to Elvis who were way down at the end of the hall, starting towards us. I was telling this guy he had to leave, but he started blowing off steam, and I realised that he was blind drunk. He was ranting about how rich he was and how there was a party he wanted to go to, and that he couldn't be treated this way.

Then all of a sudden he lurched through the door and slammed me back against the wall. Now, I'm pretty big, but this guy was huge. I was getting ready to lay into him, or at least to try, when suddenly Sonny West was there. He took three quick steps and nailed this guy with the heaviest shot I've ever seen anybody take: a massive hit. The guy crashed into the wall, blood everywhere, and slithered to the floor.

By this time security was there and they stopped Sonny from going after this guy some more. I went back into the suite to tell Elvis everything was under control. But Elvis had a .45 pistol in one hand, a Thompson submachine gun in the other, and he'd got Lisa Marie behind him. 'Where's the S.O.B.?' he demanded, thinking that somebody was coming after his daughter. I told him everything was under control, but that wasn't enough for Elvis. He was in his super-hero mode. He went down the hall and saw this drunken guy being handcuffed and taken down the hall to a suite. We followed and all the way Elvis was still snarling.

But after they put the guy on the bed of the suite, Elvis took one look at him and said, 'Oh, my God.' The guy's lip was hanging loose, he was wrecked. Elvis sat down on the bed next to him and asked, 'Why did you do this? What were you doing?' But the guy was still very upset, and all of a sudden he kicked out at Sonny and nailed him. At which point Red dropped a fist onto the guy's jaw. Pow! It was like a gun going off. The jaw just shattered and he fell back, blood gushing. Elvis grabbed one side of him and I grabbed the other and pulled him forward so the blood wouldn't choke him.

Elvis was mad at Red. I mean, this guy was still handcuffed when Red hit him. But Elvis's anger turned instantly to pity. He helped the guy out of there, talking to him, trying to settle him down. The guy eventually sued, of course. About a year later it was settled but it cost Elvis money. Elvis was mad at Red about the incident and eventually that played a part, I believe, in Red and Sonny being fired. At least, that's what Elvis was later to say.

On 11 May 1974, we were at the Los Angeles Forum, and right across the street was the Inglewood Hyatt Hotel. We had checked into the hotel that afternoon, then we went to the Forum. In 1974, Elvis was starting to slow down a little bit, he still had the energy but he was starting to gain weight, and his drug intake started going from 'use' to 'abuse' about this time.

Right before Elvis came out on stage, I looked out at the audience, and there was Robert Plant, Jimmy Page and John Paul Jones of Led Zeppelin. John Bonham wasn't there. Tom Hewlett, who worked for Elvis, told us that they were out there that night. I told Tom that if there was any way to pull it off, I would really like to meet them after the show.

I was so excited, I pointed out into the audience and said, 'Hey, Elvis, there's Led Zeppelin!' Vernon was standing there at the time as well.

ABOVE LEFT
The wedding of Elvis and Priscilla in Las Vegas,
1 May 1967. They are flanked by Vernon *(left)* and
Dee *(right)*. *(Photo: David Stanley Collection)*

ABOVE RIGHT
Priscilla had waited nine years to become Mrs Elvis
Presley, however, it wasn't all that she had hoped for.
(Photo: David Stanley Collection)

MIDDLE RIGHT
In the summer of 1967 we visited Elvis on the set of
Speedway in Hollywood. While there we also visited
actor Ernest Borgnine on the set of *Ice Station Zebra*.
(Left to right, back row): Vernon, Dee, Priscilla,
David, Ernest, *(front row:)* Billy, Ricky. *(Photo:
David Stanley Collection)*

BOTTOM RIGHT
When Elvis and Priscilla returned to Memphis there
was a huge reception. Here is Elvis with Ricky, Billy
and me that day. *(Photo: David Stanley Collection)*

At the International Hotel in Las Vegas for Elvis's 1969 return to live concerts. Here I am on the left, with Vernon, Dee, Ricky and Billy. *(Photo: David Stanley Collection)*

Dee had risked everything to be married to Vernon Presley. Little did she know it at the time, but he was not to remain faithful to her. *(Photo: David Stanley Collection)*

I was by Elvis's side for the last five years of his life, as his bodyguard, his confidant, and his devoted brother. My role was that of a 'lifer', to make sure that he didn't choke to death on his food, and to ensure that he got out of bed on time for his shows. *(Photo: David Stanley Collection)*

On the final tour in 1977, I took these exclusive photos of Elvis on stage, in Rapid City, Iowa. Although he was a ghost of his former self, there were still flashes of brilliance. *(Photos: David Stanley)*

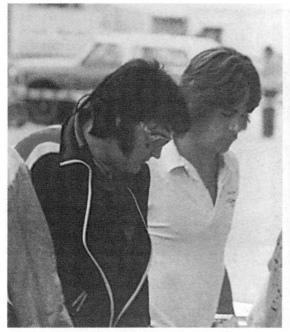

Me leading Elvis to his hotel room in 1977. His weight had ballooned, and he was not feeling well, but the show had to go on, to pay for his massive bills. *(Photo: David Stanley Collection)*

One of Elvis's prized 'TCB' necklaces, which he gave to members of his inner circle. *(Photo: courtesy of Lynn Moon, The Elvis Museum, Buena Vista, Georgia)*

Elvis in a rare moment goofing around with his buddies, playing soccer in 1977. *(Photo: David Stanley Collection)*

After Elvis's death, I found myself disillusioned with show business. I became an Evangelist preacher, but soon found myself even more disillusioned with life. *(Photo: David Stanley Collection)*

Although I was preaching to thousands of people, I felt like little more than a predator in the pulpit. *(Photo: David Stanley Collection)*

If Elvis was really alive, he certainly would have made a public appearance to voice his disapproval over Lisa Marie marrying wacko Michael Jackson. This is their wedding in the Caribbean in 1994. *(Photo: MJB Archives)*

In the 1990s with my two sons, Tyler and Austin. *(Photo: David Stanley Collection)*

Vernon piped up and said, 'Oh David, is that the group you used to listen to: Led Zipper?'

He used to kid me all the time about playing their music. I said, 'No, it's *Led Zeppelin*.' Vernon did have a good sense of humour.

So the fanfare began, and Elvis went out on stage that night and gave a phenomenal show. This was at a time when a lot of Elvis's shows were beginning to be below par. Well, that night, knowing that the new reigning rock gods were out in the audience, obviously encouraged him to give one of his finest concerts of that late era.

After the show, we went directly across the street, and back to the hotel, and Tom Hewlett of Concerts West promoters, then brought them up to the suite. Ricky and I were ecstatic, we had just bought copies of *Houses of the Holy*, which had come out at that time. They were friendly and signed autographs for us on our albums and on hotel stationery.

Then, Elvis came out of his suite, and I watched the tables turn. They were as excited at seeing Elvis as we had been about seeing them. It was at times like that that I realised Elvis's icon status.

While he was quite aware of who they were, he had never listened to a single song of theirs. He knew enough about them to appreciate who they were, but they didn't register in his mind as competition.

Jimmy Page walked up to him and told him how happy he was to meet him, and said, 'I never picked up a guitar until I heard *That's Alright Mama*.' They were truly in awe of Elvis, but he couldn't quite relate or communicate with them on any great level, because he never really had a concept of who they were.

Led Zeppelin went on to release an Anthology album in the early '90s, and in the *Anthology* copy of the booklet it tells how 'Elvis's step-brothers' introduced them to Elvis Presley.

Actually, we ran into them a couple more times. When we saw Tom Hewlett we would ask about them. Ricky and I were such fans that we would be on the Elvis tour and wearing Led Zeppelin tee shirts on the plane. Elvis was quite intimidated by them after that, seeing how Ricky and I worshipped them, like his fans worshipped him. The music that Ricky and I were into was 20 years removed from Elvis's prime era and his musical frame of reference. Whenever we started raving about someone like Led Zeppelin, Elvis would say to us sarcastically, 'Look at who's autograph is at the bottom of your paycheck.'

I would sit down with Tom Hewlett and when I looked at the rest of his booking roster I would say, 'Why are you on tour with us? You have Led Zeppelin, you have Elton John, you have Paul McCartney and Wings, you have The Moody Blues, you have John Denver. Why are you with us?'

And he said to me, 'I make more money with Elvis Presley than with all of those combined. He's our Number One client.'

The next time we saw Led Zeppelin we were playing Baltimore. We were in Baltimore airport, and Elvis was playing there that night, and Led Zeppelin was playing in nearby Washington D.C. We had landed in Elvis's 880 Convair, which was like a huge converted 707, similar to the old Kennedy presidential jet. Elvis had bought it in 1975. It originally held 129 passengers, and now it was customised to acommodate 29. There was a bedroom, stateroom, communications centre, conference room – this was a gorgeous plane.

We had landed and Tom had told us that Led Zeppelin had landed there too, and that we would probably be on the same tarmac. So, we pulled up under some mercury lights and in the soft rain that was falling they were blindingly bright. Elvis's jet pulled up on the tarmac, and all of a sudden this 707 called *Caesar's Chariot* – which was Led Zeppelin's plane – pulled up next to us.

I wish I had had a camera with me that day, because there were the jets of the two superpowers of rock and roll. What an impressive sight that was for me! The King himself and The Gods of Thunder.

This was three or four years after we had first met them. I got off Elvis's plane and I went straight over to the *Chariot*, because I wanted to say 'hello' to them. Tom Hewlett would constantly send greetings back and forth from Ricky and me to the guys in Led Zeppelin.

As Ricky and I were walking across the tarmac to their plane Robert Plant and Jimmy Page were coming across the way to greet us. We stopped in between the two planes, and they said 'David, Ricky, how are you?' That alone impressed the hell out of me. I was still a wide-eyed kid of 20 at that time.

We were talking and then all of a sudden the two of them looked up. I turned around and there was Elvis. He was wearing one of his jump suits, but he had a coat on over it. He walked up and gesturing towards their plane, said, 'Hey, that's an impressive jet.'

And they said, 'Well, we lease this from Caesar's Palace in Las Vegas. We were just admiring yours as well.'

Elvis said, 'Oh, well I own mine.' Then he looked at Ricky and me and said, 'Time to go to work, boys.' And, we turned around and walked off.

Elvis could hold his own in a crowd, and Plant and Page were not offended. They were huge rock legends in their own right, however they knew that they were witnessing The King acting like The King.

We went over to do our concert and Led Zeppelin had a caravan of 16 Cadillacs taking them to theirs and we had a stream of Cadillacs of our own. It was an awesome sight to behold this display of rock and roll royalty and their opulent carriages. It was one of those historical moments in rock history, and I wish I could have captured the whole scene on video.

It was 1975 and I had been on the road with Elvis for three years. I had grown up a lot in those three years and I had a pretty good understanding of how the image worked. If Elvis wanted to be a prick, he could be a prick. Even if he said to Jimmy Page and Robert Plant, 'I own mine,' they still respected him. He was never intentionally mean to people, and he wasn't mean to the rockers, he had a sense of leadership just to let everyone know that The King had spoken.

That same night I met Elton John. He was in Baltimore and he came to catch Elvis's act. He came up and he hugged Elvis, and Elvis didn't like that. Elton hugged him warmly but Elvis backed away and said, 'Nice to meet you.' Then he went straight to his dressing-room.

When referring to Elton's song, *Don't Let The Sun Go Down On Me*, Elvis used to say sarcastically, 'Elton should sing *Don't Let Your Son Go Down On Me*.' I thought Elton was great but he was a bit too much for Elvis.

I remember when the original Catwoman, Julie Newmar, came to see Elvis after a show. She was hitting on him big-time. Julie looked great and she was really coming on strong. Elvis took me aside, and said, 'David, you've got to ask her to leave.'

So, I went back in the dressing-room, and I had to sit down and tell Catwoman, 'We've got to go upstairs now, because Elvis has to go to bed,' and essentially blew her off. Elvis walked out just then and she was offended. You could tell that she knew that Elvis wasn't really into getting together with her.

These were the kinds of responsibilities that were put on me at an early age. Elvis would never do his own dirty work, someone else would have to be the 'heavy' so that no one was ever personally offended by Elvis. One of my regular tasks was being the liaison between Elvis and all of the stars who came to see him – amongst them Rod Steiger, Gregory Peck, Kirk Douglas, Alice

Cooper, Ann-Margret, Linda Lovelace, Three Dog Night and John Wayne.

Elvis would also entertain some of the Las Vegas Mafia figures. One night, one of the Mafia Don's daughters came in with her bodyguards. She must have had 20 of them. It was all black suits and black sunglasses and was like a scene from *The Godfather*.

Elvis had that ability to play different roles, and I was able to see them all. He could play the professional power person and get away with it. He really could have been a great actor if he hadn't squandered his screen career on all of those singing-rebel-wins-the-local-sweetheart beach blanket films.

Three Dog Night was another group I really liked at the time. They would come to Las Vegas, as would that whole L.A. crowd. This was another situation where Ricky and I were the ones in the entourage who knew who they were when they showed up to meet Elvis. He, on the other hand, didn't have a clue but later he really liked *Shambala*. As a result of meeting them that night he recorded his own version of *Never Been To Spain* and *Shambala*.

It sometimes took him a while to pick up newer groups and performers, but he would dabble in some of the new material that was out there from time to time. He recorded Simon and Garfunkel's *Bridge Over Troubled Waters*, Neil Diamond's *Sweet Caroline*, the Beatles' *Something*. Later on we influenced him into doing James Taylor's *Steamroller Blues*. It was exciting to see him meet the guys from Three Dog Night, get hip to their music, and then record a couple of their songs. He would talk negatively about the Beatles, but he'd do their songs. He did some stuff by Bob Dylan too. To me, most of the pop music covers that he did were unappealing but there were some exceptions. I really liked what he did with the Righteous Brothers' *You've Lost That Lovin' Feeling*, but his version of *Hey Jude* sucked. There were a couple of things that just didn't work, but I give him credit for trying them.

Then he had his 'saviour' music during this era. Songs such as *Suspicious Minds*, *In The Ghetto*, *The Wonder Of You*, *My Way* and all those dramatic '70s songs that kept his recording career alive. At this point, he was making most of his money from the live performances.

His records at this time weren't booming like they once did. The albums of his that were successful, and were certified 'Gold' and 'Platinum,' were the special event kind of LPs that all of the fans had to have: *Elvis As Recorded At Madison Square Garden* (1972) and *Aloha From Hawaii via Satellite* (1973).

After 1973, Elvis just didn't have any real monster songs of his own. He was beginning to feel the failure once again of his music. Groups and performers that were totally beyond him were beginning to eclipse him. He was out of touch, and he knew it. It all started to depress him.

It was at times like these when I would think back to that wonderful November evening in 1965 when I hid behind the curtains and listened to Elvis playing the piano. That was Elvis the musical genius. Where had the brilliance gone? To have seen that, and then to witness the mid '70s rhinestone jump-suited circus atmosphere that he was now settling for was very disheartening.

It was through Elvis's relationship with one particular woman that I first became aware of his racist mentality. What I am about to state is totally contradictory to everything that has been said or written about Elvis. We were in Los Angeles in 1975, staying at Linda Thompson's apartment, not far from the Mormon Tabernacle off Santa Monica Boulevard.

Elvis and I got into the car one afternoon and headed down to the local Cadillac dealership where he was going to buy a new Cadillac Seville. While he was in the showroom looking at the car, he saw a tall girl with long blonde hair and spit curls on the side of her head. Elvis told me to go and get her, and I returned with her in tow.

The words, 'My big brother, Elvis Presley, mentioned that he would like to meet you, would you mind if I introduced him to you?' usually did the trick.

I came back across the Cadillac showroom floor and before their conversation was over he had bought her a car and was moving in on her. I had learned to recognise all the signs of Elvis on the make. Here he was buying a perfect stranger a new car, followed by the statement, 'Let's stay in touch.'

So he bought this girl a Cadillac and while he signed the papers, I got her phone number. From there we went to Las Vegas, and we had been there about a week when Elvis said to me, 'Call her up.'

I called her up, and said, 'Elvis wants to see you.'

Then I gave Elvis the phone, they talked for a while, and I left the room. When I walked back in, Elvis was hanging up the phone and he said, 'Go get her.'

Dr Ghanem, the doctor in Las Vegas who supplied Elvis with a lot of his drugs, had an aviation service. He and his Arab brothers were brokers for the big oil guys when they bought their private jets. Not only was he a doctor but his Arab family was involved in all sorts of trade. As far as aviation trade and sales, they were the suppliers of North American oil for the Saudi Arabian rich.

Dr Ghanem had access to several Lear Jets, so I had them jet me to Los Angeles to pick up this girl, and to jet us back. We arrived at the hotel and I escorted her up to Elvis's room. About 30 minutes later he stuck his head out of the door of the bedroom suite and said, 'David get in here immediately.'

I rushed in and said, 'What's wrong?'

He said, 'Get her out of here.'

'What?' I said, not knowing what the problem was.

'Just get her out of here,' he said emphatically.

Without hesitation, I collected her and her things, called Ghanem and booked their jet. She and I flew back to Los Angeles, and she had no clue what was going on or what she had done wrong.

I flew back to Las Vegas, returned to the hotel suite, and said, 'What is going on here?'

Elvis looked at me with a serious look in his eyes and said, 'David, she dated a black man, so I can't be with her. I want nothing to do with her.'

I am not saying that Elvis was prejudiced or a bigot, but he certainly would not endorse an interracial relationship. I can positively say that he would have freaked out at the thought that Lisa Marie would one day marry Michael Jackson.

If anyone feels that somehow Elvis is still alive, let me tell you, that he is not. Knowing what I know about Elvis, that marriage would have brought him out of seclusion for sure!

When I was with Elvis from the ages of 17 to 19 I thought that most of Elvis's cronies were geeks. I thought Joe was cool: he wore black all of the time, and was sharp. I thought Jerry was cool. I thought Lamar was just there. I liked him, I always kidded with him.

Since I was 20 years younger than these guys, I had a different frame of reference, and from time to time, I was able to introduce them to new things they knew nothing about. I was the first one to go out and get a Sony jambox – portable stereo – and the next thing you knew, everyone on the tour had to have one. Ricky and I were the fresh blood on those tours, and we were listening to the new music that they knew little or nothing about.

Ricky and I were the ones who introduced Led Zeppelin's music to these guys. We were the ones who got this huge kick out of meeting these new and happening groups, and we were the ones who plastered our briefcases with the tour stickers of all these groups.

Ricky and I used our positions with Elvis to meet all of the rock and roll legends that we could and to get free tickets to their concerts. We were having a great time. If we wanted to go and see the Rolling Stones we'd just make a phone call, and not only would we get great seats in the audience but we would also be given backstage passes.

Elvis wouldn't come with us at all, but everyone seemed to want to get a look at his little brothers. Elvis didn't like all the rival backstage passes and stickers on my briefcase, he was threatened by this display of interest in someone else's music.

I was from a whole different generation to Elvis. I wore blue jeans, and worn Stan Smith tennis shoes. I wore tee shirts from Concerts West with my favourite rock groups' names and logos on them. I also wore a jacket with a 9 mm pistol under that. I had this rock and roll 'Starsky and Hutch' mentality. Everybody played their role to the hilt, and mine was that of bodyguard/headhunter badass guy for Presley.

I cultivated the image of the tough guy. My whole attitude was, 'Give me some coke and a fifth of Scotch, and I'm cool. But, I'm sure as hell gonna protect you.'

I was wild and crazy, but at the same time I was hip enough to pull off this role. I learned a lot from Dick Grobe, who was the head of Elvis's security and who had been a sergeant with the Palm Springs Police Department. Elvis knew him from when he had a home out there. In the 1970s, Dick went to work for Elvis. Dick was training me, as well as Red, and Sonny, and Ed Parker – Elvis's karate instructor.

Elvis would arrive at an arena about ten minutes before he was supposed to hit the stage. The lights would go down, and as long as he was on a stage that was 12 or more feet off the ground, our job was basically over. No one would be capable of jumping up on the stage if it was of that height. If the stage was no more than three to six feet high it was a nightmare, because anyone could leap that far. Usually we played coliseums where Elvis was 12 feet up off the ground and we were safe, and we could just kick back. I would go out back and smoke pot with the members of the warm-up band, and get high as hell.

After Elvis was on stage, it became a dull and routine hour for me. I would just as soon have been across town at the Led Zeppelin show, or whatever else was going on in that given town that evening.

People who had just bought tickets to see Elvis the icon would be appalled that I wouldn't be in the wings watching every show.

However, after seeing the same show hundreds of times, it became very mundane for me. I really didn't pay much attention to what he did on stage anymore.

I was never enthralled with Elvis. I thought he was cool, I was impressed with some of what he did on stage, but his act became stale for me after several months on the road.

My job on tour went through a progression. I had started out as a personal aide, making sure that he woke up when he was supposed to, overseeing the drycleaning of his stage and street clothes, making sure that his food was delivered, and basically just taking care of him.

Well, the job of bodyguard seemed much more interesting to me. When I went from aide to fully-fledged bodyguard, it felt like a real promotion within the ranks, and I was happy to have the added responsibility. In my mind, I was going to the top, I wanted to be the best I could be. I realised that at any moment I might have to save his life, and I liked the idea that my presence was needed at all times.

There were occasional bomb threats, and instances where people threatened to hurt Elvis. I was very trustworthy and responsible as a bodyguard. But, I also felt that the majority of the Memphis Mafia members were geeks. We all had fun, and we were all a tight-knit family, but with all of the girls on the road there was also an on-going ego battle between the guys. There was a constant contest to see who was going to score after the shows, so there were a lot of levels of competition that existed on the road. There was also a lot of manipulation and back-stabbing.

Just to be part of the inner-circle of the whole Elvis clan was like a big fraternity. It could also be like walking into a room full of piranhas, especially if you were an outsider. For me, that was what it was like to grow up in this atmosphere.

As I've said, for me, one of the major 'perks' that I got from working with Elvis, came with getting to meet some of my most admired rock heroes. Elvis still rented the theatre in Memphis every night of the week to watch movies. One night Jerry Schilling, a really neat guy who worked for Elvis for years, brought over Eric Clapton.

He was in Memphis and he had just played the Liberty Bowl Stadium – a big open air stadium date he played amid the 'I Shot The Sheriff' tour. It was after his *461 Ocean Boulevard* album was released and I was a huge fan of his. Well, Jerry Schilling, who worked with Elvis for several years, brought him to the Memphian Theater.

I had gone to the Clapton concert earlier that afternoon, and suddenly, here he was at one of Elvis's private late-night motion picture parties. I was totally blown away to see him there at such close proximity just hours after I had seen him on stage.

Jerry brought him over to Elvis who was very nonchalant, just saying, 'How you doing, Eric?'

Well, Eric had the look of a kid in a candy store. He looked like he was just another of Elvis's enthralled fans. 'I'm doing fine,' Eric said.

'And what do you do?' Elvis said to him with a sincere look on his face.

'I play guitar.'

'Yeah, for who?' Elvis asked him.

Eric said, 'Well, I have a band.'

'Well, my guitar player's name is James Burton, and maybe he can teach you a few things.'

I almost fell over as he totally humiliated Eric Clapton. And Clapton, with absolutely no anger whatsoever, accepted the humiliation with total class and dignity.

'Elvis,' Eric said, 'there is nothing I would like more than to play on one of your sessions someday.'

And Elvis said, 'Well, maybe someday,' as he turned around and walked off.

Colonel Parker, in those days, was a really brutal guy. He was a shrewd businessman. He knew that Elvis was making the bulk of his money from his tours. It took massive amounts of money to keep Elvis happy, content and protected and waited on hand and foot every minute he was on the road (he had 18-20 people travelling with him at all times). In addition to that, there were the people keeping up his homes, his jets, and his other collections.

Imagine the kind of money it takes to refuel a jet! We're talking about an entire commercial jet just to hop from city to city. That was Elvis's professional life, but to me the best part was what was going on behind the scenes with him.

The general public didn't have a clue in the mid '70s about what kind of person he actually was off stage. He was always hidden behind his voice, his singing and his performances.

If I were to describe the Elvis Presley I knew during this era, I would say that Elvis was a modern-day King Solomon, or King David. I think that somehow he was hand-picked to live this outrageous life that he did, as though he had a gift. The gift was not only in his singing voice but in his overall appearance, from the way he looked to the charisma and appeal he had. I think he realised that it was a gift and I also believe that he felt that he was somehow a godly person.

However, there was also a tremendous weight resting on his shoulders, and he began to feel the consequences. He always had to weigh out in his mind, 'Who loves me because I am Elvis the superstar?' and 'Who loves me because of my personality.'

This was all tempered by the 'survival syndrome' of dead twin brother Jesse. The loss of his mother, Gladys, just when he started to become successful, the introduction of a new family just as he came out of the army had all put additional weight on his shoulders. While he always knew he was someone special he was somehow uncertain who this person was underneath it all.

Elvis had a tremendous amount of presence. I use this King Solomon reference because if Elvis had lived 2,000 years ago, he would have been of that historic magnitude. Elvis lived only 20 years ago, and there are already enough books written about him to make up a pretty good Bible. His disciples – including myself now – have all written their testaments about what their lives were like with him. Everybody has their different perspective of Elvis Presley.

I was with Elvis one day at Graceland, out on the grounds where he is buried today in an area known as 'Meditation Gardens'. There was a statue of Jesus Christ there which a bunch of the older members of his Memphis Mafia troupe had given to him. It stands up very regally, and there is a big wall behind it. I have pictures of Meditation Gardens just before he was buried there.

I sat down with Elvis that day as, deep in thought, he looked up at the statue of Christ. 'Who am I?' he asked.

I realised that he was trying to figure out why there were thousands of people gathered every day at the gates of Graceland just to get a glimpse of him. He must have always thought, 'Why do all the people flock to the concert halls, and why have they always reacted so adoringly towards me? I have been influential, I have a straight, clean-cut image, but I have the frailties and flaws of life on Earth.'

Since he could never really let anyone into his inner sanctum he had to live that life. The only Elvis that you knew was the Elvis he allowed you to know. For that reason, all of the guys around Elvis had that same type of mentality – from me, to Joe Esposito, to Lamar Fike. All the guys had a protective concern towards him. They were always thinking, 'Watch out who you let into your life, and be careful of what you say to them.' That was a direct result of being around Elvis. He couldn't ever get a handle on who he was. It got to a point in his life where he would walk out in front of a crowd and he knew that he had a serious drug problem. He knew that he had molested young girls. He knew that he had manipulated families and destroyed lives. He knew that, but at the same time, he realised that everybody worshipped and adored him. If they had known about his darker side he wasn't sure they would have felt that same way. That really got to him. His image was his weakness, and eventually that started to get to him. Exposure meant death to him, so in his later years he became more secretive and more bizarre.

He realised that he could never survive the blow of his adoring fans learning the whole truth about his strange life. That whole strange episode of wanting to have Mike Stone executed, or his penchant for sleeping with underage girls, or his wallowing in a sea of prescription drugs. Any of these episodes splattered across the newspapers could ruin him in an instant.

In the 1970s there began to emerge an impending sense of self-destruction about Elvis. In 1975 things began to get tougher for Elvis to continue on an even keel. It was that year that respected American TV commentator Walter Cronkite appeared on national television announcing, 'Elvis Presley: Fat and 40.' In 1974 Elvis started putting on the weight, and by 1975, after his 40th birthday, people could really see it on him.

I saw him stuffing himself into the costumes every evening. After 1973's big Hawaiian concert, he began to see his weight balloon out of control.

When Walter Cronkite came on the air I was at Graceland. Linda Thompson came upstairs and the TV was on. Elvis went totally ballistic that day. He took a ton of drugs, passed out, and we literally had to drag him over to the bed and pull the blankets up around him.

The very idea of turning 40 had been rough on him. His mom had died when she was in her 40s, as did several of his relatives. Elvis was a product of his environment, and he was also a victim of his environment as well. From the time he turned 40 he just couldn't handle it anymore. It was as if he reached the age of 40 and gave up. We all began to realise that the party was over. It was almost as if he made sure that it was over: he doubled up on the drugs, he doubled up on indulging himself with too much food. His demise, from that point forward, became totally self-induced.

People ask me, 'How can you say that about Elvis Presley?' It's because I knew him, and I was there to witness it. I was privy to the information, and I saw it all with my own two eyes. I was part of the team who concealed the reality of Elvis Presley until the day he died.

People also ask me, 'How can you say these things now that he is dead?' Well, at least I waited until after he was dead, because I sure as hell had to keep my mouth shut while he was alive. He was an image, a big image, and he couldn't hold up that flag anymore – it became too heavy for him. He couldn't cope with the reality of what he had become. He simply got tired of keeping the whole façade upright. If you are a jerk, and realise that you are a jerk, you end up being eaten up from within. If you have skeletons in your closet that you don't want anyone to see, and your every bit of energy goes towards making certain that no one learns your secrets, it becomes an impossible task.

He knew things about himself that he was genuinely ashamed of and realised that they would ruin his career instantly. He was walking on thin ice and it became a really dangerous way to live. That was how Elvis was living, and his conscience couldn't take it.

From that point on, he really loaded up on heavy drugs. Reality was crashing in on him, and he couldn't handle what he had become. The task of keeping all of his secrets consumed him. To take him further and further away from the reality of it he took more and more drugs.

Elvis was anything but stupid. Any logical human being with any sense knows that taking those amounts of drugs on a day-to-day basis spells eventual death.

I think that over his final two years, Elvis consciously killed himself. And, I think that he killed himself because it was his last great act of humiliation towards himself. I think that Elvis killed himself just to prove to himself that he was just a human being. This was a situation where he had everything except peace within himself. His death finally humanised The King of Rock and Roll.

In spite of the fact that living with Elvis was kind of like sitting on a lifeboat watching the *Titanic* slowly going down, life at Graceland did continue to have its amusing moments. We were up in the house at Graceland one night when Uncle Vester called from the front security gate and said there was this big box for Elvis. We asked him what it was and he told us, 'The delivery man said it was some dogs, Russian wolfhounds or something?'

When Elvis was informed of this, he called down, and Vester told the delivery man, 'Elvis said we didn't need no more dogs, and to send them back.'

So, Vester told the truck to go away, and it did. It turned out that in the box were two girls from Mississippi who had decided they would be a surprise birthday present for Elvis and had packed themselves inside. I guess they started banging on the box or something and the driver let them out. They never did get inside to see Elvis.

At first it looked as if Elvis might just pull it together and kick his drug dependency. He would go into the hospital every once in a while and dry out and then it would be fine for a time.

At the end there were five of us whom I would call the 'Lifers' sharing the job of watching over him. It is my term for Elvis's faithful servants who were there at all of the worst moments, right up to the end of his life. In that category, there was myself, my brother Ricky, Al Strada, Dr Dean Nichopoulos, and Steve Smith. But the core 'Lifers' were Ricky, Al, and me because we'd been with Elvis so long. Basically the job of the 'Lifers' in the last couple of years of Elvis's life was to give him the drugs he demanded and to watch over him. At the end it got to the point where somebody had to be there 24 hours a day because he was taking so many drugs. Elvis would go to bed with 33 pills and wake up with amphetamines and sometimes liquid cocaine. This was what he was up to in the 16 months leading up to August 1977. Almost everything he took was prescription. We'd have to go to Baptist Hospital to pick up the stuff and it would be in everybody's name but Elvis's.

The irony is that even now, with his own life almost totally out of control, Elvis would come into my room two or three times a week, catch me smoking a joint and fire me on the spot. And while he was firing me, he'd be ranting about 'druggies' and how they were destroying the moral fibre of a great country and saying they should all be locked up. I guess you could say he was in what they now call 'denial'.

The 1975 New Year's Eve show at the Silverdome in Pontiac, Michigan was massive. At the time it was supposed to be the largest turnout for a solo headliner ever recorded, at 62,500 tickets sold, garnering a phenomenal $816,000 earned for one concert. And, it also turned out to be a wild one. Suddenly in the middle of it this guy was seen running toward the stage from the football field carrying a gun. It was my job to stop this sort of thing, which

I did. I took him out of the arena, nice and clean, and the cops carted him off. Incidents like that didn't scare Elvis; he wasn't a fearful guy at all. They just pissed him off.

About a week or so later, Elvis called me in and said he wanted to telephone the guy who came after him. 'John O'Grady gave me the guy's number in Detroit,' Elvis said. 'He's already out on bail." Now my first reaction was, 'Oh, no, here's trouble, because Elvis is all drugged up.'

Elvis got on the phone and said, 'Hey, buddy. You know who this is? I'm your worst nightmare. I'm gonna blow your brains out.' He was stoned as a moose, eating quaaludes like they were sweets, and just going on and on about it. The volume of his voice was going up and up and he was yelling into the phone. That was when I grabbed it and hung up.

'Elvis,' I said, 'you're getting yourself in a heap of trouble.'

He stared at me hard and said, 'Call the plane. We're leaving for Detroit.'

In Elvis's state of mind that night, he had every intention of flying to Detroit with his guns waving. Super Elvis was shifting into high gear. I realised that I had to put an immediate end to this crazy scheme. Glancing out of the window gave me an idea, and my brain kicked into action.

'Elvis,' I said, 'there's a snowstorm outside and we're not flying out of here tonight to go kill this guy in Detroit.'

'Oh, yes we are, damn it!'

Of course we didn't go anywhere, but I bet there was a guy in Detroit who didn't get too much sleep that night.

It's important to note that Dr Nick wasn't the only one prescribing drugs to Elvis. Dr Elias Ghanem also prescribed massive amounts of drugs and others who prescribed for Elvis included Dr Max Shapiro of Los Angeles and Dr Thomas Newman from Las Vegas. What would happen was that one doctor would say, 'No way, not anymore,' and another one would go ahead and give the prescription. Until right to the end, Dr Nick would say 'No' a fair amount of the time when Elvis pressed him for drugs.

Elvis had bought Dr Nick a $750,000 home and had invested in something called Center Court Racketball, which Dr Nick and Joe Esposito were involved with, and which collapsed and was a total financial disaster. Nick was way into Elvis for money so at the end, Elvis had him right where he wanted him.

When Elvis didn't get what he wanted he was a dangerous man. I remember one time we were in Los Angeles at Linda Thompson's apartment and Elvis asked me, 'Do you have any drugs?' I told him 'No,' but that I was trying to find Dr Elias Ghanem, his doctor in Las Vegas.

Just then, Ghanem called me up and said, 'What do you want?'

And I said, 'Elvis needs his drugs.'

And Ghanem said, 'No, David.'

I was practically begging him, because I knew how mad Elvis was when he didn't get his 'medication'. But Ghanem flatly refused and hung up.

Well, Elvis just blew a fuse. He jumped onto a table with two .45 pistols in his hands and started blasting bullets into the ceiling. 'I'll buy a goddamn drugstore if I have to.'

This was not a one-time deal. The exact same incident happened at least four times just with me. I remember another time in Denver when I went into his room when he was really zonked out and said, 'I'm gonna take your drugs, Elvis, this is crazy.'

And he said very evenly, very calmly, 'No, you're not.' I walked across the room and picked up the kit of drugs and the next thing I felt was the cold barrel of a gun pressing against my forehead. I looked at him and said, 'You don't have the balls.' I knew he wasn't going to kill me, but I gave him his drugs back.

Long-time friend John O'Grady took his family to one of the Sahara concerts, and Elvis was having a bad night, forgetting the lyrics to his songs in the middle of the act, and stumbling around the stage. O'Grady said later that he 'cried' after seeing Elvis in that condition and that he 'thought he was going to die that night.'

So, he went to Elvis's attorney, Ed Hookstratten, and they cooked up a plan to confront Elvis about his problems – what's now called an 'intervention'.

They told him that since he was the first to do everything, why not be the first to check into rehab? Can you imagine what Elvis would have been like coming out of rehab clean? He could have accomplished anything. He'd have become even bigger than he'd ever been. Imagine how his fans would have responded, 'Elvis has a problem and we can help.' Lord, they would have loved that.

But it wasn't to be. According to O'Grady, Elvis told them all to 'drop dead'. He was busy avoiding reality. And as he was with so many things he did, he was world-class at it.

I also had abuse problems of my own. My drug problems were with 'street drugs', whereas his were 'prescription drugs.' This is how he could justify his own addictions and still be one of President Nixon's narcotics agents.

Meanwhile, after all of the years that they had been together, and all that they went through to be married, Mom and Vernon were having some serious marital problems. It was really Vernon who caused the split. Out on the road with Elvis and all of us guys, Vernon too was cheating on his marriage.

I remember very distinctly the first time I ran into Vernon and his girlfriend, Sandy Miller. At the time, Vernon was still married to my mother. That was a very bizarre feeling.

Mom was becoming painfully aware of the fact that her idyllic marriage to Vernon, and introducing her boys into the world of Elvis, was turning into a sad nightmare. As Elvis had treated Priscilla, Vernon was now living a separate life from her while he was on the road. Broken-hearted, she was to look back on this era and explain, 'It seemed that everything I had wanted for my boys, all of my hopes for them, had been taken away. Everything that had happened to them only disillusioned me more about what I had done. I never felt that when they were young, but then they grew up idolising Elvis. I was so shocked when I learned that Ricky was taking drugs and when he was arrested [for possession] I almost died. Billy was so hurt by Elvis [sleeping with his wife] it made me cry just to see what was happening, and then my youngest, David, was out there with a gun, ready to die for him. I never forgave them for that. I'd been hurt bad on occasion in my life, but the deepest hurt was when my sons left to go off with Elvis because then they could no longer come home and share their lives with me. They couldn't tell me about the drugs and the women.'

Vernon suffered a heart attack in February 1975 and it was Sandy Miller who was there by his side. Mom remained a devoted friend, although he was cheating on her. While Vernon's life hung in the balance, Mom began seriously to rethink her life, and the obvious mistakes that she had unwittingly made. Vernon recovered, but their marriage did not.

Elvis and Vernon had ruined my father's life in the late '50s. Now they were inadvertently doing the same thing to my mother. The dreams that she had for us boys growing up in the lap of luxury had turned into a never-ending nightmare, and now Vernon was cheating on her. Who did she have to turn to? She decided that calling her ex-husband, Bill Stanley Sr., was going to solve everything. He would come to the rescue. She was sadly mistaken. Finally the tables had turned, and it was Dee who was begging him for help.

At first she found a sympathetic ear in Dad. She called him in Jacksonville and pleaded with him to come back to Memphis and to her. He was happily married to his second wife, Lois, and after a short stint of managing a dinner theatre in Florida, he was back working at a hospital and was very stable. He had no intention of ditching his wife and his job and returning to the woman who had hurt him beyond belief.

Mom even flew down to Jacksonville with Billy to beg him to reconsider. According to Dad, 'Dee pleaded with me to come back to Memphis with them and make our family circle complete. She painted a rosy picture for me. I wouldn't have to work, I could be a companion. This really put me at my wit's end. I couldn't tolerate this act any longer. I told her I had a wife of 11 years whom I loved very much, and a wonderful family. I had a good position at the hospital and I didn't want her or anything to do with her. I wasn't playing games. Life was a serious business. Mine was finally firm and stable. I intended to keep it that way. She started to cry, and I looked at her running make-up. She was such a sight. If I wasn't so disgusted, I could feel sorry for her. I was thinking she had missed the boat on life. How could she have the nerve to come back to me these many years later and assume I would go with her? I thought about my wife home in bed because she would go to work again that night, and she had no idea I was sitting in the [Jacksonville] airport having this conversation with Dee. My statements had to be strong enough to finish this charade once and for all. I meant that.'

Somehow, Mom's plan for the perfect life had backfired on her, and fate was playing some sort of cruel joke. Originally, Dee had thought that life with the Presleys and all of their money was going to spell unlimited happiness for her and for her three sons. Instead, Vernon had grown into a philandering old fool, Ricky was a heroin addict, Billy was emotionally scarred by Elvis's incestuous affair with his wife, and I too was mired in the quicksand of Elvisland.

Things only became more and more complicated with Vernon and Dee's divorce in 1976, and my choosing to be loyal to Elvis. At this point, my main objective was to protect Elvis, even though I saw him destroying himself. My intention was never to hurt Mom, but I was so embroiled in the whole Elvis scenario, that my perspective was becoming totally distorted as well.

It wasn't long before Elvis lost Linda Thompson. Linda loved Elvis, she really did. Of all the women around him, I think she was the only one he really allowed to love him. But towards the end it was rough, when you love a guy and you have to drag him from room to room unconscious. Linda couldn't live with that anymore. Finally, by 1976, she'd had enough of the craziness, and she left him.

This brought the total to two women in a row – Priscilla *and* Linda – who had walked out on him. Elvis was really at sea after Linda left. He'd accomplished everything any man could want, but he was missing the simplicity of spending time with someone, of being able to communicate. He was still looking for love. Even now, at the end, he was still searching. That's when his final girlfriend, Ginger Alden came in. But she couldn't help him. Those last two years – 1976 and 1977 – were all downhill. He kept taking drug after drug after drug, and the cancelling of shows was becoming more pronounced.

He could never talk about what was happening to him. He just had no ability to do that. In some ways he was even boring to be with because of his inability to talk in depth, or about anything of real substance. Sitting in a room with people talking, Elvis was like a prostitute in church – he'd be that uncomfortable. Communicating was so hard for him that eventually you could see that he was just giving up. He was becoming more and more withdrawn and uncommunicative with all of us. That was another huge eroding part of the demise of Elvis.

9

The Last Days of Elvis

In 1976, things indeed started falling apart in Elvis's inner circle. The Memphis Mafia was heading for a big split. On one hand, there was Lamar Fike, Charlie Hodge, Billy Smith, Joe Esposito and Al Strada. All of them were witness to Elvis's self-destruction, but for whatever reason they could not and/or would not confront Elvis and tell him he was the screwed-up mess he had become.

On the other hand, there was Red and Sonny West. Red especially, and almost single-handedly read Elvis the riot act. Out of the caring and devotion that he felt for him, Red was able to look him in the eye and tell Elvis exactly what he thought – regardless of the consequences.

Red was getting more and more frustrated with Elvis. There were cancelled shows, there'd been a couple of incidents of passing out. He would confront Elvis and say, 'You're doing too much dope, pal.' When that wouldn't work, Red would say, 'You son of a bitch. Get a grip!' Nobody talked to Elvis that way. Nobody ever did. And, to be perfectly honest, it was about time that somebody whom he would listen to did just that.

I tried, but he wouldn't listen. I was just a kid. But Red and Sonny were his contemporaries, his equals, and Elvis couldn't blow them off, couldn't ignore them the way he could do with me. I think Elvis's last bit of conscience lay in Red West. Red was the last link between what Elvis ought to be, and what he was becoming.

On 13 July 1976 Vernon fired Red and Sonny, citing some lame 'financial' reason. The actual reason however was the fact that they were upsetting and offending Elvis by telling him the truth about himself.

With regard to their firing, I think, Elvis may have been unconsciously thinking, 'I've got to get rid of my conscience.' And since Sonny would join in with his cousin Red, he had to go, too. These guys were his last connection with reality. With them gone, Elvis didn't have to confront what he was doing to himself. Since he could rationalise that I was just his little brother he could justify totally ignoring anything that I could possibly say to him.

On 23 July Elvis began the fifth leg of his extensive 1976 American concert tour. That night in Louisville, Kentucky, 19,400 people were in attendance. He performed 11 concert dates in 12 days, and then flew back to Memphis. On 21 August RCA officially announced that Elvis had sold in excess of 400 million records since the start of his recording career.

From 27 August to 7 September we completed the seventh leg of the 1976 tour, throughout several cities in the South. While the crowds loved him, the reviewers were slaughtering him. Variety said in a review from this era, 'His attempts to perpetuate his mystique of sex and power end in weak self-parody . . . Elvis is neither looking or sounding good. He's 30 pounds overweight: he's puffy, white-faced, and blinking against the lights.'

Elvis had taken to singing in his concert shows his world-weary version of Frank Sinatra's *My Way*. Squeezed into a rhinestone-spangled skin-tight jump suit, he would say, introducing the song, 'I'd like to do this song for you, ladies and gentlemen . . . Don't know all the words . . . but I'm gonna read 'em off this sheet . . . hope y'all don't mind.' Elvis was doing things *his* way, in spite of the consequences.

The real highlight of that particular leg of the 1976 tour was the fact that Ricky and I were able to get in contact with our real Dad and to meet up with him on the road, where he could spend some time with us.

We arrived at our hotel in Jacksonville on the night of 31 August 1976, following the Macon, Georgia show. Dad came and met us there. He was later to recall, 'I joined them about midnight and joined the party, which lasted all night with members of Elvis's show group. By this time I knew very few people there. I was excited at being invited into the group, because I knew they had to get permission from Elvis. I knew security was very tight, and I was lucky to be allowed in. I had a good chance to talk to David, my youngest. We had not really talked for several years. Looking at him I saw the image of myself when I was young. He is tall and big, looks so much like me. I was pleased to hear he had married, and his expression told me as much as words that he really loved his wife. I thought she must be a fine girl. He related some hopes for the future, and I got the feeling he would make it.'

The next morning, Ricky and I went with Dad to the hospital where he worked. His wife, Lois, joined us for coffee in the hospital dining room, and we chatted for a while. I gave her four tickets in the fourth row, for that evening's concert. My first wife, Angie, flew in for this particular show, as I was anxious for her to meet Dad.

Dad recalled, 'We attended Elvis's show at the Coliseum that night backstage. The crowds and excitement brought back so many memories of my days in Germany. I thought back to the times I had been offered a job and realised what it meant on a full-time basis. I had experience in crowd control, but this was mania. The crowd was quiet and orderly during the first part of the show. There was a feeling of expectation in the Coliseum. You knew everyone was waiting for the King to appear, and when he did it was bedlam. So many people had tried to get tickets when they had been on sale two weeks earlier. Every person in the installation of the Coliseum felt lucky to be there. Elvis had to be the most popular entertainer even after so many years. It seemed like waves of people surging forth in mass to get as close as possible to touch him. When he threw scarves [into the audience], it was wild. I saw first-hand, just how tight security had to be.'

Dad drove to Lakeland, Florida, that night so that he could spend some more time with us the next day and evening. We all lounged by the hotel pool that day, and it was good to have him around. According to him, 'That evening I accompanied the first group to the auditorium to catch the [opening acts] that I had missed in Jacksonville. When Elvis arrived, I stood with his security to get him from the bus to his dressing-room unharmed. Such utter bedlam has always seemed unbelieveable to me. People will do anything just to get a glimpse or a touch. A few minutes later, David came and told me Elvis wanted to see me. I entered his dressing-room as he was getting ready for the show. He asked me how I was and if I needed anything. I told him "no". He seemed to have divided attention, and I wondered why he had sent for me just before a show. I knew he took a long time getting psyched up for a performance, and not wanting to hinder his thoughts I excused myself.'

There was the feeling that Elvis might want Dad to come to work for him as a bodyguard. Dad claimed that some of the members of the troupe gave him the impression that if he did come into the organisation, that it would be to replace one of them. However, no formal offer was made.

Dad stayed with us, as we bounced from city to city in Florida, and was to explain, 'I remained with the group for two more days, visiting with David and Rick as much as possible. They were on the job, so they had duties. I felt lucky to be allowed to stay with the group. The entire troupe was fantastic. Everyone was so friendly and accepted me as a special person. Being the father of David and Rick was special. They were well liked by everyone. When they left Florida, I left for home, taking with me many memories, especially those relating to my boys, who were finally men. I shall never forget those days.'

Elvis's constant concert touring continued throughout the rest of the year, throughout the Midwest, the Northwest, West Coast, and back to the South. In December 1976 Elvis met and fell for the last of his long-time girlfriends, Ginger Alden. She was a former beauty queen, who held the title of Miss Memphis Safety of 1976. She was only 19 at the time and very taken by the idea that Elvis Presley was in love with her.

Unfortunately, it wasn't until she was too deeply embroiled with him, that she realised that life with Elvis was no picnic. In spite of the fact that she was a lovely girl, with a very optimistic outlook, she found herself on the downward turn of a fast moving roller coaster. She was to be with Elvis up until the very end of his life.

Since Elvis was perpetually interested in teenage girls, his girlfriends were increasingly closer in years to my age than to his. When Ginger first arrived on the scene, we were all a little apprehensive about her motives. In his drugged state, it would have been easy for him to be highly susceptible to 'gold-diggers'.

After getting to know her, I had to admit that I liked her very much, and enjoyed talking to her about all sorts of things. In fact, I got along so well with Ginger, that Elvis became suspicious that I was making a play for her, if I wasn't actually having an affair with her. He also confided this deluded line of thinking to Vernon, which later led to problems for me.

The reason Elvis suspected me of such a thing was that Ginger and I were close in age and had a lot in common to talk about, including the latest music – which Elvis didn't have a clue about.

I was just being nice to her, because she was my big brother's girlfriend, and because she and I had a lot to talk about. It wasn't long before Vernon was sticking his nose into the middle of things, and confronting me about whether or not I was sleeping with Ginger. I was not. It was just that in Elvis's drug-induced paranoid state, he was getting suspicious of everyone.

While on tour in Mobile, Alabama, in 1976 Elvis called me in my room. He was crying, really crying, and he said, 'David, I need to see you now.' I walked into his room and he was sitting in the middle of the bed, and I'll never forget it, it was the loneliest thing I ever saw. He was sitting with his legs crossed, face in his hands, and he was surrounded by all the guys and nobody was saying a word. It was a weird scene and I just thought, 'Lord, what's going on here?'

I said, 'Does someone want to fill me in? What the hell's going on here?' And Elvis just held up a manuscript and said, 'My life is over. I'm a dead man.'

The manuscript was a book called *Elvis: What Happened?* It was by Red, Sonny and David Hebler. John O'Grady had got an advance copy from the publisher.

'What the hell is this about?' I asked.

Elvis just started blurting out what Red and Sonny had said in the book. That he was taking drugs. That he had tried to have Mike Stone, Priscilla's boyfriend, killed. On and on, and all of it 100 per cent true.

He was acting in a bizarre manner. One second he'd be crying and saying, 'How could Red and Sonny do this to me, we were in school together, we were friends. I love those guys.' The next second he'd be cursing them, saying, 'Those dirty bastards, I want to kill them!' These were the guys he thought were as close to him as anybody and much to his disbelief they had turned on him. Now, in some ways this was typical Elvis – seeing things from his perspective only and conveniently forgetting that he had fired them.

But they didn't have to write a book about him. They called it a plea to Elvis to get his act together, and I'm sure it was. They had not only been fired but dumped on – dropped like a bad habit – after 20 years of loyalty and dedication. They felt betrayed, and this was their chance to vindicate themselves.

Even if they were wrong about Elvis, you can never convince me that Red West didn't love him. You can never convince me that Sonny didn't care for him. They sincerely wanted him to get better. I don't have any doubt of that, and I never will.

But their book was completely devastating to Elvis, and I don't think they had any idea what effect it would have on him. This was in the days before celebrities were praised for dealing with their drug problems, and middle America considered most rock musicians a bunch of dope-smoking degenerates. Elvis was held to a higher standard. As far as his fans were concerned, he could do no wrong: he didn't cuss, smoke, drink, chew, lie or lust. Well, the big 'reality check' was about to take place.

It was this all-American image that separated him from stars like John Lennon and all those 'druggies' who embraced the hippie culture. Elvis never did; he was a patriotic American with traditional Southern values, and here was this book calling him a junkie. It was the beginning of the end for Elvis. After Red and Sonny wrote their book, his life was never the same. With them gone and all his secrets out on the street, it was as if the wing had come off of a 747 mid-flight. There was no more gradual descent, Elvis plummeted straight downward after that.

New Year's Eve 1976 was spent in Pittsburgh, where 16,049 fans helped him ring in his last year at the Civic Center Arena. Elvis celebrated his 42nd birthday on 8 January in Palm Springs, California. On 26 Jaunary he presented Ginger with a huge diamond engagement ring, professing his intention to marry her the following Christmas.

In February 1977, RCA Records were desperate to get some new material recorded by Elvis. To accommodate him, they set up a makeshift recording studio in the den of Graceland. Elvis however, claimed that he was feeling too ill to record, and refused to leave the bedroom. At a relentless pace, Elvis continued to consume prescription drugs, and perform concert after concert.

When I think of all of the stories I heard about rock and roll decadence when I was growing up, Elvis still takes the cake. When you consider all of the rock star drug busts, and Led Zeppelin and The Who throwing televisions out of the windows, and the stories of John Lennon and his heroin addiction, that's all part of their anti-establishment legends. Then, you have right-wing, gospel-singing, family-oriented, flag-waving, All-American Elvis, with his untarnished record, and all of that nonsense about being deputised by President Nixon as a Narcotics Officer. From the outside, his public image was still miraculously totally unblemished.

However, in reality he was the most screwed up one of all. You should have heard him go on about 'all those dope-smoking hippies' and how they should all be arrested. Yet here he was, the biggest hypocrite and the biggest dope-head of them all.

I had been such a smart-ass when I joined Elvis on the road at the age of 16. No one could teach me a lesson back then. I was a cocky know-it all. I knew where the best cocaine was, I knew where to find the hottest girls, I knew where to score the best pot. In my mind, I was the hip kid on tour with the King of Rock and Roll, and for me it was nothing but a long entertaining ride.

But, while I was on this ride, I was watching someone I really cared about slowly and effectively taking his own life. Now, in the spring of 1977, there he was, on his way out. He was so fried that he couldn't even exist on his own, without someone to hold him up, or drug him up.

It was 1 April 1977, the day following the debâcle that occurred in Baton Rouge the previous night, which I described at the beginning of this book. Right then and there, with both of us in the hospital, it really hit me that Elvis was soon going to die.

I checked myself out of the hospital the next day and went home. A couple of days later, amid his week-long stay at the hospital, I went to visit him.

I went into his room and I was so offended. He was lying on his bed and I looked at him and laughed. Joe Esposito came up to me and said, 'I want you to leave.'

I said, 'Why is that?'

And he said, 'You just need three or four days off.'

When Elvis got out of the hospital, he went back to Graceland. I went to Graceland to visit him three days later. I walked into the room, and I said, 'You couldn't stand me looking at you could you?' What a disappointment I felt.

I realised right then and there that this guy was unreachable. At this time he was so stoned that he couldn't function. That doesn't mean that he wasn't a human being, and that doesn't mean that he was a bad person, but he was a victim of circumstance.

In his final months, I was so shaken up by what I saw Elvis doing to himself, that I vowed never to let that happen to myself. While I can be thankful for that fact, I can honestly say that Elvis had no one who came before him, who could put him on the right path.

All of the drugs that Elvis was taking brought him an escape from reality. I was taking recreational drugs for a good time, but Elvis didn't take them to get happy. He took them to get unconscious. In fact towards the end, he often said, 'I'd rather be unconscious than miserable.' Whether he was dealing with himself or other people, if he didn't want to face something or someone, he'd just go inward. He wouldn't read books or magazines or newspapers – other than mystical type books, stuff on numerology and Scientology, and books on death. But I think his favourite book was the *Physicians Desk Reference*. He knew that book as well as he knew the Bible. Elvis was like a pharmacist, with himself as the only patient. He'd go through the *PDR* and pick out combinations, mixing a drug cocktail that would be just right for him.

At the end, Elvis had a trailer in the back of Graceland where a full-time nurse lived. Her name was Tish Hinsley. In that trailer was a complete drugstore full of pills. Every night about 12 or 1 a.m., we'd give Elvis what we called 'Attack 1'. It was a package of 11 drugs, including three shots of Demerol, and then Elvis would eat. After that, you had to stay with him, because sometimes he was so stoned that he'd choke on his food. Then, after he fell asleep, you'd have to sit there and watch him. About three or four hours later, he'd wake up and take another package of drugs which we called 'Attack 2'. After several more hours of sleep, Elvis would wake once again and take 'Attack 3'. It was total madness.

If Ginger wasn't there, one of us would have to be with him 24 hours a day. It was absurd but no one knew how to break the cycle. It was like the story of the Emperor's New Clothes, and everyone was afraid to tell the Emperor that he was a pathetic junkie.

Towards the end of Elvis's life, even Ginger just couldn't handle it anymore. It was like a fantasy that turned into a living nightmare. She didn't stay with him that much anymore. It was all too much for her to deal with. She didn't know what she could do to help. And no one could blame her. She was in over her head – just like the rest of us.

Elvis continued to tour right through the summer. He had again resurrected himself from his hospital bed, and was back on the road. On 19 June he appeared at the Civic Auditorium in Nebraska, which was filmed by CBS-TV for a special to be called *Elvis In Concert*.

On 25 June at Riverfront Stadium in Cincinnati the evening was plagued with problems. In addition to some technical difficulties with the equipment, Elvis was late getting on stage. He blamed some dental work that he had had. The following night he was in Indianapolis, where he sang to 18,000 fans at Market Square Arena. It was to be his final concert performance.

After that, Elvis spent most of July 1977 in seclusion in Graceland. The month of August began with the publication of *Elvis: What Happened?* by Red West, Sonny West, Dave Hebler, and Steve Dunlevy. Once the public got hold of this book the charade was going to be over.

Lisa Marie, now eight years old, had come to visit Graceland for several weeks. On 8 August Elvis rented out Liberthland Amusement Park, and threw one of his all-night private parties. Throughout the day, however, Elvis vacillated over whether or not the event was going to happen. Finally, at the urging of Lisa Marie and Ginger, the event went ahead as planned.

On the nights of August 10 and August 13, Elvis rented out the local theatre, and had a couple of his movie parties till dawn, just like the old days. According to Ginger, Elvis was in good spirits on the 13th. The next day, Elvis was wolfing down diet pills and water, in an attempt to lose weight. Another tour was due to start on the 17th, and Elvis's weight had ballooned to 260 pounds. His usual performing weight was usually between 200 and 220 pounds, so he was bigger than ever.

The last day I saw Elvis was during his last 48 hours. Our last conversation was on 14 August 1977. Among the things we discussed was that Angie was divorcing me. The last thing that he said to me was, 'David, I want to say goodbye.'

I said to him, 'What do you mean?'

And he answered, 'The next time you see me, I will be in a different place, a higher plane.' I didn't take him seriously, I figured that it was just another bout of his drug-induced rambling.

I came in to Graceland at noon on 16 August and we were due to leave Memphis for a 21-day tour. I was in the pool room with a friend of mine, Mark White. Lisa Marie and Amber, Ginger Alden's niece came into the pool room and said, 'Uncle David, Daddy's sick. He's asleep on the bathroom floor. We can't wake him up.'

Thinking that this was another of Elvis's ploys to cancel the tour, I wasn't immediately concerned but I knew that my day was about to get busy. I took Mark to the front gate. As I was at the gate an ambulance was coming in – I realised that this was serious and raced back up the drive.

I went upstairs just as the paramedics arrived. The minute I saw him, I knew he was dead.

'You son of a bitch,' I yelled. Elvis was lying there, with pills and empty syringes all around him, and I had no doubt what had happened; none whatsoever. And it just pissed me off. It hurt, but it made me mad too. Damn it, Elvis! But I didn't spend a lot of time hurting right away, because it was so instilled in me to take care of business. And that's what I did, picking up syringes, picking up pills. And I've received a lot of heat for that. But I didn't care. All

I knew was that an ambulance crew was about to walk through that door and there was stuff lying all over the place, and I had to clean the place up then and there. So I grabbed everything I could and stuffed it in my pocket and then moved over to Elvis. He was lying face down, kind of all curled up. We turned him over and his eyes were rolled back in his head. His face was blue, bloated, and his tongue was sticking out of his mouth, black, and half bitten off. He was obviously dead.

However, once the paramedics arrived and whisked him off to Baptist Hospital in Memphis, they continued to make attempts to save his life. Joe Esposito, Al Strada, Billy Smith, Charlie Hodge and I were standing in a waiting room while all efforts were being made to revive Elvis. A doctor came in and Joe asked, 'How long has Elvis been without oxygen?' The doctor's response was too long in coming. Joe said, 'I guess we should hope he's gone, otherwise he would just be a living vegetable.'

Moments later, Dr Nick walked into the room and just lowered his head. We already knew, but Elvis was officially pronounced dead. At that moment time stood still. My mind flashed back to 22 November 1963, when President John F. Kennedy died. Family and friends much like us were the first to hear the news that would forever be inscribed in the minds of the whole world.

As soon as the news hit, crowds began setting up a vigil at Graceland. Officially, the cause of death was listed as being a 'heart attack'. I immediately suspected that it was a drug overdose, having been privy to the knowledge of what kind of substances he had been taking by the handful.

The funeral was surrealistic. My brothers, Billy and Ricky and I walked up to the open casket, and I put my hand on his, and it hit me so fundamentally that Elvis was truly gone. We were all choked up. There was a feeling of disbelief and unreality, but also a sense of acceptance and even relief. And a tremendous feeling of peace. If anybody ever deserved a rest, it was Elvis. Those of us who had seen him in so much pain through the last months of his life were thankful that his suffering was over.

After the funeral, I remember coming out of Graceland and looking down the hill at this enormous sea of people. All kinds of people, some crying, some screaming, others just solemn and sad. It was like a Presidential funeral, a universally shared grief. When we got into the limousines, I remembered one of Elvis' favourite songs called *Long Black Limousine*. It was a song about life's last long trip, and here Elvis was doing just that at last. The show was finally over.

When Elvis died the estate didn't want anyone to think of his death as anything other than death from natural causes. No one can tell me that he did anything but commit suicide. Yes, it took him two years to finally do it, and yes, his heart did give out, but it was suicide, plain and simple.

The estate didn't want anything to do with that kind of explanation, because it threatened to destroy their claims to the insurance companies. They wasted no time getting Elvis's doctors to determine that the cause of death was 'heart failure', and insisted that there was no autopsy to prove otherwise. A fortune was at stake, and there was no way they could permit anyone to prove that Elvis had essentially done himself in.

There were millions and millions of dollars wrapped up in Elvis's various insurance policies. If they even got a whiff of the theory that Elvis died of a self-induced drug overdose then a fortune was at stake. At the time that Elvis died there wasn't a lot of cash flowing in. He had to tour towards the end simply to pay the bills.

The bills that he incurred going out on tour were just phenomenal. If he didn't drag himself out on stage those last months, he was going to find himself in big financial trouble. There were no more movies, the record sales had dwindled, and the bills just kept mounting up.

With a morbid sense of curiosity, fans began buying Elvis Presley albums by the handful. RCA Records had to step up production at their album pressing plants just to keep up with the demand.

After Elvis died, one of the most bizarre things happened. I went and talked to my stepfather, Vernon. He looked at me and said, 'David, I got to ask you a question. Did you kill my son?'

I couldn't believe my ears, so I said, 'Excuse me?'

And Vernon repeated the question: 'Did you kill my son?'

'What the hell are you talking about, Vernon?'

He said, 'The last conversation I had with Elvis, he told me about you and Ginger. He said you and Ginger were having an affair.'

'Vernon,' I said, 'think about what you're saying. I loved Elvis, you know that.'

And he did. He saw how I felt when Elvis died. I was devastated. God, I was 21 years old, half drugged out myself, with my whole life pulled out from underneath me. It was hard to even get the words out when Vernon and I were speaking. But I managed, and he believed me. But it was sad that he even had to ask. I guess it just shows how strange everyone and everything had become by the end of Elvis's life.

Under the terms of Elvis's will, my brothers, my mother and I did not receive one cent. It wasn't that we ever expected anything monetary from Elvis, but it put everything startlingly into perspective.

With Elvis dead, my life was suddenly turned upside down. The only things that Elvis left me were wonderful memories, drug addiction, alcoholism and no education. Once Elvis had died, I was out of Graceland as quickly as I moved in. That same year, my marriage to Angie came to a crashing ending.

No longer living at Graceland, and without an income, I took a job at the airport where Elvis had kept his personal jet and I found myself pumping gasoline there. It was a very humbling experience.

Suddenly, with all the television and radio coverage that Elvis's life and controversial death caused, the Stanley family was pursued by the press. I appeared on TV's *20/20* and was interviewed by Geraldo Rivera. This was the first time I publicly stated that Elvis didn't die of a heart attack, but of a drug overdose. Elvis's doctor, Dr Nick, was brought up for charges by the Medical Board of Examiners.

During the months following Elvis's death, I was completely lost. Everywhere I turned I saw memories of Elvis and the kind of life that I once lived. I lived with Mom and I began drinking and drugging at an alarming rate. One night, unable to cope with my depression, I began taking handfuls of Valium like they were M&Ms. By the time I was finished, I had consumed 70 Valiums. I staggered into her room delirious.

Mom was later to recount, 'At the time he said he wanted to die. And, when he came in, I could see that he meant what he said. I just thank God that someone was there with me at the time to help me rush him to the hospital. I was worried that we weren't going to make it, but we got there in time. They pumped his stomach and kept him overnight. I thank the Lord we got there in time.'

Lying in my hospital bed, I was convinced that the spirit of Elvis was in the room with me saying, 'David, look at you. Haven't you learned any lessons from me? You look like me, and I don't like that.' From that point on, I started resurrecting my life. Although the partying continued, that suicidal urge vanished, and I was able to go on with my life.

Not long after Elvis had died I wrote several magazine articles about my life with Elvis. Along with my brothers and mother, we wrote the book *Elvis: We Love You Tender*, which was scheduled for publication the following year. We were able to vent some of our pain and frustrations over the death of Elvis onto its pages.

While the writing of that book was underway, Vernon's health was failing. Ever since Elvis died, his will to live had gone right down the tubes. On 26 June 1979, Vernon died of heart failure. Mom was later to say, 'Vernon Presley died when Elvis died. The amazing thing was how long he was able to live with such heartbreak. He was a strong, beautiful man. I shall always love him.'

The day of Vernon Presley's funeral, my former sister-in-law Priscilla and her daughter Lisa Marie flew in from L.A. For moral support, Priscilla came with her younger sister, Michelle. I hadn't seen Priscilla since Elvis's funeral, nearly two years before. When I saw her and realised that she was more beautiful than ever, it reminded me of the crush I had on her when I was growing up at Graceland.

The whole family had gathered together once again. I had a strange sense of *déjà vu*. Unlike Elvis's funeral the gathering that day was just the family. My brothers, Ricky and Billy, were also present. The previous year, Rick had married his wife, Robin, and they both had been 'saved', by rediscovering their Christian religious roots. He was now a practising Southern Baptist Evangelist, and he travelled throughout the country spreading the gospel of Jesus Christ. In fact, that was all he talked about. This in itself was a miracle. The last time I had seen him, he had a $300 a day heroin habit, weighed just over 110 pounds, had hair down to his waist, had bloodshot eyes, and was strung out. Now he stood before me, 70 pounds heavier, with his hair cut short, wearing a three piece suit, and carrying a King James version of the Bible.

Billy, on the other hand, like me, was still a party animal. He lived in Memphis with my mother, while I was staying in Memphis in a small studio apartment. Since Elvis's death, I had continued to work at the Memphis International Airport.

The first thing that Priscilla said to me when we met was, 'I'm so glad that greedy son-of-a-bitch Vernon is dead. He never cared for you, and you know he changed the will, and left us all out. But don't worry, I will take care of you boys.'

Michelle was acting like Priscilla's secretary that day and she carried a black briefcase. Reaching into the briefcase, Priscilla produced a fully prepared 'release' form for Billy, Ricky, my mother and me to sign. It concerned the rights to Elvis's personal home movies, in which we were all featured. She explained that she wanted us all to sign this particular release, claiming, 'This will make us all very rich.' It struck me as odd that nowhere in the release was there any mention of monetary compensation. What struck me even harder was the fact that she had the gall to discuss business, while my step-father's body was laid out in the next room – barely cold. What immediately came to mind was Elvis once saying to me, 'She's nothing more than a greedy gold-digger.'

Not only did it seem to be highly inappropriate to be discussing this at a funeral, but I was amazed by her total attitude that day. We were all appalled at her insistence in producing these documents in the middle of a funeral. I finally said to her, 'Hey Priscilla, give it a break. We'll discuss this later.'

Priscilla respected our wishes – for the moment, but her persistence didn't let up. Watching her that day, I noted that she seemed oddly flirtatious towards Ricky. When Ricky didn't react, I knew he had truly embraced God, and was immune to her aggressive behaviour. I thought to myself, 'If she tries this with me, I'll fuck her brains out!' The next day, the day of the actual funeral, I was surprised to find that she did indeed turn her affections towards me.

That night, after burying Vernon in the grounds of Graceland, Priscilla asked Billy and me to join her and Michelle for dinner at an Italian restaurant in town. Still wanting to get me to sign the video release that she had brought to Memphis, she really turned on the charm. Over dinner she reminisced about all of us growing up together, and how the tragedy of both Elvis's and Vernon's deaths had split us up. I kept thinking to myself, 'It wasn't really Elvis's death that did this at all, it was the fact that she divorced him.'

The more we drank, the more frank and bizarre the conversation became. As the wine flowed that night she told me how Elvis wouldn't have intercourse with her, and how she would spy on him while he masturbated, and how that frustrated her. I felt sure that Priscilla was telling me this in order to seduce me.

From the Italian restaurant we proceeded on a trail of serious bar-hopping. We were all pretty tanked by the time we arived at The Cock-Eyed Camel. While this was happening, Billy and Michelle were starting to get pretty friendly with each other as well.

The evening, however, was not over. When we moved on, Billy got into the driver's seat of my car, with Michelle sitting next to him and said, 'Where to next?' Wasting no time, Priscilla spoke up and said, 'Let's all go swimming!'

'Great!' I said, 'Where shall we go?'

'Back to Graceland,' Priscilla answered.

Instead, we kept a tiny percentage of our dignity and went to McKeller Park, which had a lake and was an old hang out of Billy's and mine. When we got there, we got out of the car, and Billy and Michelle proceeded to the edge of the lake, which was only a few feet away. Michelle took one look at the water, and said, 'This isn't happening, the water's disgusting.'

Since the water in the lake was pretty unappealing, when Michelle asked, 'Where shall we go instead?' Billy and I both answered in unison, 'The pool at the apartment complex,' referring to the place I currently lived. Both Billy and I were determined not to let the moment end. This evening was a fantasy come true.

It was approximately 3.00 a.m. when we arrived back at my apartment. As we stood at the edge of the pool, I said, 'O.K., who's first?' With that, I pushed Priscilla into the water with all of her clothes on. I proceeded to peel off my shirt, and began to remove my breeches. As I did so, Michelle pushed me into the water, and Billy pushed her in after me. By now, Billy, who was buck naked, dived in after us.

After swimming around in the pool, we thought it was time to proceed to my apartment. When we got there, Priscilla and Michelle took a shower together. All the while, Billy and I kept laughing to each other with regard to the overtly sexual tone the evening had, proclaiming 'This is unbelievable!'

Michelle came out of the bathroom first, with a towel wrapped around her. Just then, Priscilla yelled out to me from the bathroom doorway, 'David, do you have something dry I can put on?' I reached into my drawer and threw her my favourite University of Tennessee jersey. When she came out of the bathroom, she was wearing nothing more than the jersey. She filled out that white jersey with the orange 'Tennessee' across it better than any cheerleader I had ever seen before!

Priscilla left town the next day. Needless to say, the release contracts that Priscilla had presented to Billy and me had been signed.

10

A Predator in the Pulpit

A week later, in July 1979, I went to Los Angeles and stayed with Larry Geller, Elvis's personal hairdresser and spiritual advisor. Priscilla had said to me, 'Come out to L.A. and I'll help you in any way I can.' I called her when I got out there, and took her up on her offer. She sent me to Holly Hire's Commercial Acting school, with the idea of my embarking on an acting career. I went through the two week course, and almost immediately landed a Purolator Courier television commercial.

After three weeks in L.A. I returned to Memphis. I often spoke to Ricky on the phone, and he kept trying to talk me into going down to Florida and following the path he had taken: working for Evangelist preacher, Moody Adams. With nothing to lose, I went down to Ft. Walton Beach. I was especially curious to investigate the cause of Ricky's visible transformation.

While there, he persuaded me to accompany him to Toronto, Canada in September 1979 for one of his revival meetings. When I saw Ricky in action, I thought to myself, 'I can do this!' Ricky talked me into appearing with him on the Evangelical TV show *100 Huntley Street*.

He tried to convince me to take a job with one of his Evangelistic associates – in a non-preaching capacity. He wanted me to be 'saved', but he made it clear that he didn't want me as competition on stage. As part of his programme, he advertised under the tagline: 'He served The King of Rock and Roll, now he serves The King of Kings.' It was a slogan I could easily use myself. Over the next couple of months, I considered his idea.

In January 1980 our book was released. Ricky, Billy, Mom and I all went to New York City for a book signing, and while there we appeared on several TV shows. We went off across the country as part of the book release media tour and when we returned I wondered what I was doing with my own life.

In April Ricky called me from Florida and told me that an associate Evangelist named Freddie Gage was going to be preaching in Memphis. He suggested that I go and listen to him speak, which I did.

At the time, Ricky had been featured on several crusades of James Robison's. He informed me that James had a TV special coming up and he wanted me to tune in and watch him in action. He also told me that there was a job available with Robison as the Director of Communications, and that he had suggested me for the position.

Curious, I watched James's broadcast and was impressed by his message and his boldness and decided that this was right for me. When James said on TV, 'Pray with me,' I did exactly that and felt better after I did so. At this point I had tried everything but God and made the decision right then and there. 'Why not?' I thought to myself, 'I have nothing to lose, and everything to gain.'

The following week, with a friend, Larry Inman, I went to meet Freddie. The only reason that I went was because I needed the job and wanted the position with James. Larry and I smoked a joint and got good and stoned before the meeting. I stood there in the meeting with Freddie and he said to me, 'I understand last week you made a decision for Christ, because of James's telecast.' I told him my story, and he invited me to speak at his Memphis crusade that evening. I said, 'Yes!'

There I was, stoned out of my mind, in front of a crowd of 2,000 people. Somehow I pulled it off, and Freddie gave a 20 minute speech, finishing with: 'Tonight we have reached into the Graceland mansion, and have gotten David Stanley to give his heart to Christ, and what God has done for him can happen to you. Before long we can also get Priscilla and Lisa Marie.'

Then he asked for the audience's offering, using me as that night's 'star trophy'. I was desperate for 'anything' in my life because I was at a low point and I went along with it. I figured that I had tried everything else and still felt lost. It also triggered my memory of my mother's church influences as a kid. I decided to 'Try God'.

I had no idea at the time what I was getting myself into. Freddie went back to Texas, and the next week I received a call from James

Robison's office, stating, 'If you want a job, get out here immediately.'

In May 1980 I was off to a new life. I grabbed my only two pairs of blue jeans, my toothbrush, gassed up the car and headed for Euliss, Texas – in the Dallas/Fort Worth area. When I arrived, the James Robison Organization had arranged for me to stay with a very wealthy family who were one of James's biggest contributors. They were members of what was called the Inner Circle, a sort of millionaire's club within the structure of the ministry.

The house I stayed in was phenomenal. It reminded me a lot of the Beverly Hills house that Elvis once owned. They were in the antique business, and the house was Louis XIVed to the hilt!

The following day, when I went to James's office I was greeted by Diane Fraley, James's shapely personal assistant, and she announced my arrival. I walked into a huge luxurious office that would have befitted a very successful businessman. It was like visiting the office of a movie studio head. James's passions were hunting, fly-fishing and golf – the decor of the office reflected all three. Stuffed deer heads, prize fish he had caught and his golf clubs were conspicuous within the office. Before I arrived there, I expected his office to be filled with portraits of Jesus and religious paraphernalia. I couldn't have been further off base.

I had seen him before on television and the TV cameras didn't do justice to his massive stature. I expected a much shorter man, as he appeared on camera, and I was surprised how tall he was. I anticipated that as a minister he would ask me about my finding God, and would be curious about how I was doing personally. Instead, he spent the majority of our conversation talking about himself, his mastery as a flight pilot, and how he wanted to send Priscilla and Lisa Marie copies of his own personally published *James Robison Bibles*. He also bragged about my brother Ricky, and talked about what a great speaker he was.

James Robison is a real fireball of a Southern Baptist minister. He was regarded as having the potential to become the next Billy Graham. There was not a question that he was and is a master communicator and that his ambitions were vast. His sense of self-importance, however, was so phenomenal that it was eclipsed only by those of his staff members.

James wasted no time announcing in his weekly newsletter how he had 'reached into Graceland to save the brother of Elvis Presley'. He made me feel like one of the trophies that hung – stuffed and mounted – on his walls. I expected him to ask me about the state of my soul, and instead he seemed more interested in showing me off like the unfortunate deer and fish that had crossed his path.

When it came time to talk about the job I was about to do, he said to me, 'The soundman that I have at the moment is the best in the business, and I expect nothing less from you.'

I said to him, 'James, I've been in every major concert hall in the country, I don't think it will be a problem.'

I had walked into his office expecting to be very 'buddy-buddy' with him. Instead of finding a friend in James, I found an ego as large as Texas itself. Very quickly I sized him up, and – though he was my ticket to a new life – I wasn't about to take any crap from him.

Suddenly, David Meckley, the soundman I was replacing was called in to meet me, and James was off on his way to his other office – the golf course – which was actually more holy than his organisation.

It was David who took me on the grand tour of the offices. As I walked through the building, I was treated with celebrity status, and as I met everyone, it was clear to me that this was less a church, and more like a multi-million dollar corporation.

The organisation was a vast machine. There were two huge corporate buildings as their headquarters. There was a vast video facility, in which to film, edit and broadcast television programmes and a mobile tractor trailer for location shooting. Also in the building they were in the process of completing a brand new studio from which they would produce prime-time TV specials, and James's weekly TV show.

As I walked through the building, I noticed a framed photograph of two impressive aircraft, which obviously belonged to the organisation. Emblazoned on the tail of both of them were the initials 'J.R.'

I said to David, in an effort to make conversation, 'Are these owned by the organisation?'

David said, 'Yeah, we have two full-time pilots on the staff.' Right then and there I could see where all of the money was going. Instead of feeding the hungry and the needy, James was feeding the organisation and his ego.

As appalled as I was at the gross display of wealth before me, I thought to myself, 'This sure beats working as a bouncer in a strip joint.'

Also on my tour of the complex, I met several of the other

'executives'. Two of the men who left the most lasting impression on me were James McKinney and Jim Rogers. They impressed me mainly because they were two of the biggest power hogs I've ever met!

I couldn't believe the degree of fear they instilled in their staff. People literally shook when it was announced that either Jim McKinney or Jim Rogers wanted to see them. Even when they walked into the building, people cleared out of the way like the parting of the Red Sea.

At one point they actually had the nerve to ask me to mow their lawns for them. Upon that suggestion I simply replied, 'I don't think so.'

Very quickly I began to see the interworkings of this money-making factory. In addition to James's crusades travelling around the countryside, there were also several other touring factions. There was Associate Evangelist Freddie Gage, and his crusades. Gage was a former Houston street punk, who found God later in life. He stood only 5feet 4in tall, and had the typical 'short man' complex.

There was also Musical Director John McKay, who would give gospel concerts at churches. I always liked John, as he was very straightforward and nice. I found out that he shared some of the same opinions about the staff that I had. In addition, there was Jeannie Rogers, a female vocalist who would go out on the road and give her own concerts. Like most religious singers, she couldn't cut it in the secular world, so she acted like a prima donna to hold on to this gig. Both John and Jeannie raised money at their appearances as well. After every concert there was of course an 'offering', where the audience would be asked to 'dig deeply into your pockets.' My brother Ricky would occasionally be brought in as a guest speaker at James's crusades. But, since he wasn't 'saved' through James's ministry, I quickly took that position.

As I was introduced to this whole new world, I was struck by the similarities between this organisation and the rock and roll world. It was complete with obvious female groupies, hangers-on, and 'yes' men, and the awed charity cases. I could see that my initial perceptions were right on target.

At this time, James was embroiled in a huge controversy. He got involved in a public battle against the local gay rights community. The Dallas gay organisations literally shut down James's weekly TV broadcasts. This only gave him further fuel to fight with. He even got noted right wing conservative and gay opponent, Anita

Bryant, to come in and speak on his show. He eventually got back on the air. He used the slogan, 'God created Adam and Eve, not Adam and Steve.'

While he preached with fervour, about 'honour' and 'fidelity', it wasn't long before I discovered the entire organisation was riddled with deception and hypocrisy.

On my way out of the office that first day, I again ran into Diane, who was very warm and friendly to me. As we spoke she said to me, 'Why don't you come over to my house for dinner?'

She was gorgeous – blonde hair, blue eyes, and was a former track star, so her body was trim and in shape. Over dinner I asked her about her relationship with James. She told me that she had been working for him for two years. She explained that her job was as James's personal assistant. She also told me that James had 'rescued' her from a very bad marriage, and that he had literally taken her under his wing.

When she spoke of James, I could see that she was excited, which made me wonder about their relationship. He definitely sounded like her knight in shining armour.

She then asked me, 'Are you really Elvis's brother?'

I said, 'Sure. Why, don't you believe me?'

She replied, 'It's not that I don't believe you, it's just that a guy posing as Gene Simmons, the bass player of the rock group Kiss, came to the organisation and took us for a very expensive ride, especially me.'

I got a huge charge out of this. I said to her, 'No, Diane, that's not the case here. I don't feel like I have to prove anything.'

After dinner, she excused herself and went into the bedroom. Moments later she appeared in the doorway wearing only an unbuttoned men's white Oxford shirt. She had a fifth of vodka in one hand and a glass of ice in the other.

I was in total shock as she said to me, 'Welcome to Evangelism, David, I hope you enjoy the ride.'

Because of the comments about Gene Simmons, and the fact that she put James up on such a high pedestal, the first words out of my mouth were: 'Are you sleeping with James Robison too?'

She said, 'I'm not.'

With that, I sensed that James was indeed sleeping with someone within the organisation – other than his wife. I also instinctively sensed that under James's charm was a mean and vindictive man who had several skeletons stashed in his closet.

The shock of seeing Diane standing in the doorway quickly

subsided, and I stood up and followed her to the bedroom . 'Yes,' I thought to myself, 'this is going to be quite a ride!'

This was the beginning of a five month relationship that I had with Diane. Within the next couple of weeks, I could tell that James sensed that Diane and I had become close, he just didn't know how close. I later moved into the same apartment complex as Diane.

Within the organisation there was a woman named Betty Godwin. She was one of the coordinators of the 'Inner Circle'. She had a son, Mike Godwin, who worked in the organisation as an errand boy. He was my age, a handsome guy with whom I became friends. One afternoon I went out for a lunch break with him and, to my surprise, he produced an ounce of grass. I couldn't believe that I had a drug connection and smoking buddy. I was amazed how this whole organisation totally paralleled my Elvis years in terms of drugs and sex.

My responsibilities for James included working as a soundman at his crusades, concerts, and other functions. This is where I learned the tactics and techniques of Evangelical fund raising. The objective was to have the corporate 'Wall Street' image. There was slick professional packaging on everything. The ministry had its own monthly glossy magazine, and there were also several products to sell at every performance, including books, tapes, brochures, posters, tee shirts and buttons.

In addition, once the organisation got hold of a donor's address they were put on the computer and constantly asked for more money. 'If you don't contribute, our ministry will collapse . . . ' James would wail with such conviction that the money would somehow miraculously pour in.

There were the concerts, five major crusades a year, two major prime-time TV specials a year, associate Evangelist meetings, all designed to generate literally millions of tax-free dollars. In addition, there was an annual Bible Conference for preachers and their families, which was a four day mega event held in Ft. Worth.

I very quickly learned that James's main concerns were not how many souls he could save, but how big the audience was and how much money was coming in. As part of the technical crew, I was privy to James's prime concerns on TV. The camera angles on him were very carefully planned to make him look like an imposing and authoritative figure. He had his own personal make-up woman, as he was very vain about his looks. It was very important that a camera never show a vacant seat in the audience. There was also a

There was also a conscious effort to group all of the young people together, the reasoning being that if you could draw the kids, you could get to their parents' wallets. Cameramen were always instructed to look for displays of emotion in the audience, particularly tears.

Dramatic sound effects were also attention-getters. James made certain that there was always a microphone under the stage, so that whenever he stamped his foot to make a point, it resounded. For extra measure, the 'reverberation' dial was always turned up to the max.

Watching him strut around like a peacock on stage was fascinating whether you believed a word that came out of his mouth or not. It was P.T. Barnum show business at its best. Somehow it appealed to the frustrated actor in me and he became my mentor. I not only wanted to be like him, I was convinced that I could be better than him.

To have a truly effective presentation, you had to have a scapegoat. 'What's heaven without hell?' 'How can you appreciate angels without devils?' James of course would pick his own devils as if he was put on Earth personally to judge people. One of his main focuses was to appeal to the real gung-ho patriots and flag-wavers, pontificating about, 'If things continue like this, there will be no more America in ten years.' He really knew how to push their buttons.

Because of his controversial nature, and finger-pointing, he had his share of public hecklers. When he went back on the air, he made it seem as though he had conquered the entire gay community, which only inflated his own ego. He didn't defeat anyone, he simply bought his way back onto the airwaves with more cash from his wealthy supporters.

He constantly said to me, 'You bodyguarded for Elvis, I need you to bodyguard me.' James had become inflated by his own out-of-control ego. In one of his self-important moments he again harped on to me about how I was to protect him from his evil enemies.

I told him, 'James, you aren't worthy of being a target. You're James Robison, not Elvis.' Finally to placate him, I said, 'I'll keep my eye out for you.'

Watching this, I realised that I was capable of achieving the type of power and influence that James had. In the years with Elvis, I could never hope to become the next Elvis. However, with James, I began to see that I could indeed become bigger and better than him. From this point on, I began to formulate my own plan for my own crusades.

1980, being an election year, found James putting a huge focus on getting involved in it. To gain active involvement, he became part of what was called 'The Religious Roundtable'. Other members included Jerry Falwell and various members of the so-called Moral Majority. There was a taped and broadcast TV special which wielded an immense amount of power. I was the technical director for this. James was the keynote speaker who introduced Ronald Reagan. I realised just how powerful the religious movement was.

Slowly, I began to get more on-stage experience. I was travelling around the country with John McKay, and he was using me more and more as a speaker. Eventually, I graduated to speaking at James's crusades as well. I was testing my wings as an Evangelist preacher in my own right.

It was around this same time that I met Kandis Linear, a pretty girl who was a Southern Baptist virgin. She was working as a secretary in James's organisation.

As far as Diane was concerned, she and I were finished. My brother Billy had moved to Texas, and he had taken up with Diane after we broke up.

In December 1980, I received an unexpected phone call from my mother. She said to me, 'David, I know you are hurting.'

I said, 'What do you mean?' I hadn't been anywhere near a radio or television in hours. She told me that my rock and roll idol John Lennon had been shot and killed. This was traumatic to me, second only to Elvis's death.

It was seven months since I had started working for James Robison. Up until then I had just worked as his soundman. Finally, at a massive crusade in Huntsville, Alabama, I was going to be used as a speaker, to give my testimony as to how I had been 'saved'.

James had no problem drawing a crowd and there were 15,000 people seated in the audience. What he did have a problem with was garnering enough press to placate his ego and to turn him into a true media phenomenon.

I had flown into Huntsville earlier that week in James's private aircraft. I remember thinking that although this was impressive, it was still several notches down from the 880 Convair jet from Elvis's personal fleet.

I couldn't help but think back to the time five years earlier, when I was in this same coliseum with Elvis. I kept expecting to hear

Elvis's trademark opening *Theme From '2001'*. But tonight, the lights were going to be on me and not Elvis. Finally this was my turn to be in the spotlight. As I was standing in the wings of the Von Braun Auditorium that night, hearing James introduce me, I was struck with a last-minute case of stage fright. Could I really pull this off?

I walked up to the pulpit, amidst polite applause. 'Ladies and gentlemen,' I began, 'the first thing you must know is that I'm not a celebrity. There's nothing special about me. I'm just an old sinner saved by grace. And I'm not here to lift up "The King of Rock and Roll", but to preach "The King of Kings: Jesus Christ". I'm serving a risen saviour.' With that the crowd went wild, breaking into a thunderous round of applause, and an in-unison 'Amen!!' I *could* do this!

'I was here in this auditorium five years ago with Elvis Presley, but now I am under new management. You could have never told me at that time that I would be standing here before you tonight.' From there I proceeded to relate my life story, which in effect was my testimony: how I had escaped my life of sex and drugs and rock and roll, and ended up standing on that stage.

As I spoke, I emulated my two mentors – Elvis Presley and James Robison. Years before I had seen Elvis filming *Speedway*, and had been impressed with the way he would pause after making a dramatic statement. I punctuated my performance with this same ploy. From James I had learned the importance of dramatic effect, such as driving a point home by pounding my fist on the pulpit when I wanted to emphasise something.

After speaking for about 15 minutes, it came time for the wind up. Standing there, looking at the faces of these thousands of people, I knew that I had them right where I wanted them. They hung on my every word. They laughed, they applauded, and at several points I had actually driven people to tears. You could have heard a pin drop as I soared into my closing statement. Standing centre stage, and looking out at the audience, I raised both my arms as if I was about to ascend into heaven that very moment and said, 'Ladies and gentlemen, Elvis gave me money, fortune, fame, power and prestige. But Jesus gave me peace, love, joy, and everlasting life. To God be the glory! Thank you.' Although my motive was wrong, in my heart I truly believed this.

As I turned to walk off the stage, the crowd exploded into a thunderous screaming and cheering standing ovation. While hollers of 'Amen' and 'Praise God' spilled forth from the crowd,

James met me halfway towards the wings and threw his arms around me, exclaiming, 'David, that was incredible!'

'James, I've been wrong for so long, but I'm right tonight,' I said in his ear.

As I walked off the stage I was met by press photographers and reporters. Betty Robison, James's wife threw her arms around me to greet me. Several of his followers were running up to me and telling me what an awesome job I had done on stage. Even James Rogers and Jim McKinney, who had previously treated me like an errand boy, came up to greet me.

Now I knew what it felt to be in the spotlight. This exhilarating rush was better than any drug I had ever taken. I thought to myself: 'This is it! I can have a real good time doing this!'

After the first rush of success settled in, I went backstage for a Coca-Cola and to relax. I spent ten or 15 minutes answering the questions of the press, and posing for photographs.

While I was doing this, James was up on stage 'taking' the customary 'love offering', which was nothing more than asking for money. I wandered into the 'green room', where the local 'finance chairman' was being supervised by members of James's staff.

After my brief moments of glory following my presentation that night, I saw something that literally brought me crashing down to the ground in a flash of cold, hard reality. There before me I saw bucket after bucket of cash, cheques and offering envelopes. Using cardboard buckets from the local Kentucky Fried Chicken franchise, I watched one assistant after another dump tens of thousands of dollars out on the floor before me, until I stood in front of a mountain of money over three feet high.

As I stood there my mouth dropped open. I thought to myself, 'This is "Evangelism T.C.B." – Taking Care of the Business we were in.' Now that I saw this vision before me, my stomach began to turn. I had poured my heart out on stage to the audience that night and now I realised that this was a straight-line business: deliver the sermon, pull their heartstrings, collect the money and leave town.

On 6 March 1981 I married Kandis, thinking that this would totally change my life. I had seen the same thing happen to my brother Ricky, as his wife Robin helped to keep him in line.

By 1 April I had begun getting in gear to leave James. I had already started printing up press kits and tapes of my testimony to sell wherever I spoke. Finally, in May I made my move. I had received some money and used this to do a mass mailing to different churches. Almost immediately I had booked dates throughout the entire year.

That summer, Bob Tilton, another television evangelist from the Word of Faith Church, called me up and asked me to be a part of his faith healing service. He and his wife Marty sat me down and told me to join them, and their crusades, because like them I could make millions of dollars. I passed on their offer, because I did not trust them. (In 1992 they both became the subjects of a huge ABC-TV Prime Time exposé.)

In the fall of 1981 I began attending Tarrant County Junior College in Ft. Worth. This was all due to Kandis's credit, as she encouraged me to better myself. She had talked me into taking a high school equivalency test, to obtain my 'GED', to make up for the schooling I had skipped out on when I ran off with Elvis.

I carried an 18 credit hour semester load, and a change came over me. Although I still smoked a little pot and had a couple of beers with my buddies, I didn't cheat on my wife. For me, this was big news.

Travelling across the country as one of the star speakers at one crusade after another was quite a crash course in the business. I often had preachers ripping me off when it came time to pay me, telling me that they had taken in a fraction of the cash I had witnessed pouring out of people's wallets and pockets. I also had several preachers' wives come on to me sexually. I always refused.

I also had several parishioners come up to me after hearing me speak, only to tell me that they wished that I was their preacher, which fed my ego and gave me more confidence. Because of this, I had several preachers become quite jealous of me.

There were all kinds of politics and back room double dealing in the business. I watched how James turned his back on the Southern Baptists, to align himself with the Charismatic movement. As soon as he did, I watched his empire start to crumble.

The highlight of my life came on 22 December 1982, when my son Austin was born. My education was continuing, my ministry was growing, and several offers were coming in to me. I appeared on the popular religious TV show *The 700 Club*, and I was invited to appear on Jim Bakker's *Praise the Lord* show.

Seeking more religious guidance and a better education, I enrolled in Baylor University, the largest Southern Baptist University in the country. I thought this was going to be different and inspiring. Instead, I found that this was the most party-going of schools in the country. I thought this was going to be a college that held the Bible as infallible. I was crushed to find out that this was not true and I argued with my professors constantly about this.

I transferred to North Texas University and changed my major to Communications. Unbeknown to my wife, I was back up to my old tricks of living life in the fast lane. I was at that time becoming very disillusioned with the whole ministry scene. Ironically, I found myself becoming bigger and more popular – in terms of bigger churches, and greater amounts of money that I was being paid.

In Washington D.C. I attended the National Religious Broadcasters' Association. I worked as an Associate Producer for James's TV broadcast, and one of my more off-the-wall responsibilities was to interview the famed faith healer, W.V. Grant. My first question to him was, 'Do you really heal all of those people, or are you just in it for the money?' He got up and walked out on the interview!

I was beginning to have more second thoughts about what I was doing with my life. Evangelism was beginning to become nothing more than a job for me.

At this point, Priscilla Presley was becoming a regular player on the TV series *Dallas*, playing the role of Bobby's ex-girlfriend, Genna Wade. While she was in town doing some location filming, I took Priscilla out to dinner with Kandis and her brother Lindy. That evening Priscilla said to me in private, 'Be leery of anybody who does anything in the name of Jesus.' She also warned me about James Robison, and told me how she had joined the religious cult of Scientology.

I went out with Mike Godwin one day, and the two of us copped a buzz on some great reefer. When I confessed it to my preacher he simply said to me, 'No problem, I used to smoke a couple of cigars whenever the pressure got to me.' I was obviously falling back into some of my old ways, and no one in the organisation cared what I was up to behind closed doors, because they all had some sort of sexual misbehaviour or substance abuse problem of their own.

By the end of 1985, I was doing six to seven gigs a year with Evangelist Bailey Smith and his new musical director, John McKay. I was also doing five to six gigs with Freddie Gage, although we were arch enemies. By this time I wouldn't get on stage and clear my throat for less than $1,500. I remained with it strictly for the money I was making.

At the end of 1985, I was approached by a publisher to write a Christian book called *Life With Elvis*, which I decided to do. It was scheduled for publication the following year.

Meanwhile, I became friends with Wayne Lee, who was the chairman of the deacons of the Church I attended, the First Baptist Church of Euliss. He invited me to preach on a crusade in Vancouver, British Columbia. He also invited two singers to perform on the show: Billy Taylor and Donna Smith.

As the year progressed, I found myself in a position to invite singers to perform with me, and I enjoyed Donna's company. Since her husband, Steve, was a good friend of mine, he had no objections to her accompanying me across the countryside.

On 9 July 1986, my son Tyler was born. When I visited my wife in the hospital, I also ran into Donna there, as she had become good friends with Kandis. Steve, Donna, Kandis and I were all good friends at this point, and we were often in each other's company in different combinations.

On the ninth anniversary of Elvis's death, 16 August 1986, *Life With Elvis* was released, and I enjoyed the fruits of cross-promoting the book on my crusades, and my crusades on my book tours. Financially, I was really on a roll now.

By the following spring, Donna had become my regular musical coordinator and Steve had become one of the directors of the new non-profit making organisation which I was setting up. I had become very close to both of them, and found myself becoming more and more attracted to Donna.

In April 1987 Donna and I were both in Greenwood, South Carolina. On a long walk around town, I confessed to her that I was in love with her. I didn't know what her reaction was going to be. I half expected her to leave me right on the spot, but I hoped she wouldn't.

She then turned to me, and said, 'David, I'm in love with you.' This was one of the happiest moments of my life. We still didn't know how this was all going to manifest itself. That night after the crusade meeting, I kissed her on the cheek, said 'goodnight', and we both went to our separate hotel rooms.

After we flew back to Dallas the following day, while Steve was in the Seminary, Donna and I went out to play tennis together.

I said to her on the courts, 'Donna, what are we going to do?'

She said to me, 'I don't know David. I know this is wrong – a sin – but I want to wallow in it.'

My preaching was becoming stronger and stronger, and my draw was becoming more and more powerful. On 21 April 1987, I was booked to appear on one of Bailey Smith's crusades, in

Mesquite, Texas. At the time he was the President of the Southern Baptist Convention.

He had already started the crusade on Sunday, drawing only 2,000 to 4,000 people a night. I spoke on Tuesday, and the crowd seated well over 10,000. This was usually the case when I appeared, which was generally the crusade's 'Youth Night'. I became a necessary evil to him, because I always drew a bigger crowd to his crusades. Although he deeply resented me, he always gave me 40 minutes for my segment. On that particular night, as we sat on the platform, he leaned over and announced that he was only going to give me 12 minutes.

I said to him, 'That is a big mistake – you'll lose your audience the minute I leave the stage.'

'You are getting a little cocky, aren't you?' he said to me.

I spoke for exactly 12 minutes, as requested, and when I was finished, he returned to the microphone. Just as predicted, he looked out into the audience, only to see thousands of people get up and leave the crusade while he spoke. It gave me great pleasure to witness that.

On 24 April Donna and I both appeared at a Mid-Cities Crusade in Euliss, with Rosevelt Grier. We couldn't have cared less about the crusade, as Donna and I couldn't keep our eyes off of each other the entire time. The following Saturday, Donna and I left for a four day crusade in Cooper, Texas. Our restraint was wearing thin. I said to her that weekend, 'If I ever get in you, you are in trouble!' She just melted, as Steve never spoke to her that way.

We were together in Hendersonville, North Carolina, from 23 to 27 May. On the 25th, I told her that I had a surprise for her after the revival meeting. When I got inside of her that night, the affair was on, with unstoppable velocity. I wore a condom, but soon thereafter I had a vasectomy just so we could continue our affair without worrying about birth control.

Eventually, my best friend Steve approached me and took me aside to ask me for my advice. He said to me, 'I feel that Donna is slipping away from me physically. We've been married for 18 years, and she's never been like this. What do you suggest I do?'

Being the cool-as-ice character that I was capable of depicting, I just said to him, 'Oh Steve, it's just your imagination. You have been so busy studying at the Seminary, and you've been so overworked at church lately, I think you're just stressed out.' Talk about a soap opera!

In June of that year, Kandis wanted us to take a family trip. She wanted my two boys to go to Florida to see my real father. I told her that I wasn't interested in going since I hardly knew him, but realised that it was important for the boys to know their grandfather. So, I said, 'Why don't you and your mother go to Florida with the boys. You'd enjoy it much more than I would. Besides, I hardly even know my father, in fact I still call him "Bill". I really don't feel like sitting down and shooting the breeze and listening to his stories about what really happened between him and my mother 30 years ago.'

Much to my surprise, my ploy worked. Meanwhile, a couple of weeks later, Steve came to me and told me that Donna and their two teenage boys, Chad and Ryan, had their heart set on a family vacation to West Virginia to visit her mother and her brothers. But he couldn't go with them, as he felt it was more important to attend the Southern Baptist Convention. He asked if I could take them. There was no way I was going to miss this opportunity. I of course said 'Yes!' My only concern at the time was, 'What the hell am I going to do with their boys?' But I was certain that Donna and I would think of something.

Our trip took us through Nashville. Along this 18 hour drive to West Virginia, Nashville semed like the logical half-way point to spend the first night. While we were there, I stayed in one room and Donna and the boys stayed in another. Donna and I went out to dinner and I told her, 'I want *in* you tonight.'

This excited her so much that we didn't even finish dinner before we went back to my room and made passionate love all night. This was all done with Donna and Steve's two boys in the very next room.

Our physical escapades continued throughout the entire trip: we had sex everywhere we could find a moment to be alone. We did it in the car and on top of mountains.

When we returned from our trip, Steve Smith asked me to come into the Singles Meeting. Donna sang and I spoke about the evils of fornication and adultery. It wasn't hard to cite examples, since I was so experienced in both matters.

On 31 July I took Donna to a Kenny Loggins concert. I had aproached Steve earlier, announcing, 'I have backstage passes for the show, would you mind if I took your wife?' He was thrilled to let me.

Donna came to my office unannounced on 11 August and when I hugged her she stiffened her body. When I asked her what the problem was, she said – referring to my vasectomy – 'You clipped your wings for me, I've had my breasts lifted for you!'

I was so excited that we got on the floor and got it on right then and there. At one point she moaned, 'Oh, Steve!'

I said, 'Excuse me?!?' We laughed it off and continued with our love making.

On 16 August 1987 my book *Life With Elvis* was released at a big gala in London. Donna told me that she was insanely jealous that I was taking my wife, and not her.

As my affair with Donna continued, preachers kept making comments about our obvious closeness. I kept dismissing it as ridiculous gossip. We were so happy when we were together, but neither of us wanted to hurt Steve or Kandis. Donna had confessed to me that she had never climaxed having sex with Steve. Throughout this period, I kept emotionally separating myself from Kandis, yet Donna didn't seem to be cutting off her relationship with Steve. This frustrated the hell out of me.

By 1988, Donna and Steve's sons were already very fond of me. On one occasion, Donna and Steve went off to Hawaii, and I stayed at their house with the boys. My relationship with Donna and Steve was getting so awkward that I began to call my mother and ask her what it was like when she and Vernon were carrying on. She simply said, 'You're making a big mistake. She'll never leave her boys.'

That spring, the Jim and Tammy Bakker scandal blew up in the faces of all of the television Evangelists. Misappropriated funds, graft, sex scandals and backstabbing was suddenly the business of the day. As Jim Bakker's empire buckled, Jerry Falwell screwed Bakker over and pulled a power play to take over the PTL organisation and Bakker's prize theme park: Heritage U.S.A.

I was at a crusade with Bailey Smith when he told me that he was part of Falwell's operation and was about to take over the theme park. I stared him coldly in the eyes and said, 'It seems like you screwed him too, Bailey.' That was the end of my working relationship with Bailey Smith.

In March 1988, I went with Steve to Tucson, Arizona, for a Singles Session of preaching. I was then scheduled to go to New York City, and had plans to take Donna along with me. I received a phone call from a pastor in New York, informing me that Jimmy Swaggart had been caught in a sex scandal with a prostitute and that I was not to bring my female singer to the meeting.

Instead, I flew to Los Angeles and the following day I picked up Donna at LAX airport. She pretended that she was going to L.A. to see her grandmother, when in actuality we finished the trip with a stay at the Century Plaza Hotel.

The Jimmy Swaggart situation put a whole new light on what I was up to, and seriously cramped my relationship with Donna. The Southern Baptist church organisations jumped all over both Bakker and Swaggart – making them the scapegoats for problems inherent in all the money-greedy Evangelists. Jim Bakker ended up spending several years in prison for tax fraud, and Swaggart's career was ruined.

Not long afterwards, Pastor Billy Weber was caught in adultery – on the desk of his office, no less. I had seen him years before flirting with a young girl in a Washington hotel elevator, so it came as no surprise to me. If caught at the wrong moment, this kind of scandal could ruin me as well.

In December 1988, I celebrated Christmas with my wife and boys, but by New Year's Day 1989 I had split with my wife. Kandis volunteered to go for marriage counselling, but I explained to her, 'Counselling can't save our marriage – we have drifted too far apart.'

As soon as I announced my impending divorce, I was immediately washed up with the Southern Baptist church. All my engagements vanished instantly. I found myself progressively going broke. Finally, my friends Donna and Steve took me into their home. At this point, Steve still didn't have a clue that I was sleeping with his wife behind his back. It was just like the strange affair of Vernon, Dee, and Bill Stanley, 30 years before. I thought to myself, 'What have I become?'

I continued to attend First Baptist Church in Euliss, Texas, where I ran into my old nemesis, Freddie Gage. He came up to me and said, 'What are you doing here? Why don't you go the Charismatic Church, they'll take anybody.'

I looked him in the eye and said, 'Freddie, you're right. They're a lot like Jesus Christ, aren't they?'

Since I didn't have many options, I decided to turn to the Charismatic church, because they will allow their members to divorce without turning their backs on them. In July 1989, I found that my preaching career had come full circle, and I appeared on James Robison's television programme. After the programme was over I found that I had 20 fresh invitations to speak at Charismatic churches.

In March 1990, I met a beautiful girl named Jennifer Nicholas, and I started going out with her. At the same time I was still involved with Donna, but our physical relationship had ended. I realised that Mom was right, she wasn't going to leave her family. I continued to see her throughout the year, but unlike Dee had done for Vernon, Donna was not willing to divorce her husband.

That spring, I assisted writer Albert Goldman in penning an article for an upcoming issue of *Life* magazine, about Elvis. In the article I asserted in greater detail why I felt that Elvis had lost his will to live, and had effectively taken his own life. When the magazine was released in June of 1990, with the cover story entitled 'Down at the end of Lonely Street', it sold a record number of copies.

For me it was my way of 'letting go' of the personal trauma which his death had caused. I had settled his life and his problems in my mind, now it was time for me to do the same for the charade that was my life. In my mind Elvis lived a lie and died a lie. I didn't want that to happen to me. I felt that my life at the time had become much like Elvis's was when he died: a façade.

In July 1990 Donna and I were in Dallas, playing tennis as we had done over the last three years. We got into a disagreement about the tennis game and a 'bad call' about the last ball. I looked at her and said, 'Donna, you always have to be right. I'm tired of this.'

She said, 'I don't have to put up with this,' and turned to walk off the court.

I said to her, 'If you walk off, don't turn around and walk back. This will be the end.'

She walked off, and there I stood. My three and a half year relationship with her had cost me my ministry, my marriage and my kids. Needless to say, I was furious and I certainly paid the price for my devious actions.

I stormed over to Kandis's house and told her that I had something to tell her. All the while she had blamed herself for the demise of our marriage. I couldn't let her do that. 'Are you on drugs?' she asked.

'No,' I said, 'I have been having an affair with Donna.' From that point on, I began dealing with the truth.

As a result of my new-found conclusions, I began to break away from the instilled negative actions of my past. In the previous ten years in organised Evangelism, I had spoken in literally thousands of venues proclaiming the Gospel. While I spoke of 'saving' others, it was I who was 'lost'. It wasn't very different to travelling with Elvis, except for the fact that there were more backstabbing thieves in Evangelism than I ever met in rock and roll. I knew I had to escape.

11

I am my Father's Son

On 14 September 1990, Jennifer and I were married. With my marriage to Jenny, I brought along all of the demons of my past to our union: the guilt, shame, anger and the hurt. However, we both went into this marriage with our eyes open.

Just prior to leaving the ministry, I was in Edmondton, Canada, in the autumn of 1991. I got a phone call that my father was sick. I flew for 18 hours just to get to him. When I arrived in Jacksonville, Florida, Ricky and Billy were there, and my wife Jenny had driven down from Washington D.C., where we were living at the time.

When we walked into the hospital, there lay this six-feet-four-inch, 245 pound man. The first thing Jenny said to me was, 'God, he's even big lying down!'

He had intravenous tubes in his arms, and tubes up his nose. He had developed diabetes and it had destroyed his circulation. Because of the diabetes, he had had to have one of his legs amputated a couple of years before.

Although he had been married to Lois all of these years, and had finally had a happy home life, obviously the scars of the past had left their mark on him.

Ricky and Billy and I all sat on the bed with him, and Jenny was there at my side. He grabbed Jenny by the hand and said, 'She sure is a pretty thing.'

She stepped back, and each one of us boys told him how much we loved him. I took him by the hand and kissed him on the cheek, and told him that I would always love him, and then all of us began to cry together. It was a very emotional time.

We were down there for several days. It was during this visit that I made a decision that I wanted to know who my father really was before it was too late. It really struck me as I saw him lying there that I knew so little about his history and all that he had gone through before I was born. I also wasn't aware of what really happened between him, Vernon and Dee – although I always wanted to know.

I returned to Washington D.C. Jenny was working for the Treasury Department of the government, and I was working on a video project with a group called Cabin Fever.

In February 1991 I was at my apartment, when the phone rang. It was my brother Billy, and he told me that Dad had died. I didn't know how to feel. I was still calling him Bill. From this point on, I have always referred to him as Dad.

I hung up the phone, sat on the side of the bed and I began to cry. Jenny came up, I told her the news, and we cried together. She comforted me through all of my mixed emotions and pain.

His death only intensified my quest to know my Dad. I continued to speak as an Evangelist preacher through most of the rest of the next year and a half.

My last speaking engagement was in November 1992. It was in Calgary, Canada. I remember standing in the pulpit, in front of the crowd, and I said, 'There is something I want to share with you: this is the last time I'm going to preach. There are things in my life that don't measure up to the position of Evangelists. Evangelism has become a business to me, and it has been a way for me to get through the last 12 years. Although it is very important for you to know that I do believe in God. I do believe that Christ died for me. It was He who has gotten me through the perils of the last 16 years since Elvis died. He has been there for me. It isn't God or Jesus I have any doubt in, it is just that I can't deal with the politics. The politics between Evangelists is no different than being on the road with Elvis Presley. Through this experience, I have learned to look "up" instead of looking "at". I encourage you to do the same thing. Don't misunderstand me folks, there are some great men of God out there, and there are great leaders out there who preach, who are to be admired. In the words of our Lord: "Let he who is without sin cast the first stone." We all have sin in our lives, and if we didn't, Christ would have died in vain.' And with that I left the pulpit for the last time.

I left Canada, and I came back to live in Ohio. I have lived near Dayton ever since I married Jennifer in September 1990. When I came back, I was resolved that I truly had had enough of preaching.

In the spring of 1993 I was offered a contract to write *The Elvis Encyclopedia*. As I began to put that together, it was a fresh reminder of all of my memories of big brother Elvis Presley. While working on it, I realised that I had never dealt with the problems in my own life, from growing up at Graceland and with Elvis. There was still a lot of emotional baggage that I was carrying around with me.

It was having an effect on my third marriage. I should have dealt with a lot of these issues back in 1978. I had finally come to realise that I had several unresolved issues in my life, and it continuously extracted an emotional toll. By all rights, I should have marched myself into a therapist or a counsellor in 1978, to sort out all my mixed-up feelings, pain and frustrations.

When Elvis died, I wasn't equipped to deal with the real world. I've let circumstances control me, instead of taking control of the circumstances. I realised that I had a lot of problems.

I carried around a lot of resentment and anger. I was angry when I saw him lying in his casket at Graceland in 1977 and I had buried that rage all of these years. I had watched him self-destruct and I took his death personally.

It finally hit me: how could I go on for 12 years preaching Evangelism, and not taking to heart what I was preaching? I was not practicing what I was preaching. I was so incensed by all that I had learned about the backstabbing and double-dealing in Evangelism, that I tried to write a scathing exposé on the church, called 'Predator in the Pulpit'.

Instead, I decided to write this book because I realised that it would be a cathartic experience for myself. In the writing of this book, I have been able to do just that.

One of the questions that I have asked myself over and over again has been, 'What would it be like if Dad had raised me, and not Elvis and the Presleys?' At that time, I began to embark on the journey of discovery: 'Who was Dad, and what did he really do?'

When I was working on *The Elvis Encyclopedia* I looked at some of the other books written on the life of Elvis. This really made me want to set the record straight on several matters.

I looked at what some of the members of the Memphis Mafia have written. They have been mainly negative towards Elvis. As you read this book you may think, 'Well, isn't this a matter of "the pot calling the kettle black?"' I feel that I am approaching the subject of Elvis from a totally different perspective. Besides this is my autobiography, not his. I was never jockeying for position, I was secure in being Elvis's little brother, and I never had to do anything to secure or better my position within the inner circle.

Soon after Dad died his widow, Lois, sent me a copy of his memoirs. On a note she wrote, 'Your Dad wanted you to have this.' Finally, in 1994, I decided to confront my Mom, and ask her some of the details about Dad's life that I never knew.

'Oh, he was just an alcoholic,' she said, 'and I wanted a better way for you boys.'

As I spoke to her on this subject, I could sense the conviction that she obviously felt. I could also see that she did love Dad, and that she did care about him. Clearly she herself had regrets.

I told her that I had been reading his side of the story, and had just found out that he was a veteran of the battle at Omaha Beach and that he marched across France and was in the Battle of the Bulge. 'All you ever told me was that he was General Patton's bodyguard.'

So, Mom said, 'Son, he drank a lot, he was full of fight . . . '

And, as she spoke, I could sense that the war had done to Dad what the Presleys had done to me. They had warped my perspective of life and reality completely.

I said to her, 'I feel like I am a lot like my father'

'You're just like your Daddy,' she said. 'You look like your Daddy, you walk, you talk like him. You are authoritative, and a strong individual . . . ' But she never was able to give me the information I really wanted from her.

I called my brother, and said, 'Hey, Billy: let's go up to Ft. Campbell,' which is right outside Nashville. We drove up to Ft. Campbell, and walked through the base. We were very taken by seeing where Dad was stationed, right after he had been shipped back from Germany, where he was in the thick of it.

After that, I came home, and I wrote a letter to the government, requesting a list of my Dad's medals and his complete dossier. I freaked out when I saw the size of the package that I received. Usually a dossier on a soldier is about ten pages. Dad's file was in the vicinity of 110 pages long. It had details of everything he had ever done, and listed all of the medals he had ever received.

Reading all this material, I realised that in five months – June 1994 – it was going to be the 50th anniversary of D-Day. I became obsessed with the idea of learning all that I could about the battle that Dad was involved in. In a matter of months, my library of books on World War II quadrupled, as I got more and more enthralled by it.

I announced to Jenny, 'On 6 June 1994, I want to go to France for the 50th anniversary of D-Day. I don't know how I am going to do this . . . but I'm going.'

Sure enough, I juggled my time and obligations, and found myself boarding a plane bound for France. I was wearing an army jacket which was covered with my Dad's medals and patches all over it. Jenny even made a little sign for me to take there that said, 'In Honor of William J. Stanley.'

I stayed in Paris for a couple of days, then I went over to Normandy. I was there on 6 June. Dad had hit the beach at six thirty in the morning. Exactly 50 years to the day and the exact minute I was walking that very same beach that Dad had risked his life to land at.

In my mind I could feel the ghosts of the past. I could imagine the screams, the stench of burning flesh, and the sound of the guns. Since I had read everything I could get my hands on about this, the images were very clear to me.

This moment was interrupted by a man who had been in Dad's unit on the fateful day 50 years before. As tears rolled down his cheeks he said, 'You look just like your father. You're Billy Stanley's son, aren't you?' Overwhelmed with emotion, the man proceeded to tell me how my father had dragged two of his wounded comrades to safety amid the chaos. My eyes became misty as I listened to this man and I knew I was in touch with my true heritage.

Standing there, the tears began to roll out of my eyes, and I really began to miss Dad. I swelled with pride as I asked myself, 'How different would I have been if Dad had raised me, instead of Elvis and the Presleys?'

I decided that I really wanted to get to know who I am, and not in relationship to Elvis Presley. I don't want to live in the shadow of Elvis, and I don't want to go down that road anymore.

I came to the conclusion that somehow I wanted to tell my Dad's side of the story. I wanted people to know that Elvis might have been the King of Rock and Roll, but Bill Stanley and his buddies were the ones who laid down their blood for the principles of freedom that we all enjoy.

Today, my Mom still lives in Nashville, Tennessee. She is basically retired. She lives alone, and still has a lot of spunk, although she is now in her 70s. I love my Mom dearly. And, in retrospect, I can see the regrets that Mom has for not sticking with Bill Stanley. She was very supportive throughout my whole quest to know more about Dad, and we remain very close. I fully understand that she made certain choices in her life, just like I do in mine.

My brother Billy is living in Nashville with his wife Laurie and his daughter Brooke. He is working with a group out of Dallas, who are steering him into automobile racing. Ricky is the true miracle of the family, as an Evangelist minister. What I was trying to do as a business, Rick takes literally. He is destined to become the next Billy Graham. He lives in Atlanta, Georgia, with his wife Robin, and his daughters Brittany and Betheny.

My sister-in-law, Priscilla, is in Los Angeles where her acting career has blossomed into more television and movie roles. She and I had a huge falling out in the mid-'80s and haven't spoken since.

I haven't seen Priscilla since December 1985 when I was in Los Angeles with her and Lisa Marie. Lisa was asking me a lot of questions about her father, Elvis. Priscilla seemed to have a problem with this whenever I was around. Priscilla consistently put Elvis down whenever Lisa Marie inquired about him. Amid one of my stories about Elvis, Priscilla said, 'Don't tell her that David, don't try to elevate him: he was no good.'

Well, Lisa was genuinely curious. I told her, 'Your Dad wouldn't have approved about your getting involved in Scientology, because he was a Christian.'

Lisa Marie wanted to show me what Scientology was all about, and I said, 'I'll go with you to a Scientology meeting.' I went with her and as we left the meeting, I said to her, 'That's nothing but a high-priced philosophy. Your Dad would have no part of that, I'll tell you that right off the bat.' Priscilla didn't care too much about that, but she just let my comments slide by.

After the meeting, we went back to Priscilla's house. At the time, Lisa was living at the high-priced Scientology hotel in Hollywood. I went over to the hotel with Lisa Marie and her first husband, Danny Keough. Danny and Lisa were really loving all of the stories that I was telling them about life with Elvis.

The more that I told her about her father, the more she wanted to know because she was so young when he was alive, and she missed out on most of what was really happening back then. We were in Lisa Marie's suite, and we decided to go up onto the roof of the building. Before we went to the hotel we had picked up a couple of six-packs of beer, and we were just talking and shooting the breeze. Well, I reached in my pocket, and I found half of a marijuana joint. I pulled it out of my pocket, and Danny and I were smoking it. Lisa declined to smoke any of it.

We stood up on the roof of the building for quite a while laughing and talking. Not long afterwards, I left and went back to Larry Geller's house where I was staying. The next day I got a phone call from Priscilla and she was absolutely livid. 'You call yourself a Christian,' she started yelling at me. 'You're up on the roof of the Scientology building, smoking pot – you drug addict – you son-of-a-bitch! You betrayed me like Red and Sonny betrayed Elvis. How dare you do this to my daughter?!'

Although she had a point, I couldn't believe this. She was someone who used to party with the best of them and here she was jumping all over me about smoking half a joint on the Scientology building.

I haven't seen or talked to Priscilla since then. The bottom line wasn't the marijuana, although I knew that was wrong, it was the fact that I was telling Lisa Marie about Christianity, and it was conflicting with what Priscilla had told her about her cult of Scientology – and she couldn't take it anymore.

From that experience in 1985 and the request from Lisa Marie to know about Elvis, I realised that one day Lisa Marie was going to rebel. In 1994, when Lisa Marie suddenly divorced Danny, and married Michael Jackson, in my mind the motivation was simple: she did it to rebel against Priscilla.

Over the last 20 years since Elvis's death, I have dealt with the constant question from fans: 'If you were Elvis's bodyguard, why didn't you do anything to save his life?' Dr Nick even went so far as to accuse me of killing Elvis by giving him a karate chop to the neck. What nonsense, it was Elvis who killed himself, with the drugs that the doctors gave him!

As I finish this book, I am closing the last of my Elvis chapters. It is time to put an end to the Elvis within me. I have learned a lot, seen a lot, and I thank God that I have survived all of this.

Through living vicariously through my father, and looking at life through my father's eyes, I feel that I have an objective perspective for the first time. I have made the first big step in my life.

In this book I have exposed all of my past mistakes. To get my life together further, I have gone through counselling. This was a major step for me. Through counselling, I am facing all of my own personal demons, in the hope that I can become the truly rounded person I know I can grow to be.

I have lived my first 40 years behind the shadow of Elvis Presley. It is my goal to live the next 40 as a fully-developed person unto myself. I intend to put the past behind me, and to get on with my life. I loved my life with Elvis but he has been dead and gone for two decades now.

I don't hate Elvis. In revealing all of the unattractive aspects of his life, I haven't tried to rip him apart, I merely wanted to explain who he was and how he affected me. He was a person who had it all but was unhappy with what his wealth and fame brought to him. This is not what I want to happen to me, or to anyone else.

Elvis was afraid to let people see who he actually was behind the public image. I grew up in Graceland being taught to keep all the details of my life a huge secret. In this book, I have tried to expose my deepest secrets, to get them out into the light of day, deal with them, and put them all behind me. By finally writing this book, and going through counselling, I have done that and I feel stronger and better than ever because of it.

When all is said and done, I am more proud of being the son of Bill Stanley Sr. than I am of being Elvis Presley's step-brother. I can finally say that I am truly proud to be who I am: my father's son.

Bibliography and List of Sources

Elvis Albert Goldman; McGraw Hill Book Company, New York, 1981

Elvis And Me Priscilla Beaulieu Presley; G. P. Putnam's Sons Publishers, New York, 1985

The Elvis Encyclopedia David Stanley; Virgin Books, London, 1995

Elvis We Love You Tender Dee Presley, Billy, Rick and David Stanley; Delacorte Press, New York, 1979

Living In The Shadow Of The King Bill Stanley; Vantage Press, New York, 1987

Priscilla & Elvis Carolyn Latham; Signet Books/New American Library, New York, 1985